BLUEGRASS
AMBASSADORS

SOUNDING APPALACHIA

Travis D. Stimeling, Series Editor

TITLES IN THE SERIES

Songwriting in Contemporary West Virginia: Profiles and Reflections
Travis D. Stimeling

Folk Songs from the West Virginia Hills
Patrick Ward Gainer; Foreword by Emily Hilliard

*50 Cents and a Box Top: The Creative Life of Nashville
Session Musician Charlie McCoy*
Charlie McCoy with Travis D. Stimeling

BLUEGRASS AMBASSADORS

THE MCLAIN FAMILY BAND IN APPALACHIA AND THE WORLD

PAUL O. JENKINS

West Virginia University Press • Morgantown

First edition published 2020 by West Virginia University Press
Printed in the United States of America

ISBN
Paper 978-1-949199-68-0
Ebook 978-1-949199-69-7

Library of Congress Cataloging-in-Publication Data
Names: Jenkins, Paul O., author.
Title: Bluegrass ambassadors : the McLain Family Band in Appalachia and the
    world / Paul O. Jenkins.
Description: First edition. | Morgantown : West Virginia University Press,
    2020. | Series: Sounding Appalachia | Includes bibliographical
    references and discography.
Identifiers: LCCN 2020008820 | ISBN 9781949199680 (paperback) | ISBN
    9781949199697 (ebook)
Subjects: LCSH: McLain Family Band. | Bluegrass musicians—United
    States—Biography. | Bluegrass musicians—Travel.
Classification: LCC ML421.M425 J46 2020 | DDC 782.421642092/2 [B]—dc23
LC record available at https://lccn.loc.gov/2020008820

Book and cover design by Than Saffel / WVU Press
Cover images courtesy of the McLain Family collections, Peter Taylor (*top left*),
and Rick Goodfellow (*bottom left*)

To Owen, who loved how Ruth "beat up on" her bass.

CONTENTS

McLAIN FAMILY TREE

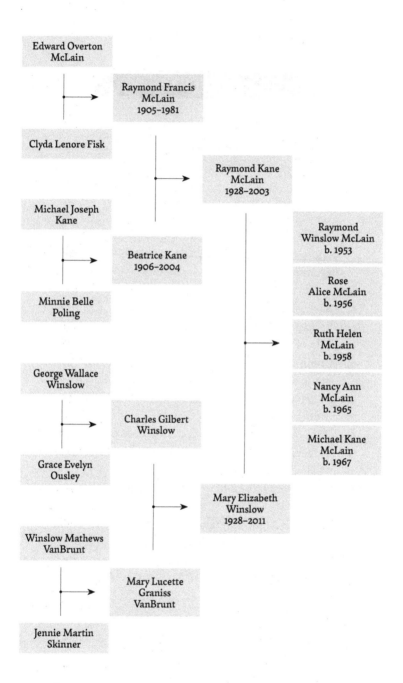

Edward Overton McLain

Raymond Francis McLain 1905–1981

Clyda Lenore Fisk

Raymond Kane McLain 1928–2003

Michael Joseph Kane

Beatrice Kane 1906–2004

Minnie Belle Poling

Raymond Winslow McLain b. 1953

Rose Alice McLain b. 1956

Ruth Helen McLain b. 1958

Nancy Ann McLain b. 1965

Michael Kane McLain b. 1967

George Wallace Winslow

Charles Gilbert Winslow

Grace Evelyn Ousley

Mary Elizabeth Winslow 1928–2011

Winslow Mathews VanBrunt

Mary Lucette Graniss VanBrunt

Jennie Martin Skinner

FOREWORD

ith their sunny personalities radiating from the stage, the McLain Family Band has brought energetic, joyful, and distinctive music to local, national, and international audiences since their formation in 1968. Organized by a musical father, the Kentucky-based band has shared stages with great musicians of many stripes: folk, blues, old-time, country, classical, and—especially—bluegrass. Over the decades the band evolved as children grew up, married musical spouses, had children, and moved around the country.

The McLains play traditional bluegrass instruments (banjo, fiddle, guitar, mandolin, and bass), occasionally in the past adding an accordion played by the family patriarch Raymond K. McLain. While they have always performed bluegrass favorites, the McLains have also featured their own songs and tunes, as well as pieces adapted from unexpected sources.

As Raymond K. McLain put it, "I loved Bill Monroe's music, but with our group, there was no way we could have copied his sound. So, we went with something different." For example, on their first recording—a single 45 rpm disc—they sang a bluegrass rendering of the Coasters' 1959 rhythm and blues hit "Charlie Brown (He's a Clown)" complete with a startlingly advanced banjo break.

The McLains are lifelong learners. Son Raymond W. recalls playing a festival that included the famous Ernest V. Stoneman Family. After the McLains' set, he was descending the stairs leading down from the stage when he heard a slightly sarcastic female voice declaring, "Well, you're a pretty good banjo player, aren't you!" It turned out to be Roni Stoneman, banjo-playing comedienne on the Hee Haw television show. Startled, Raymond was unsure how to respond. "Well, thank you, I guess . . . ," he replied.

"And you think this audience has come just to look at the top of your head, don't you!" Roni went on. Suddenly Raymond W. got it. Without realizing it, he had always bent over his banjo, watching the fingers of his left hand as they roamed the fingerboard instead of making eye contact with the crowd. After graciously thanking Roni, Raymond resolved to improve his stage presence and quit staring at his fingers. Since then, there has been no one better at forging and maintaining an enthusiastic bond between audience and bluegrass band than Raymond W. McLain.

Music fans delighting in a stage performance can't be expected to appreciate the real-life backstory. The reaction of many is, "You sure are lucky to make your living just traveling around playing such great music!" What is missing from this picture for many musicians is the absence of health insurance, lack of paid vacations, job insecurity, no pension upon retirement, low pay (sometimes promoters even stiff the artists), exhaustingly long travel to and from shows in cramped quarters, irregular time at home, and resulting strain on relationships. At the conclusion of one highly successful McLain performance, the promoter had the nerve to say, "That was a great show and we'd like to do it again next year. How much less could you do it for next time?"

On another occasion, the McLain family emerged from their van after a particularly arduous journey to a festival, rushing to change clothes and do a quick cleanup for their imminent appearance on-stage. A weary but game Ruth McLain thoughtfully summed it all up with the perfect bumper-sticker motto for a musician's road vehicle: "If it weren't for the music, I bet we wouldn't be doing this!"

Jack Tottle,
emeritus professor and founder of the East Tennessee
State University bluegrass, old time, and country music program

y intention in writing this account of the McLain Family Band is to discuss their innovative contributions to blue-grass music and explore the most important aspects of their *professional career*. My discussion of the group's career is not strictly chronological. Rather, I have divided the text into broad thematic blocks that highlight their contributions to the genre of bluegrass music. While on occasion I have included appropriate and pertinent details of their personal lives, I have otherwise concentrated mainly on the band members as musicians. I trust that by including excerpts from letters, diaries, and interviews, the distinct personalities of band members emerge, and that my approach presents the reader with a vibrant portrait of them as individuals.

Biography is, of course, a tricky business. Published accounts of events sometimes contradict memories of those actually involved in them, and each of us recalls shared experiences in different ways. The McLains have been very generous with their time and have provided me with feedback throughout the project. This book would not have been possible without their willing and enthusiastic contributions. Any mistakes I may have made result from judgment calls I was forced to make when presented with differing accounts.

Another issue I feel obligated to address here is the availability of McLain Family Band recordings. With few exceptions, the albums the group made for their own label, Country Life Records, are not yet obtainable on CD or via streaming services. Plans are in the works to release a collection of their best material on CD sometime in the near future. In the meantime, interested listeners can find many of their performances on YouTube, and the original LPs are often listed for sale on eBay. Finally, the solo recordings band members made are representative of their sound as a family unit and are all available on CD and in electronic formats.

ACKNOWLEDGMENTS

I am deeply indebted to the following family, friends, musicians, and associates whose assistance helped make this work possible.

Katie Hoffman conducted numerous interviews for an oral history project about the McLain Family Band and graciously allowed me to use them for this book. She also served as a reader and alerted me to the talents of Sam Gleaves.

Anne Chase, former director of the Berea College Library, made me aware of Katie's work and thus brought us together.

Jill Wixom, Amy Horton, and Lisa Wiley at Franklin Pierce University and Char Gildea and Eileen Wedig at Mount St. Joseph University provided vital assistance in obtaining interlibrary loan books, articles, and recordings.

Sharyn Mitchell and all the staff at the Berea College Archives were patient and helpful as I sifted through their extensive holdings on the McLain Family Band.

I am indebted to Sam Gleaves, Sharon and Cheryl White, Rhonda Vincent, Nathan Kiser, Sonny Osborne, Lauren and Leanna Price, Michael Johnathon, and Tim Stafford for consenting to be interviewed for this project.

Hearty thanks to the following people who helped me obtain permissions: Harry Rice, Kopana Terry, Doug Boyd, and Kevin Slick.

The book is enriched by photographs taken by Peter Nash, Emma White, Rachael White, Peter Taylor, Terry Vaught, Fred Park, Rick Goodfellow, and members of the McLain Family.

Amanda Combs and Maggie White shared their views on Michael McLain's teaching style and philosophy.

Nancy Cardwell provided an updated list of undergraduate institutions that offer bluegrass music education programs.

Craig Ledoux read the manuscript and offered shrewd insights into how the work might be improved.

I wish to thank Travis Stimeling and Derek Krissoff of West Virginia University Press for their guidance and support. Charlotte Vester was extraordinarily helpful as the book's gestation period neared an end. Copy editor Lee Motteler cleaned things up nicely.

Andy Cunningham helped with photographs.

I acknowledge Ralph McTell, George Harrison, Steve Moore, Jeff Hillard, Matt LeTissier, Dennis Bergkamp, and Roger Federer for their artistic inspiration.

Ron White helped with his general knowledge of bluegrass music.

I thank my parents, Owen and Barbara Jenkins, for their love, support, and use of the family hi-fi system from 1965 through 1983.

Thanks to my siblings, Hugh, Carol, Doug, and Clay, for helping to shape my musical tastes. And to Doug for being my third brother.

I would be a nowhere man without the love and patience I receive every day from my wife, Mary.

My son, Tom, helps me to remember the meaning of life.

My stepdaughter, Glenna, reminds me how to laugh and smile.

And, finally, thanks to all members of the McLain Family Band for letting me share their foolish pleasure for so many years.

INTRODUCTION

You don't choose your family. They are God's gift to you, as you are to them.
—Desmond Tutu

This is the story of a family whose talent, industry, and inventiveness combined to change bluegrass music. First as performers, then as bluegrass ambassadors, and finally as educators, the McLain Family Band has enriched this uniquely American genre and left an indelible mark on both audiences and fellow performers. From their formation in 1968 until their retirement as full-time performers in the late 1980s, the band performed in the United States and more than sixty foreign countries. Family patriarch Raymond K. McLain (1928–2003) arranged most of their songs and laid down a solid rhythm on his guitar. Raymond W. McLain (born 1953) was the band's virtuoso, dazzling audiences with his inventive banjo work and creative fiddling. Alice McLain (born 1956) played mandolin and bass and sang lead in a clear, high voice that recalled the mountains that surround the family's central Kentucky home. Ruth McLain (born 1958) sang and played mandolin but is best known for her innovative work on the bass. Later in the band's career, Nancy Ann McLain (born 1965) played bass, while Michael McLain (born 1967) contributed lead guitar and banjo. The group enjoyed considerable acclaim throughout their career, performing at venues such as the Kennedy Center for the Performing Arts, the Lincoln Center, the Grand Ole Opry, and Carnegie Hall. In 2013, the International Bluegrass Music Association (IBMA) recognized the

McLain Family Band's many achievements by bestowing on them a Distinguished Achievement Award. Three years later the group received a similar honor: the LEXI Lifetime Achievement Award. This recognition stems from a unique process where both music fans and industry professionals nominate artists who hail from the Lexington, Kentucky, area.

Any honors the band received reflect their many contributions to bluegrass music and the innovative way with which they approached it. As I discuss below and throughout the entire book, the McLain Family Band respected the genre's traditions, but they were not afraid to experiment and augment the music their predecessors created. The McLains collaborated with classical composers and performed with symphony orchestras. They established a festival designed to show-case the talents of family bands like themselves. The group introduced bluegrass music to thousands of international listeners during their numerous foreign tours. Compositions penned by members of the band display a distinct ingenuity, especially in their lyrical cele-bration of the powers of music. Their experiences both as classroom teachers and program directors have left a lasting mark on the field of bluegrass music education. And, finally, the group's joyous attitude has impressed critics, influenced fellow musicians, and inspired their listeners.

I first heard the McLains in 1979 when my father, an English pro-fessor with a penchant for Mozart, came home one day with a handful of LPs. Eighteen at the time, I'd grown up with the Beatles and Simon and Garfunkel, so I was familiar with pop harmonies. The McLains, however, combined their voices in a manner altogether new to me. After listening repeatedly to my father's haul (*Country Life, Kentucky Wind, 7th Album, On the Road*, and the *Family Album*), I moved on to the giants of the genre—Bill Monroe, Flatt and Scruggs, the Stanley Brothers—but soon realized that the McLains remained my favor-ite bluegrass performers. I began to wonder what it was about their sound that so intrigued me and why they had not joined the pantheon of bluegrass greats.

In 1988, I moved to Cincinnati to take my first professional po-sition at the College of Mount St. Joseph. Now a mere one hundred miles from Berea, home of the McLains, I eventually decided to learn more about the band. After watching them perform at the Carter Fold in Hiltons, Virginia, I decided to introduce myself. When I told Ruth how much her interpretation of "Fair and Tender Ladies" (which they had not performed that night) moved me, she smiled and started singing it to me. As I listened, I noticed that members of the audience were engaging other members of the band in friendly conversation. In short, I learned that the family was just as engaging as I'd imagined.

After completing a number of other scholarly projects, I decided to more seriously pursue my research of the McLain Family Band by making two-hour drives down I-75 to Berea College. There I began to sift through the family band's remarkably complete archive. During my research I discovered that another scholar, Katie Hoffman, shared my interest, and together we began a series of interviews both with members of the McLain family and with musicians including Rhonda Vincent, Sonny Osborne, and Sharon and Cheryl White. Coupled with the visits to the Berea College archives, these conversations form the basis of the pages that follow.

OVERVIEW

In the ensuing chapters, I explore why the McLains left such an impression on thousands of music fans in the United States and around the world. I use the term "music fans" instead of "bluegrass fans" here because my experience mirrored that of so many others: the McLains served to introduce many of us to the genre. We came to the band enjoying many different kinds of music but left with a new appreciation of one with which we had not previously been familiar. It was the music that Raymond K. McLain described so vividly as containing "the sincerity of the Anglo-Saxon ballad, the hoopla of the minstrel show, the sociability of the singing game, the loneliness of cowboy life, the sass of ragtime, the fervor of the camp meeting, and the pathos of the blues."[1]

In order to understand the band's ethos of teamwork and their willingness to take on any challenge, in this work I first explore the family's cultural and spiritual DNA, tracking the educational career of Raymond F. McLain. In chapter 1, I describe his tenure as president of three universities. I then show how his son, Raymond K. McLain, inherited much of his father's drive by describing his time as executive director of the Hindman Settlement School. It was there that McLain and his wife Betty began coaxing latent musical skills out of their five children.

In chapter 2, I describe Raymond K.'s move from Hindman to Berea College. After providing an overview of that institution's history and unique mission, I examine the formation of formal bluegrass music education. At Berea, McLain faced the daunting task of establishing the first courses in the genre ever taught at the college level. That he succeeded is testament to his character, determination, and belief that the music merited such attention. I then return to the band's formative years, including their "big break": their discovery in 1971 by Italian composer Gian Carlo Menotti and his subsequent invitation to them to perform at his annual music festival in Spoleto, Italy.

A tight-knit group whose togetherness was apparent in more than just their close harmonies, the McLains were one of many family bands to grace bluegrass stages. Chapter 3 profiles the likes of the Stonemans, the Lewis Family, the Cox Family, the Whites, and more contemporary performers such as Cherryholmes and the Wells Family Band. This section of the book concludes with a brief history of the Family Band Festival, which the McLains hosted on their property from 1978 to 1988.

Chapter 4 is dedicated to the McLain Family Band's forays into classical music. Composer Phillip Rhodes played an important role in introducing the group to this genre. Rhodes was immediately intrigued by the McLains' charm and musicality and struck up a close relationship with Raymond K. As he came to know McLain better, Rhodes hit on the idea of writing a bluegrass concerto expressly for the family band to perform. Much of the chapter describes the composition of the piece, the recording made of it, and performances with symphony orchestras across the country. To conclude this section, I note the band's subsequent attempts to merge bluegrass and classical music and how these innovative projects influenced other bluegrass performers, most notably the Osborne Brothers.

The book's fifth chapter includes an overview of the band's recordings. I begin by recounting the formation of Country Life Records, the label that the group established in 1972, before examining their early, middle, and late albums in general. Many of the band's early recordings featured songs composed by Rosemary McLain, Raymond K.'s sister. Chapter 6 is a detailed discussion and analysis of the nature of her songs and how well they suited the group's talents and outlook on life.

One of the band's most important roles was that of bluegrass ambassadors. Chapter 7 details the group's experiences as they toured sixty-two foreign countries from 1972 to 1978, often under the auspices of the U.S. State Department. As early as 1975, *Bluegrass Unlimited* writer Walter Saunders hailed them as "America's bluegrass ambassadors to the world." [2] Rhonda Vincent, the current queen of bluegrass music, agrees with this assessment. "They were ambassadors, around the world, for bluegrass music. I don't think they set any limits for themselves. It was almost like their duty to introduce bluegrass, to say 'here's a music you will love.' " [3] Many sources inform my account of these tours: letters sent home by family members, missives mailed to Kentucky from foreign audience members, and official reports from embassy staff noting their appreciation. The most important source I draw on, however, is the lengthy diary Alice kept during the band's 1975 tour of Alaska and the Far East. This document provides key insights into the McLains' daily life on the road and the many remarkable experiences they met with abroad.

Chapter 8 is devoted to the thirty-two tracks composed by Raymond K., Raymond W., and Ruth. In both musical style and lyrical content, these numbers show the McLain Family Band at their best and form an important part of their legacy.

One key element that distinguishes the McLains from other bluegrass performers is their involvement in education. Chapter 9 examines the teaching careers band members pursued after the group ceased performing on a regular basis. Raymond W. became director of bluegrass music programs at Eastern Tennessee State University and then at Morehead State University. Ruth joined her brother there and, along with Nancy Ann, helped bring juvenile literature to thousands through her work with Usborne Books & More. Alice took her love for children to its natural conclusion, working for twenty-six years as an elementary schoolteacher in Berea. Her husband, Al White, still leads the bluegrass ensemble and mariachi band at Berea College, while Michael taught bluegrass music for thirteen years at his alma mater, Nashville's Belmont University.

My work concludes by recounting the band's return to the road in 2018 to mark their fiftieth anniversary as a performing unit. Here I discuss their return to the studio by examining new and best-loved songs included on their *Celebrate Life* album. Finally, I make the case for the band's enduring legacy by describing the many innovations and lasting contributions they made to bluegrass through their international tours, original songs, and educational careers.

Appendix A is included for readers interested in exploring how the McLain Family Band interpreted instrumentals and songs that stem from traditional sources or the pens of songwriters other than themselves. Appendix B details solo recording projects band members embarked on between 1992 and 2018. These seven albums are musical cousins to the recordings of the McLain Family Band, sharing the same kind of vibrancy, optimism, and joy so characteristic of the group's work.

A DIVERSE VOICE IN BLUEGRASS MUSIC

Though generally recognized as practitioners of bluegrass music, the McLain Family Band's repertoire and performance style were more diverse than those of their peers. Critics and reviewers often pointed out that their recordings and concerts displayed elements of country, folk, and even pop music. Though this was sometimes perceived as a weakness by bluegrass purists, most fans and writers recognized that such diversity distinguished them and formed part of their charm. Blue Highway's Tim Stafford notes that their occasional stylistic departures from the traditions of the high, lonesome sound served as a gateway to bluegrass, both for him and other listeners. He makes the point that newcomers to bluegrass "sometimes can't take the nasally singing" that characterizes traditional approaches to the genre. The McLain Family Band was one of the first bluegrass groups Stafford heard, and while previously he hadn't enjoyed traditional vocalists like Bill Monroe or Ralph Stanley, the band's "singing was a little more accessible to a fourteen-year-old kid from the suburbs" [4] like himself.

Those well acquainted with the genre know it is fiercely protective of its roots, and that debates over what constitutes "true bluegrass" are taken quite seriously by critics and aficionados. In an article written in 2012 for *Popular Music*, Joti Rockwell describes the extent of such passion. "The world of bluegrass music is notable for its heated, hackneyed and inconclusive debates over self-definition. The question 'What is bluegrass anyway?' is cliché enough to have received its own acronym, 'WIBA.' " [5]

As Rockwell notes in his essay, dozens of scholars have attempted to define bluegrass music. In *The Bluegrass Reader*, Thomas Goldsmith offers the following elucidation: "It is an expansive, twentieth-century, acoustic string-band music based in traditional styles, including fiddle tunes, blues, and southern church music, and it features high-pitched lead and harmony singing and emphasizes instrumental virtuosity on fiddle, banjo, mandolin, guitar, and acoustic bass." [6]

Neil Rosenberg's definition is quite similar. He classifies bluegrass as a subset of country music, further noting that it is a music "in which singers accompany themselves with acoustic rather than electric instruments, using the fiddle, mandolin, guitar, five-string banjo, Dobro, and bass." Like other scholars, Rosenberg compares bluegrass to another musical genre born in America. Its "emphasis on individual virtuosic self-expression led some to call bluegrass the jazz of country music." [7]

It is perhaps most accurate to categorize the McLain Family Band as a bluegrass group that extended the range of the genre. With few exceptions, they performed on the stringed instruments associated with bluegrass. Their virtuosity is unquestioned. Raymond W. was recognized by his peers as one of the best banjo players on the circuit, and Ruth's prowess on the bass earned praise from every quarter. The subject matter of the band's songs, both original and from the tradition, celebrate the genre's core values: love, home, and faith.

It is principally the group's vocal stylings that have sometimes led critics to question their place in bluegrass. If not always "high and lonesome," the McLains' vocals do consistently feature another characteristic of bluegrass: harmony singing. Cheryl White explains one reason their sound was so distinctive. "They could sing songs so many different ways because they were all good lead singers. That's very uncommon." Cheryl's sister, Sharon, elaborates. "Sometimes they would utilize all four voices and there wouldn't be a bass part, maybe doubling one of the girl's parts. That was different. Nobody else did that in bluegrass. The McLains never backed away from anything."[8]

Sonny Osborne, who together with his brother Bobby created some of the most famous harmonies in the genre, is impressed if also somewhat mystified by the harmonies the McLains could fashion. "Their harmonies were different. I can't explain to you why because I don't know what they were doing. They were so well rehearsed. Their harmony was worked out to the fraction."[9] Some examples from the McLains' repertoire that feature the kind of harmonies Osborne praises include "Sweet Rivers of Redeeming Love," "Sail Away," "Pretty Flowers," "Foolish Pleasure," "Lonesome Day," and "Straightaway to Jesus."

In a 1980 interview with Marilyn Kochman for *Frets*, later reprinted in her *Big Book of Bluegrass*, Raymond K. explains how the group worked out harmonies and arrangements for particular songs. "There are a whole series of decisions that have to be made with every new piece. It's partly the excitement of it. If it's a song, you decide who should sing it and how to harmonize it. You can't start making decisions with the whole group because that would be too overwhelming. Generally, we start with two people. If there are just two, we find the key by trial and error somewhere in the range of our voices. Then we use a guitar or mandolin to outline the harmony."[10] In McLain's words, they attempted to keep their sound as "bright" as they could. "We put it as high in the range as we can without straining. You always want to give the impression that you could sing higher or lower if you wanted to, or could play faster or sustain the note longer if you wanted to. You never expose your limits."[11]

As if in answer to those who questioned whether their music truly fit into the genre, various members of the McLain Family Band offered their own definitions of bluegrass. Raymond K. explained bluegrass in a way that hints at the group's varied repertoire. "Bluegrass music first and last is fun. Its proponents are often unschooled musically so communication is direct. It is 'people's music' today. The popularity of bluegrass betrays the yearnings of the public for simpler times."[12] He also recognized the reasons for the growing popularity of bluegrass. "This kind of music is very basic. It's the kind of music that I think anybody can understand. There are very few chords in it. Most pieces just have three different chords, tonic, sub-dominant, and dominant. Some songs, of course, have minor chords and secondary chords. But mostly it's very simple. The rhythm is very simple and driving and yet, with all this simplicity, there's a complication in the orchestration. That is, the instruments are very busy and they are doing lots of things. You can add all kinds of embellishments to make it exciting. I think it's the kind of music that you don't have to have a musical education to understand."[13]

McLain's daughter Ruth echoes her father's opinions, but she also stresses another aspect of bluegrass: how it can unite its listeners. "It's a happy music, it's a friendly music. It's easy to listen to. It's not too complicated. Yet it's busy. It's exciting. It's the kind of music that appeals to many different kinds of people and brings us closer together. If you go to a bluegrass festival you'll find older and younger people and the middle-aged people in cut-off jeans and the ladies in their fancy dresses and hats and gloves, all enjoying the same kind of music."[14]

At times, elements of the McLains' sound resemble old-time, or mountain music, a genre closely related to bluegrass. In their 2014 bestseller, *Wayfaring Strangers*, Fiona Ritchie and Doug Orr cite old-time musician Ron Pen to help differentiate between the two styles. Bluegrass, Pen maintains, is more up-tempo than old-time music. It features the finger-picked instead of the clawhammer banjo style and emphasizes harmony singing to a greater degree. Furthermore, "the emphasis in old-time music is generally on rhythm, while bluegrass is more note dense."[15] Al White, who married Alice McLain in 1977, offers further distinctions. "I acknowledge the fact that the people involved in both kinds of music don't always see eye to eye on certain things, but I don't know. There's power and beauty and great picking in both kinds. I guess bluegrass is just slightly more commercially oriented, and people nitpick the harmonies a little closer."[16]

Raymond K. points out that, far from being static, tradition is ever evolving: "We have ideas about tradition, and consider ourselves to be a traditional band. All traditional bands have been very creative, and there's a great place for creativity within tradition. One of the great things about tradition is change, appropriate to the time and place. It's important to keep blazing new grounds with material and performances."[17]

On stage and in the studio, the McLain Family Band tapped into various genres of popular music. They featured old-time pieces like "Shady Grove," "Married Me a Wife," "Fair and Tender Ladies," and "Pretty Polly." Their recordings of "Milk Cow Blues" and "Columbus Stockade Blues" indicate their familiarity with the blues. They were firm admirers of the Carter Family, recording "The Storms Are on the Ocean," "You Are My Flower," "Worried Man Blues," "I Never Will Marry," "East Virginia Blues," "Working on a Building," and "Sweet Fern." They paid tribute to other giants in country music with their covers of Ernest Tubbs's "Walking the Floor Over You," Fred Rose's "Bringing in the Georgia Mail," Jimmie Rodgers's "California Blues," and Patsy Montana's "I Want to Be a Cowboy's Sweetheart."

The band began its career playing for dances, and their *Country Dance* album is a collection of tunes for such occasions. Gospel music was also an important part of the McLain Family Band's repertoire. *Sunday Singing* features exclusively gospel numbers, and earlier albums include the likes of "Darkest Hour," "I Saw the Light," and "Turn Your Radio On." When he joined the band, Alice's husband Al White brought western swing songs like Bob Wills's "Take Me Back to Tulsa" to the group. Raymond K.'s love of jazz and ragtime is reflected in tracks such as "Beaumont Rag" and "Peacock Rag." The band even chose to record two marches: Josef Wagner's "Under the Double Eagle" and John Philip Sousa's "Stars and Stripes Forever."

It's safe to say that the diversity of the band's music reflected their personal beliefs. "You always have to sing and play from your heart," said Raymond W. "I could never be Bill Monroe or Jim McReynolds.

You have to play in your own style. You can be inspired by them, but you have to make the songs your own."[18] If they showcased a variety of musical approaches, however, the majority of the McLains' numbers are still best considered bluegrass. They performed a number of Bill Monroe songs ("Footprints in the Snow," "Rose of Old Kentucky," "Kentucky Waltz," "Blue Moon of Kentucky") through the years, and while he sometimes employed old-time clawhammer style, Raymond W.'s three-finger banjo usually dominated proceedings. A good many of their original pieces were performed in straight bluegrass manner: "Silver Creek," "Raymond's Breakdown," "On the Road," and "Troublesome Creek." Numerous traditional pieces from their repertoire, like "Shuckin' the Corn," "Two Dollar Bill," and "Rabbit in a Log," also qualify strictly as bluegrass.

The father of bluegrass music, Bill Monroe, was quite fond of the McLains and consistently lent them his considerable support during their career. "I remember how he felt about the McLain Family Band," says Sharon White. "He always invited them to be part of the big finale. We could tell he loved to see Raymond play; he loved to see those girls sing and play."[19] And yet, as Tim Stafford observed earlier, the McLains were so much more than simply a bluegrass band. Writing about the group for the *New York Times*, George Vecsey echoes Stafford's sentiments. "One of the most impressive things about the McLains is their big appeal to audiences who would not usually like bluegrass music. For sheer exuberance and inventiveness, they come closer to Paul McCartney than to Merle Haggard."[20]

Sharon White notes that the McLains kept her excited about what bluegrass music could be. "You'd be at a bluegrass festival and every band would be doing their version of the same stuff, and then they'd do something like 'Stars and Stripes.' That kept me excited. They were the original change of pace band."[21] Rhonda Vincent agrees. When asked to describe the group, she says, "The first thing that comes to mind is uniqueness. You didn't know what type of song they might sing. I don't think there was anything that was off limits. They weren't like anyone else. When you heard them you knew it was the McLain Family Band. And that's something that influenced me. I loved that they did not just follow the path."[22]

A LIGHTER APPROACH TO BLUEGRASS

While critics and reviewers generally were full of praise for the McLain Family Band, at times they questioned how well their approach fit into a genre known for its rather doleful songs. In her treatment of women in bluegrass music, *Pretty Good for a Girl*, Murphy Hicks Henry acknowledges this apparent shortcoming. One critic, she notes, wrote of "the complete lack of pain and intensity" in their music.[23] Another stated that even their sad songs sounded happy and that they lacked a certain edge. Henry nicely summarizes two ways to view this issue, quoting John Hartley Fox's claim that "the dark and haunted side of bluegrass is completely absent from the music of the McLain Family; some people see this as a plus, others as a minus."[24] Certainly most listeners understand that there is no prescribed approach to any genre of music. Individual practitioners are welcome to perform the music as they see fit, taking advantage of natural inclinations to present a genuine and heartfelt product. And while the McLains may have struck some as rather too cheerful, such criticisms ignore the fact that their repertoire also included performances as moving and powerful as any of their peers. Here one can point to traditional pieces like "Fair and Tender Ladies," but more particularly to original·compositions like "Let Time Walk By," "Kentucky Wind," "Our Song," and especially the achingly emotional "Sail Away."

Indeed, pieces written by Raymond W., Ruth, Raymond K., and his sister Rosemary constitute the best of their repertoire and are an important ingredient to their status as bluegrass innovators. In a genre known—and even occasionally lampooned for—its somewhat gloomy lyrics, these original songs present an alternative approach. While a more in-depth treatment of these numbers follows in the ensuing chapters, it is prudent to cite a few examples here. "Wild Honey" acknowledges the risks but concentrates on the rewards of harvesting the by-products of industrious bees. "Come On Out Tonight" is a joyous invitation to a country hoedown, citing numerous homespun reasons to abandon one's cares and hit the dance floor. "You're Why I Try" is dedicated to the many people behind the scenes who make professional performance of music possible, calling them as it does "my reason for pleasing." "Take One Step at a Time" is a gospel number with an infectious beat whose inspirational sentiment to confront life's problems in small segments would appeal to the stoutest unbeliever. "Can't We Get Together Once Again?" is a song with considerable appeal to every performer who has ever trod the boards, granting the sadness felt at the end of an appearance but simultaneously anticipating the next time musician and audience will become one.

It is perhaps in Raymond K.'s three tributes to music, however, that the McLains' uniquely sunny views are best shown. "Foolish Pleasure" notes that "wild harmonies we never learned in school" account for the narrator's gleeful admission that when it comes to playing music, he's "an ever-ready fool." "You Sing for Me" states a universal truth: "It takes sweet music every day to keep those lonesome blues away." "My Name's Music" invites its listeners to "enter if you dare this sensuous affair" known as music. As Rhonda Vincent notes, "The McLains created their own style, their own songs, and they're some of the most unique songs you've ever heard." [25]

THE MCLAINS IN THE EXISTING LITERATURE

The McLains' eclectic approach to their music may be one reason why they have been given relatively short shrift in the literature. Music critics often ignore groups whose work is not easily categorized. Neil Rosenberg's *Bluegrass: A History* is often regarded as the most comprehensive and influential work on the genre. His book covers every important figure in rich detail but makes only brief mention of the McLains' pioneering role in performing with orchestras and their family band festival.

A Bluegrass Odyssey by Carl Fleischhauer is mainly a pictorial work, but its brief sections of text by coauthor Neil Rosenberg are thoughtful and include an excellent discussion of family bands. Again, the McLains are briefly discussed, and Raymond K. is pictured twice. In two works, Stephanie Ledgin gives the band their due by going into greater detail. In her *Homegrown Music: Discovering Bluegrass*, she discusses the McLains' international tours, their forays into classical music, and Raymond W.'s work as a teacher at Eastern Tennessee State University. Ledgin's *From Every Stage: Images of America's Roots Music* mentions the band a half-dozen times and includes a picture of them in performance. Marilyn Kochman's section on the band in her *Big Book of Bluegrass* constitutes the longest treatment of the McLains in published books. Here the band is given free rein to discuss everything from how they arrange their material to which make of instrument they favor.

In the above-mentioned *Pretty Good for a Girl: Women in Bluegrass Music*, Murphy Henry includes a short chapter on the contributions of Alice, Ruth, and Nancy Ann McLain. In a work of great interest to anyone with even a passing interest in the genre, she documents the lives of more than seventy female performers, many of whom have hitherto been neglected. Henry's book is a wonderful reminder that contemporary stars such as Alison Krauss and Rhonda Vincent did not emerge from a vacuum, and that the McLain sisters were in the vanguard of the inclusion of women in bluegrass music.

The McLains figure more heavily in the periodical literature. *Bluegrass Unlimited*, generally recognized as the genre's most influential journal, has published four articles on the band over the years, the most important of which are Marty Godbey's lengthy 1981 profile and Chandler Davis's 1972 cover article that served to introduce the band to the bluegrass world. Short pieces on the group also appeared in *Frets* and *Pickin'*, while dozens of newspapers wrote stories about the band when they came to town.

In 2017 the McLains published a pictorial history of the group titled *The McLain Family Band: 50 Years of Music*. The book, distributed by the Berea College Printing Services, includes an introduction by Sharon White and short essays that describe individual family members, the band's beginnings, its foreign tours, its performances with symphony orchestras, and the family band festival the McLains hosted at their farm for eleven years. The heart of the work, though, is a vast collection of photographs that shows the group performing by themselves and together with musicians including Bill Monroe, Jean Ritchie, and Ricky Skaggs. Shots of the McLains with the likes of Walter Cronkite and Phyllis George indicate that their notoriety extended beyond the world of music. This pictorial history forms an introduction of sorts to my project.

Here I attempt to better acquaint readers with a group of individuals who have entertained audiences the world over for more than half a century. While certainly a popular group, the McLain Family Band deserves even greater exposure than they have received to date. It is my hope not only that this work will remind existing fans of the unique charm they brought to their albums and concerts, but that it will introduce lovers of all kinds of music to performers whose spirit expanded the reach of bluegrass and brought joy to all those fortunate enough to have heard them.

CHAPTER 1

Beginnings

⟐•◆•⟐

s he stood in the wings at Carnegie Hall in 1982, waiting to take the stage with his family band, Raymond K. McLain found himself reflecting on a far different evening. Shortly after celebrating Christmas with his family in 1968, he had driven from his home in Hindman, Kentucky, to serve as music director for the weeklong Christmas Country Dance School in Berea. After playing for the final dance on New Year's Eve, McLain received a phone call informing him that the family home in Hindman was in flames. He returned to find the house in ruins, ravaged by fire.

Years later, his son Raymond W. recalled the events of that momentous evening.[1] Initially he and his mother believed they could contain the blaze themselves and called neighbor Luther Bentley for assistance. They quickly realized, however, that additional help would be required. The fire had spread from the laundry room to other areas in the house. Soon the entire family was in action. Barefoot and in pajamas, twelve-year-old Alice McLain and her younger sister Ruth hurried to escort the youngest members of the household, Nancy Ann and Michael, outside. Raymond W. grabbed a pile of instruments still stacked by the door from the group's last show and joined his siblings. Looking back at the house from safety, they could see that flames were already issuing out of the upstairs windows.

Hindman had only recently established a fire department. The McLain fire would, in fact, be the first one they faced. The outdated fire truck had trouble starting, and once it did, the vehicle stalled in the creek near the home. The volunteers labored to push the vehicle through the water. To make matters worse, the crew discovered that the hoses had frozen to the side of the truck. Once everything was finally in place, it was too late to save the house. The fire crew was able, however, to stop the conflagration from spreading to the out-buildings and nearby woods. Besides the instruments Raymond W. had managed to salvage, none of the family's possessions were saved. The house was a complete loss.

"All we got out of there was ourselves and our instruments," Raymond K. remembered. "We thought it was terrible then, but we realize now that we got out all the things that really counted for us."[2] Faced with such adversity, many families would have struggled to regain their equilibrium. The McLains regrouped immediately, though. The very next evening they performed on their weekly WKHY-TV program, their smiles masking the pain they must have felt. Such resilience and calm typified the group and, in many ways, reflected the family heritage. After all, Raymond K.'s father, Raymond F. McLain, had faced even graver crises.

In 1956, Raymond Francis McLain, then president of the American University in Cairo (AUC), found himself in the middle of the Suez Canal crisis. Israel, allied with British and French forces, was attempting to seize control of the canal and topple Egyptian president Nasser's government after Nasser had asserted the right of his country to control the waterway, a vital link between the Mediterranean Sea and the Indian Ocean. The United States, the Soviet Union, Great Britain, and France all had strategic interests in the Canal Zone, and as tensions grew, the American Embassy on October 23 advised all American employees at AUC to evacuate. Many AUC faculty questioned the necessity of the edict, but on October 30, Raymond F. strongly urged "all Western staff to avail themselves of the evacuation facilities arranged by the embassy."[3] On October 31, French and British planes began dropping bombs on Cairo, destroying the airport, a major hospital, and the war college. The following day nearly 1,500 evacuees boarded the USS *von Chilton*, escorted by a naval destroyer. After the *von Chilton* docked in Naples, the AUC staff traveled to Geneva, where they opened a "university in exile."[4] Once he knew his faculty and staff were safe, Raymond F. and his wife, Beatrice, chose to remain in Cairo. A ceasefire was declared on November 7. As the country struggled to return to normal, the university did what it could to help. A blood donation program was organized, and President McLain made the first contribution.[5]

Before assuming his post at AUC in 1955, McLain had already enjoyed a successful career, serving in a number of leadership roles. Born in 1905, he became president of Eureka College (Eureka, Illinois) at the age of thirty-one. In 1939, McLain moved on to the presidency of Transylvania University, a private institution in Lexington, Kentucky. During his twelve years there, he strengthened the university both academically and financially. Transylvania's link to the Disciples of Christ made it a good fit for McLain, who was raised in that branch of Protestant Christianity and had pastored several churches in Ohio earlier in his career.

After leaving Transylvania in 1951, McLain became the first president of the Henry Clay Foundation, an organization established to promote and ensure the legacy of its namesake. McLain's next role was as general director of the Committee on Higher Education of the National Council of Churches. One of his most important contributions to this organization was to direct a project designed to examine the philosophical underpinnings of Christian higher education.

When the presidency of AUC became vacant in 1954, McLain was one of many candidates considered for the position. On first becoming acquainted with the institution, Raymond F. was a bit wary. Although he felt that "given the right circumstances, . . . AUC can continue to be of (and perhaps extend) tremendous significance in the Middle East and therefore . . . in the world at large,"[6] he also found the university's character a bit uncertain and not fully established. Was it secular, he wondered, or was it more of a missionary school?[7] It had been founded in 1919 by Americans who wanted to further education and service in Egypt. Its first president, Dr. Charles A. Watson, established the institution as both a prep school and a university. Initially open only to men, Watson allowed women to enroll in 1928. Though the school had expanded over the years, AUC's financial condition also concerned McLain. Still, the positives outweighed the negatives, and when the Board of Trustees offered McLain the position in January 1955, he accepted.[8] AUC's executive secretary, Ward Madison, found the McLains "very genuine people, not at all flashy."[9] In his history of the university, Lawrence Murphy paints a glowing portrait of McLain. "The new president's warm, polite manner won him numerous friends and a local reputation as a sensitive, compassionate man, and a superb host."[10]

In his nine years at AUC, McLain accomplished a great deal. Most importantly, he shored up the institution's finances. After the Suez crisis, contributions by American supporters had dropped precipitously, but McLain was able to restore their confidence during his tenure. He also made major revisions to what we today would call the university's mission statement. Believing that the Board of Trustees, many of whom had never seen the campus, needed to become more familiar with the institution they helped govern, in 1958 McLain convinced them to meet on-site in Cairo for the first time. According to Murphy, "The meeting was a spectacular success, infusing trustees with a more hopeful spirit and increasing their understanding of the environment in which the school operated. A series of presentations show how much the McLain administration has accomplished."[11] Finally, McLain made structural changes to the institution's organization, consolidating disparate branches and making the university more cohesive and efficient. During this time, the McLains did not forget their Kentucky roots, even bringing renowned Kentucky author Jesse Stuart to Cairo for a year as visiting artist and lecturer.

In 1962, while en route from Cairo to the United States on a fund-raising trip, McLain suffered a heart attack. These health concerns, coupled with frustrations with the State Department's limited funding of AUC, led McLain to resign as president in 1963. He remained as chancellor until 1965, before returning stateside to become dean of International Programs and vice president of Academic Affairs at the University of Alabama in 1967. Besides his administrative duties, Raymond F. also taught a printing class at Alabama, instructing others in a craft he had practiced for years and would later put to use on McLain Family Band album covers.

Wherever he went, Raymond F. was ably assisted by his wife Beatrice, known to the family and friends as "Bicky." At AUC, McLain appointed his wife dean of Student Affairs. "Through hard work and boundless enthusiasm," Murphy writes, "she developed many important, popular student services: she scheduled regular social events, established counseling and advising programs, and introduced new scholarship programs."[12] At the University of Alabama, Bicky put her experiences in Egypt to good use by serving as a foreign student advisor. When Bicky died in 2004 at the age of ninety-eight, numerous former students whose lives she had touched came forward to testify to her qualities. John Bealle wrote, "It is impossible to overstate how remarkable she was during her time at the University of Alabama. There was no one remotely like her, and she had a profound influence on all those with whom she came in contact. I know all of her students feel that way."[13] Debbie Boykin echoes Bealle's words: "Not only was she a challenging, rigorous teacher, but she took the time to know me as a human being as well as a student. She was also the first person who encouraged me to play music with other people, giving me one of the great pleasures of my life."[14]

Folk music and folk dancing were integral parts of Bicky's life. While in Alabama she also worked as director of the Center for Southern Regional Folklife Studies. She had been an acclaimed folklorist for years and relied on her experiences to help lend the center new leadership. A longtime member of the International Folk Music Council, she accompanied a group of dancers to a festival in England and continued to work actively with the English Folk Dance and Song Society for many years. Her connections there proved vital to the McLain Family Band's 1974 tour of the United Kingdom.[15]

Raymond F. and Bicky had two children: Raymond Kane, born on April 18, 1928, in Alliance, Ohio, and Rosemary, born on July 12, 1934. Rosemary would eventually become a very important part of the McLain Family Band's success, writing many of their best-known songs and giving the group the advantage of having original and age-appropriate material in their repertoire from the very beginning.

Like his father, Raymond K. knew how to take charge of any situation and never lacked direction. He received a BA in music theory from Denison University in 1950, before pursuing graduate work at Harvard (in music composition) and the University of North Carolina (in folklore).

Though he did not finish advanced degrees at either institution, McLain did publish two books after his formal education ended. In 1955, Schirmer issued his *Come, the Recorders*, a collection of pieces arranged for soprano, alto, tenor, and bass recorders. Of the thirty-five pieces included, five ("Slow Piece," "Matthew, Mark, Luke and John," "Over the Water," "There Was a Piper," and "A Cat Came A-Fiddling") were Raymond K.'s original compositions. In 1957, Raymond K. served as one of four coeditors for a collection of regional folk songs titled *Songs of All Time*. Published in conjunction with the Council of the Southern Mountains, the work contains lyrics and basic musical notation for favorites such as "Cock Robin," "Frog Went A-Courting," and "Lonesome Valley." In its early days, the McLain Family Band performed many of these songs, and they eventually recorded another selection from the book, "Shady Grove," on 1978's *Family Album*.

Mary Elizabeth (Betty) Winslow was born in Chicago on November 8, 1928, the daughter of Charles Gilbert Winslow and Mary Lucette Grannis VanBrunt. She grew up in Wisconsin and as a girl took eight years of piano lessons. Her musical studies, however, were hindered by hearing difficulties, the result of a bout with scarlet fever. Graduating from Oberlin College with a degree in psychology, Betty hoped to find work related to recreation or social work. She learned of a position as recreation director at the Hindman Settlement School in Hindman, Kentucky, and was hired for the job. Part of her duties there included going to nearby communities to organize activities, games, relays, and folk dancing in schoolhouses. To learn more about folk dancing, Betty attended Berea College's Christmas Country Dance School, but it was while dancing at the Craftman's Fair in Gatlinburg, Tennessee, that Betty first met Raymond K. They became friends through their shared interest in folk dancing, and eventually their relationship blossomed into love. After being drafted, Raymond K. was stationed at Fort Sam Houston near San Antonio, Texas. Betty moved to San Antonio to be nearby and got a job as program director for teens at the local YWCA. While still in Texas, Raymond K. and Betty were married on December 27, 1952, before returning to North Carolina so that he could continue with his master's studies.

Raymond Winslow McLain was born on December 18, 1953, and shortly thereafter Raymond K. and Betty decided to move their young family to Hindman, where she had so greatly enjoyed working. The Settlement School was far from unknown to her husband, too. When his father had been president at Transylvania, Raymond K. had visited Hindman, and memories of its charm lingered. Though he had been chided by one of his professors for creating compositions that too closely resembled folk music, McLain realized that this "lesser" branch of music was where his true passion lay. His interest in folk music motivated him to explore its roots, and what better way to continue his research than to move to the region and immerse himself in its culture? When Betty's old position as recreation director at Hindman became vacant, Raymond K. applied for and won the post.

The first school of its kind in the region, Hindman was established in 1902 by May Stone and Katherine Pettit. Besides offering area children an education, Hindman also provided rudimentary health care and social services. Its general goals were "to reform mountain education and to initiate a broad range of programs like those offered in the northern settlement houses."[16] Today its mission remains to "provide education and service opportunities for people of the mountains, while keeping them mindful of their heritage."[17] As its reputation grew and needs in the area evolved, the Settlement School also hosted countless workshops on a wide array of topics for those interested in Appalachian art, culture, and literature.

In the years that followed at the Settlement School, the McLain family grew to include four other children. Rose Alice arrived on August 14, 1956; Ruth Helen on May 18, 1958; Nancy Ann on January 8, 1965; and Michael Kane on March 20, 1967.[18] Raymond K. never forced the children to play music, but they came by it willingly and naturally. Their father's relaxed attitude to music no doubt contributed to the joy each child felt while playing their instruments. "Daddy never put the instruments away," Raymond W. remembered years later.[19] "He always left them out because he wanted us kids to know that the instruments were there to use." From the very beginning, music was a natural part of the children's lives. "My earliest memory," says Raymond W., "is sitting on my dad's lap while he was playing ragtime tunes on the piano. I also remember riding on his shoulders when he would dance sometimes."[20]

Alice also has many clear memories of her childhood and the role music played in it. "At the Hindman Settlement School where we grew up, my dad led the students in dance and music parties every Friday night," she recalls. "And so we were hearing those old songs and dancing traditional mountain dances before we, in fact, could read."[21] Alice remembers how her father would immerse his children in the music of the area, taking them to hear it in many forms and settings. "My parents wanted us to realize how valuable it was. So my parents didn't worry about the fact that there wasn't indoor plumbing."[22] She remembers attending sleepovers where her friends' families might all sleep in one or two rooms together. "They weren't trying to separate us from the culture. They were immersing us and helping us to feel that that was the way people lived. I'm grateful for that. It helps me now that I'm a teacher. It helps me to teach my students that everything has value."[23]

Though Betty was somewhat hard of hearing, she also played an important role in the children's musical upbringing. "What she was singing to us was what was around at that time," Alice says. "They were Ritchie Family songs. They weren't things that her mother would have taught her."[24] It is important to remember that neither Betty nor Raymond K. came from Appalachian families. Their jobs and their interest in the local culture brought them to the region. A memory from Alice's childhood sheds light on this fact. She recalls that in Hindman she had two ways of talking. At home her parents required that she and the rest of the children spoke "the very proper American English," but "when we were at school we needed to speak with a Kentucky accent."[25] The fact that she was not from the area was made clear when she was asked by her teachers to pronounce the word "oil" for the class to hear how it should be spoken. "We were always the outsiders, because in order to really fit you'd needed to be there for generation upon generation. We were not *of* Hindman."[26] According to Ruth, the combination of growing up in the Appalachian Mountains and having parents who had formal educations later became a tremendous advantage for the McLain Family Band. This background helped during many aspects of their career: touring overseas, working with arts councils, performing with orchestras, and later leading and teaching traditional music programs at the university level.

Once they settled in the area, Betty and Raymond K. embraced its culture and made it central to their children's lives. Music was, of course, what they concentrated on, and though gifted with natural talent, the children still had to work hard at mastering their craft. Raymond W. recalls a vibrant music community at Hindman. "In Knott County, we were in the middle of some of the best mountain musicians ever. Fiddler Hiram Stamper and his family were renowned as master players and carriers of ancestral musical traditions. He and Ray Slone's family, Mal and George R. Gibson, Banjo Bill Cornett, Marion Sumner, Morgan and Lee Sexton, Marion Martin, Jack Chaffins, Burl C. Ritchie, Columbus Brewer, Jethro Amburgy, Billy Ray and Gene Triplett, Katie Combs, and the Ritchie family were kind and generous, taking time to teach, inspire and include us."[27]

Alice recalls how family members honed their skills. "Learning to sing on pitch was not something that came really naturally to all of us," Alice admits. "As we were learning to sing, we spent a lot of time with our ears next to the speakers of the phonograph player."[28] The children listened to performers like the Osborne Brothers, trying to hear how Bobby Osborne was singing above his brother. "We were trying to pick out parts," Alice recalls. "We were very earnest about all this!"[29] As often as he could, Raymond K. would also take the children to see performers like Ralph Stanley and Bill Monroe, whether they performed on courthouse steps, at drive-in movie theaters where listeners would use their car headlights to get a better view of the talent, or in more traditional venues.

Throughout his life, Raymond K. often spoke about the pleasures of music. "Making music is a compulsion," he claimed. "It never is a chore to practice, but rather a privilege. I always felt that preparing ourselves as musicians was the best way that I could think of in preparation for an uncertain world."[30] At times, he waxed poetic on the wonder of music. "How do you describe a sunset? You could describe the physical: the sun goes down behind the mountain. But it wouldn't have the effect of the golden glow. So if I were to describe music, I'd talk about the feeling of it."[31] Raymond W. echoes this sentiment. "I was always taught by my father that music is made up of rhythm, harmony, and melody. But the most important ingredient is how music makes you feel."[32] The artistry the McLains brought to their work lends credence to these statements. They did not merely play the right notes at the right time. Their performances showed that music was deep within them, an impulse they could call on and transmit to their audiences.

As Hindman's recreation director, Raymond K. actively promoted the importance of the arts. He knew that a balanced education involved far more than simply mastering reading, writing, and arithmetic. Expanding upon similar initiatives undertaken by his wife during her time at Hindman, Raymond K. promoted folk dancing and ballad singing and worked tirelessly to create opportunities for Hindman students to perform on and off campus. Most appearances were at small venues, but on occasion his students also appeared on far grander stages. In 1964, for example, they appeared at New York's World's Fair.

In an article published in *Mountain Life and Work* in 1958 titled "Folk Music at Hindman," Raymond K. describes the tradition of ballad singing at Hindman, how the school helped to keep this tradition alive, and finally how three famous song collectors visited the school to gather material for their studies. In the early twentieth century, many area residents considered ballad singing a wicked practice, one that certainly did not belong in schools. Hindman founder May Stone, however, actively fought this notion. "Some of the people thought it was wrong to have any kind of music, but 'meetin' house songs.' We forgot about that and asked a boy to bring his banjo and give us some mountain music."[33] Stone encouraged singing most every night. Songs like "Barbara Allen," "The Turkish Lady," "The Brown Girl," "Hiram Hubbard," "Little Oma" (aka "Omie Wise"), "I Wished I Were Some Little Sparrow" (aka "Fair and Tender Ladies"), "Ellen Smith," "Pretty Polly," "Lord Daniel's Wife," "The Drunkard's Dream," and "William Hall" were sung in groups, both a cappella or accompanied by banjo and other instruments.

Olive Dame Campbell (1882–1954) was present at one such gathering in 1907 and heard her first mountain tune. To say it left an impression is to understate the case. Hearing the song led Campbell "deeper into an understanding of much that had been before dark to me."[34] She goes on to create a ringing endorsement of the value of folk songs. "Folk songs have lived so long, shaped by the folk over centuries that they may fairly be said to have come out of the people. They express the people, and for that reason would seem to have lasting values of satisfaction for the people."[35] While lyrics had previously been the major focus of scholarly interest in ballads, Campbell attempted to notate their melodies as well. Inspired by her experience at Hindman, Campbell began collecting lyrics and melodies around the wider region. When she learned that the famed English folk song collector Cecil Sharp was coming to the United States, Campbell presented him with her findings. Though in poor health at this time, Sharp found Campbell's work so inspiring that he made the effort to visit Appalachia several times between 1916 and 1918.

In his 1958 article, Raymond K. quotes Elizabeth Watts's account of Sharp's visit to Hindman. In his view, it was "a memorable incident in the history of the school. The night he came, he told us he was doubtful of finding anything worthwhile in a school that had been established as long as Hindman and that was located in a county seat. . . . His skepticism was an added incentive to us to have as many people sing for him as possible. Sometimes the singers came to the Settlement, and sometimes he went to their homes."[36] With his trusted assistant Maude Karpeles at his side, Sharp coaxed reticent singers to share their songs, and the Settlement schoolchildren also sang for him. To his delight, the children sang complete versions of two ballads of which he had previously heard only portions. One of those who entertained and enlightened Sharp during that visit was Jean Ritchie's older sister, Una.

McLain concludes his article by assuring readers that "to this day the Ballad Group remains a strong organization, enjoying the regular meetings fully as much as the times of participation at a May Day or other celebration. It has been one of the qualities of the Ballad Group that to belong was to share, a version of a song or ballad perhaps, learned at home, continuing the natural process by which this very material has been passed on from its rich beginnings in England, hundreds of years ago."[37]

When Elizabeth Watts retired in 1956, Raymond K. took over as executive director of the Hindman Settlement School. At the time, the campus was in great need of modernization. Just as his father had done at Transylvania and AUC, Raymond K. set to work with great energy and enthusiasm. He led by example, throwing himself into every possible task with gusto and inspiring those around him to emulate their chief. McLain became a local champion for the War on Poverty movement. Lyndon Johnson made this initiative one of the cornerstones of his administration, announcing its formation during his State of the Union address on January 8, 1964. In some ways a continuation of Roosevelt's New Deal ideas, the War on Poverty sought not only to relieve the symptoms of poverty but to help prevent it. Johnson believed the federal government needed to play a larger and more active role in education and health care to improve the plight of the poor. The national poverty rate of 19 percent distressed Johnson, but comparable figures for Appalachian regions were far higher. In 1965, for example, 295 of the 420 counties that make up the Appalachian Regional Commission had poverty rates that far exceeded the national average.[38]

Hindman had long relied on private donations, and McLain increased both the number of donors and the amount of their gifts. Thanks to President Johnson's legislation, however, he was now also able to tap both state and federal money in an effort to rebuild the campus. Most of Hindman's buildings had been built after the fire of 1910 had ravaged the campus and were quite dilapidated. One of McLain's first major projects was to build the May Stone Building. In his history of Hindman, Jess Stoddart states that McLain "presented a plan to build using student labor and his own design. The board approved a plan to start construction with the funds on hand, a departure from past practice."[39] Decisions like this demonstrate Raymond K.'s daring, as well as his firm confidence in the human spirit. Experts and professionals, it seemed, were not always necessary; teamwork and industry were ready substitutes. Begun in 1959, the May Stone Building was ready for occupancy two years later and formally dedicated in 1962. According to Stoddart, "the final audit showed that over one thousand gifts, ranging from a dozen eggs to a $17,500 donation, had paid the building's $95,152 cost."[40]

Never one to let the grass grow under his feet, McLain began work on a second major building before the May Stone project had been completed. He knew that in their reports, accreditors had noted the poor condition of many existing structures on campus. McLain always remained keenly aware of the importance of the school's history to alumni and other potential donors. Thus the new project, dedicated to the industrial arts program, was named for Stone's trusted assistant, Elizabeth Watts. Following the model of the Stone Building, McLain again utilized student labor to help defray costs. Work began in 1963 and was finished within two years. Unlike the earlier project, however, the Watts initiative ran into trouble. Its final cost of $67,381 was almost 50 percent above its original estimate. Raymond K. was forced to ask trustees to realize the necessary $28,000 by selling precious endowment securities.

McLain ran into further difficulties with a third building project. The Eastover Dormitory needed to be replaced. In 1967, McLain proposed that its replacement be named for Katherine Pettit and be placed under the responsibility of a Yale architectural graduate student who had an interest in Appalachia. In this instance, McLain's innovative ideas and trust in mankind proved costly. The inexperienced architect's plans ran behind schedule and included significant engineering mistakes. Two years after work had begun, a good deal of money had been spent, but the new dorm was still far from ready. The design proved too complicated for students to complete, and the project was turned over to professional builders. Needless to say, this spiked costs. By the time the building was finally complete, the budget had been exceeded and school trustees, including board president Yancy Altsheler, were unhappy.

Despite such occasional missteps, Raymond K. proved very much his father's son, meeting challenges directly and making bold innovations. In 1968, in fact, he made his father a member of Hindman's Board of Trustees. Earlier in his tenure, Raymond K. had followed his father's AUC example by revamping the school's Board of Trustees—expanding it from eight to fourteen members— and, in another move that paralleled his father's time in Egypt, he convinced the board to meet on-site in Hindman instead of at an off-campus location as had previously been the practice. Finally, in an effort to promote subsidiarity within the group, McLain added two Settlement School graduates to the board.

It was also at Hindman that the McLain Family Band was formed. Music had always been part of life for the McLain family. "There weren't many outside activities," Betty recalled. "I often felt when these three [Raymond W., Alice, and Ruth] were preschoolers that if they were going to have anything—if they were going to know anything, I had to teach it to them. I'd play what poor piano I could, but they didn't know the difference and we'd sing nursery rhymes and I'd read nursery stories to them."[41]

Alice provides details. "If you have instruments around, people are more likely to play them, and Daddy had instruments around for us and so it kind of made it a natural thing. And we had other friends who were also playing music. We played at home a lot. It was much easier for us to have the time to spend together and sing. I know that's why Jean Ritchie's family sang together. They would work together, and then they sang together on the front porch. Well, we weren't working out in the fields, but we would come home from school and we'd sing and we'd make our own entertainment."[42] Ruth echoes these views. "One reason that the tradition and the culture stayed so much longer in that area of the country was because there weren't a lot of other things to do, a lot of other distractions like television or movies."[43]

Raymond W. recalls some of his first musical experiences in Hindman. "The first time I remember seriously thinking that I was going to try to play something was when I was nine. A friend had left her bass at our house, and Daddy said, 'Now this is the D string and this is the A string.' I think maybe we played 'Chinese Breakdown' or something like that you could play on open strings. And I just started playing with him. He was on the accordion. For several years we played, sometimes just the two of us, but sometimes with other people too, for dances around various places."[44]

In Hindman, before the McLain Family Band was formally established, Raymond W. played guitar with a friend, Mark Baker, and together they formed a group called the Grasshoppers. He and his father would also play with Burl C. Ritchie and his wife, Veda, and Columbus Brewer and his family. Since the Perry Furniture Company sponsored the radio show on which they soon began performing, the group became known as Burl and Chris and the Perry Mountain Boys.

When he was fourteen, Raymond also took up the banjo. His first five-string was so battered that playing it entailed some challenges. "It was nearly impossible to play," he recalled years later. "So Daddy and I figured we could loosen the strings and bend the neck back, stick a pencil in between the neck and the rim of the banjo, then tighten it back up, the action would be pretty good—for a couple of days, until the pencil broke. Then you'd have to put a new pencil in!"[45] Columbus Brewer and Katie Combs gave Raymond W. his first lessons on the instrument, but it took the young musician quite some time to find his feet as a picker. "I was playing at jam sessions. I was jumping in with both feet without having the first idea of how to play the break. Daddy and I were working at home, working out breaks for various songs we were doing for shows, and we—well, Daddy—always knew the value of playing the tune. That's a wonderful lesson for any musician to take to heart. Daddy always said, 'Raymond, I can't hear the tune.' And I would say something like 'Don't you like this lick I'm playing?' And he would say 'Let me hear you play the tune first. Then if you want to play something else, you may. But I've got to hear the tune so that you don't end up just playing that fancy lick, because you don't know where the tune is.' It was a wonderful lesson."[46]

Like Alice, Raymond W. remembers listening to a good many LPs during this period. "We listened to records a lot, slowing them down to half speed. If you slow them down to half speed on a tape recording it comes out exactly an octave lower, but you can stop it and start it easily so you can get just whatever little part you want to at a time. I learned a lot of things that way."[47] Watching live performances also provided plenty of inspiration. Ralph Stanley often played nearby, as did Hylo Brown and Flatt and Scruggs.

Don Reno and Sonny Osborne also impressed young Raymond W. "Don was a powerful influence, especially in his creativity. Because Don didn't have any qualms about playing something differently than someone else did, and by playing tunes that no one else had ever played on the banjo before. . . . It was wonderful to have a role model like that, who was not tied to a particular body of material. And Sonny Osborne was another wonderful influence, too, in that same way; playing what he felt and playing what worked."[48] Such early lessons from these established role models certainly paved the way for the family's inclination to experiment and expand the boundaries of traditional bluegrass music.

At this stage of the children's development, Raymond K. made a key decision: he would not teach them formal musical notation. Years later he revealed his rationale. "There are great advantages, of course, in reading music, but there are also advantages in not reading music. A literate man can read many things that other people have done, but an illiterate man is forced to rely heavily on his memory and his inventions and cleverness. The same thing holds true for reading music. If you don't read music, why, you remember more, you invent more readily, and you're not bound by the conventions of the music literacy of the music notation system. It's a confining system at best. You can't really take lessons in this kind of music."[49] The eventual abilities of his children to improvise and take their music in new and unexpected directions prove that Raymond K.'s philosophy was well founded.

It may surprise fans of the group to learn that they did not begin as a band devoted strictly to bluegrass and old-time music. While songs like "Frog Went A-Courting" were certainly some of the earliest songs the family played together, they also played ragtime selections and hits by contemporary pop groups like the Beatles and Three Dog Night. Indeed, the first single the band ever recorded (under the group name the Bluegrass State) was "Charlie Brown," by the rhythm and blues group, the Coasters. Still, it soon became clear that Raymond K.'s heart lay with the music native to his adopted region of the country. His children found the music came naturally to them as well. "We had the advantage of growing up in an area surrounded by this treasure of deep rich culture of traditional music," Alice recalls. "It's a really unique and special way to grow up."[50]

During this period, the McLains became friends with a number of famous musicians. Charlie Waller of the Country Gentlemen was so close to the family that he entrusted his son to them for one summer when his group was on the road. The McLains also rubbed shoulders with Don Reno, Red Smiley, Bill Harrell, the Osborne Brothers, Jim and Jesse, Lester Flatt, the Lewis Family, the Goins Brothers, Ralph Stanley, Ricky Skaggs, Marty Stuart, and Bill Monroe. The very founder of bluegrass music also took the fledgling band under his wing. "Bill Monroe loved to bring us up on stage with him," Alice remembers. "He was really proud of the fact that he could bring us up and we were singing harmony with him and we could get up above him."[51]

Alice and Ruth also grew particularly close to Sharon and Cheryl White. At the time it was still rather uncommon for women to be performing in bluegrass bands. "No one else of our age was doing what we were," Alice says. "We were in a man's world, largely. There were very few women that were performing, and those that were had often a kind of an edge. Those times had to be rough."[52] Gloria Belle was one such female pioneer. Born in 1939, she is recognized by many as the first female lead singer in the genre. Though she started performing in 1957, Belle had her heyday singing with Jimmy Martin's Sunny Mountain Boys in the late sixties and early seventies.

Besides the White sisters, Alice and Ruth became friends with other female musicians of the time, including members of the Sullivan Family, Lewis Family, Marshall Family, and Calton Family from Missouri. Still, they did not feel excluded by male performers. "We got so much support. Maybe because we were younger. They couldn't help but notice that we were in the front grinning at them as they were performing. They couldn't help but see that we were major fans! And that we were studying what they were doing with an intensity that maybe other women weren't."[53]

Though the children's talents were quickly maturing, they recognized that having chops and being a good band weren't necessarily the same thing. Raymond W. explains: "Well, we realized that if we wanted to be a successful band, and wanted to pursue this as a profession (which we didn't know we were going to do at the beginning), that we were going to have to be distinctive and different. The first things we noticed as we went to our first festival was that the amateur bands playing all sounded like one or another of the important bands, the professional bands. The professionals all sounded distinctly different from the other. You could tell instantly almost whether it was Bill Monroe, Reno and Smiley and Harrell, or Ralph Stanley or Jimmy Martin, or Jim and Jesse, or the Osborne Brothers."[54] Such testimony, of course, helps to explain the formation of the McLain Family Band's unique sound.

Naturally the band's first venues were quite small. In those early days, the group performed at places like Uncle Charlie's Meat Packing Company, the local bank's Christmas party, and Lees Junior College in Jackson, Kentucky. Word of their precocious talent spread quickly throughout the region. Soon a local TV station, WKYH in Hazard, expressed interest in offering them their own show. "We started when we were in Hindman, and from very early on we were doing three shows a week," Alice recalls.[55] "We were playing at the Pike County Jamboree on Saturday night, and at Jenny Wiley State Park on Sunday afternoon, and then we were playing in Hazard for WKYH TV. They had only one guy, Chuck Rucker, that was in the control room and also on camera and he would run back-and-forth between them. He didn't have a dolly on which to put the camera, so he would set it on a ladder and get it set for us and run back in the control room and push the button."[56] Ruth takes up the story. "It was the late sixties, and the studio was up the hill where the transmitter also was. During our first show, Bill Gorman, the station owner, came driving up the hill and offered us a fifty-year contract."[57] Friends of the family would occasionally appear on the show, which ran for nearly two years. Sometimes others would appear. Ruth explains: "One time we had Bill Monroe and his band on the show. He was hosting a festival in Jackson and he came in as a guest."[58] That Monroe took the still embryonic band seriously enough to hire them to play at his festivals and to guest on their show indicates how well they could play from an early age.

With the family band progressing by leaps and bounds, Raymond K. began to reexamine his duties at Hindman. His years there had been highly productive. In addition to his building projects, McLain had doubled the number of boarding students, reduced the work responsibility of students so that they might better concentrate on academics, raised the profile of the school by bringing musical and dance performances to national stages, made necessary changes to the daily operations of the school, and increased its donor base significantly. But a new adventure beckoned that possessed great appeal. Dr. Loyal Jones, a member of the English department at Berea College, had recently been given the opportunity to establish an Appalachian Center there. Jones knew Raymond K. both as the author of *Songs of All Times* and as someone who had enthusiastically emphasized the cultural treasures of the mountains in his time at Hindman. Jones had heard the nascent family band perform on a number of occasions and sensed an opportunity. He was convinced that McLain was the right man to formally instruct students in the basics of bluegrass music. The idea was entirely new and entailed some risks. Did such music lend itself to formal instruction, especially at the college level? Would enough students be attracted to traditional music courses to make it financially viable? Despite these concerns, Berea College made the offer, and Raymond K. accepted. A new chapter in the McLains' life was about to begin.

CHAPTER 2

Berea and Beyond

hen Raymond K. accepted Berea College's offer to join its faculty, he had long been familiar with both the city and the institution. While still at Hindman, McLain had been appointed musical director of the Berea College Country Dancers. His mother Beatrice had also enjoyed a long association with the folk dance community, having been one of the founders of the Berea Christmas Country Dance School. The group had begun as an informal organization in the early 1920s before gaining official recognition during the following decade after Berea students and faculty objected to the college's official stance that social dancing was immoral. President William J. Hutchins's decision to lift the ban and afford the group official status came after he enjoyed a performance at the John C. Campbell Folk School in North Carolina. The troupe quickly became popular and sometimes performed at halftime of Berea basketball games. Under the leadership of Ethel Capps, the dancers acquired a reputation not only in Appalachia but also nationally and internationally. In the early 1960s they performed for President Kennedy at the White House and also toured Latin America under the auspices of the U.S. State Department. Raymond K. McLain accompanied the dance group to Washington as music director, playing accordion and recorder on these tours, and the Dancers' international trips may have inspired him to attempt similar ventures with the McLain

Family Band in the 1970s. The McLain Family Band often supplied the accompaniment for the Dancers, as well as contributing to the celebrated Berea Christmas dances.

During his tenure at Hindman, Raymond K. had made frequent trips to Berea to consult with his immediate predecessor, Elizabeth Watts, about Settlement School matters. As Ruth remembered years later, moving to Berea "was an easy transition because we already knew a lot of the people there. It was an easy fit." Alice concurs: "We knew about Berea and I very much wanted to come here. Even as a young child, I thought this would be the ideal place to live."[1]

The McLains had now allied themselves with an extraordinary institution, the first nonsegregated coeducational college in the South. Berea College was founded in 1855 by John Gregg Fee (1816–1901). A slaveholder's son, Fee became a fervent abolitionist and incorporated his beliefs into Berea's mission. Its beginnings were humble: a single-room schoolhouse that doubled as a church. Granted a tract of land by Cassius Marcellus Clay, a fellow abolitionist and politician, Fee dubbed the community Berea after the Macedonian city mentioned in Acts, the fifth book of the New Testament. The apostle Paul famously preached there, finding a receptive audience whose members were "open-minded" and willing to listen. Fee was similarly open-minded. He believed that everyone had a right to an education and demanded that women and men, both white and black, be eligible for admission. Author Shannon Wilson writes that "Fee preached a 'gospel of impartial love' that defined not only the early programs and policies of the college but the emerging village of Berea as well. He envisioned a school that would educate 'not merely in the ordinary branches of learning but in love as first in religion and justice as first in government.' " A sort of breeding ground for reformers, Berea would become what Oberlin was to Ohio: "antislavery, anti-caste, anti-rum, anti-sin."[2]

Fee's strong faith informed his institution's constitution and bylaws. The college would "promote the cause of Christ," and "furnish the facilities for a thorough education to all persons of good and moral character."[3] How, Fee reasoned, could students be excluded if they met this primary consideration? Furthermore, schooling at Berea should be available "at the least possible expense, and all inducements and facilities for manual labor which can reasonably be supplied by the Board of Trustees should be offered."[4]

Berea began as a preparatory school, and precollege courses continued to be offered until 1968. By 1866, the institution had fulfilled its founder's vision: in the year following the end of the Civil War, more than half its students were black. The institution awarded its first bachelor's degrees seven years later. In 1904, three years after Fee's death, Berea lost its status as a desegregated institution when the so-called Day Law (named after Carl Day, who introduced the bill) took effect. Berea objected, taking its case first to the Kentucky Court of Appeal and then to the Supreme Court in 1908. After both appeals failed, Berea trustees established the Lincoln Institute near Louisville in order to continue to educate black students. By 1950, the law had been amended to allow colleges to integrate, and Berea was able to return to its original vision.

In order to carry out its mission, Berea now relies on an endowment of more than $1 billion. This foundation allows the college the unique distinction of requiring no annual tuition fees. Instead, every student must work at least ten hours a week on campus. While most of these jobs are service-oriented, many Berea students create arts and crafts typical of the region, including weaving and woodworking. Thousands of visitors flock annually to the Berea craft store, and its mail order business is also robust. Although it reserves the right to grant exceptions, Berea generally admits only students from families whose income is in the bottom 40 percent of American households.

From its inception, Berea recognized the importance of serving students, both white and black, from the Appalachian region. In 1895, President William Goodell Frost began strengthening its extension programs to "mountain people" (as they were referred to in Berea literature). "Professors traveled in the mountains," Wilson writes, "offering lectures on selected topics such as mountain agriculture, temperance, health and sanitation, rural schools, and forestry."[5] The president's wife, Eleanor Frost, traveled the mountains on horseback, noting ways Berea might help improve the quality of life for area residents, while also gaining a firm admiration for the industry of mountain women. The aim of such visits was twofold: to provide immediate advice and help to the people and also to promote the college and recruit students. These efforts made such an impression on both faculty and administrators that in 1911 the trustees changed its constitution to designate Appalachia as the school's "sole field of service."[6]

During President Hutchins' administration (1920–1939), these efforts continued. The Southern Appalachian Studies Project, spearheaded by future Berea president Willis D. Weatherford, updated previous work. If significant challenges remained, Berea was convinced that educating the area's native population was the best way to address them. "Berea's high ideals were summarized in what Hutchins and others termed 'the Berea idea.' There was no apology," Wilson writes, "for the apparent tension between the liberal arts and professional preparation found in the degree programs of Business, Agriculture, Nursing, Home Economics, and Industrial Arts."[7] By the second decade of the twenty-first century, nearly three-quarters of the annual incoming class stemmed from Appalachia.

The year 1970, Raymond K. McLain's first at Berea, saw other new beginnings at the institution. When McLain arrived, the college had just adopted a new curriculum designed to "maintain the connections between the general education and the specialization found in the student's chosen major."[8] That same year, Berea's Appalachian Center was created. Loyal Jones, a Berea graduate and former executive director of the Council of the Southern Mountains, led the initiative. Besides recommending McLain as a valuable addition to the Berea faculty, Jones also established the Appalachian Sound Archive and a traditional music festival there. Seven years after founding the event, Jones helped organize the first Appalachian Studies Conference, now known as the Appalachian Studies Association.

If Berea's commitment to Appalachia was well founded, it had not always granted much attention to the music of the region or considered including it in the curriculum. "When Cecil Sharp, the famous song collector from England, visited Berea in 1917, he was discouraged to find that 'the singing of traditional songs was apt to be despised as belonging to a past and discarded mode of existence.' "[9] Before Raymond K.'s arrival, Berea's music department had concentrated on teaching Western classical music. When he arrived at Berea, McLain found himself in a challenging position. There was little precedent for him to follow. Bluegrass music had never before been taught for credit at an institution of higher education, and although it took him several years to develop a class specifically devoted to this musical genre, Raymond K. laid the groundwork by teaching folk music history and Appalachian music courses.

In order to put Raymond K.'s contributions to bluegrass music education in proper context, it is first necessary to review how music found its way into Appalachian classrooms at lower academic levels. Music first became part of American elementary and secondary school curricula in the early nineteenth century. Scholars such as William Channing Woodbridge (1794–1845) and Lowell Mason (1792–1872) observed how music was taught in Europe and began trying to incorporate some of the same ideas and methods in America.

In Appalachia, Katherine Pettit (1868–1936) and Olive Dame Campbell played similar foundational roles. After her work at Hindman, Pettit established the Pine Mountain Settlement School in 1913, where she built upon many of the same ideas she had employed in her work with May Stone. To Pettit, music was an essential part of an Appalachian child's education and helped legitimize the culture of his or her forefathers. In his 1978 publication, *Teaching Mountain Children: Towards a Foundation of Understanding*, David Mielke highlights these efforts, noting the previous "disservice done to Appalachian children by well-meaning teachers who have forsaken teaching Appalachian culture in favor of a kind of 'national cultural amalgam' best described as middle class white suburban values" in an effort to help children rise above their cultural background.[10] The 1907 publication in the *Journal of American Folklore* of many of the ballads Pettit had uncovered reinforced her scholarly reputation and led other folk song collectors like Josephine McGill and Campbell to the region. Campbell, in turn, collaborated with Cecil Sharp to publish the landmark *English Folk Songs from the Southern Appalachians* in 1917, and eight years later she founded the influential John C. Campbell Folk School in Brasstown, North Carolina.

If gradual advances incorporating mountain music into elementary and high school curricula were established in the early twentieth century, efforts to include it at the college level had proven less successful. In the 1940s, music professors began to teach classes on jazz, another form of music established in America, but bluegrass proved a harder sell. Before Raymond K.'s class at Berea, the only comparable course in the curriculum at the university level was Cratis Williams's *Appalachian Ballads and Songs*, taught at Appalachian State Teachers College (now Appalachian State University) in 1943. A sense of elitism may have contributed to the dearth of such courses. Perhaps Loyal Jones, interviewed by Berea graduate Joseph Dinwiddie for his 1998 analysis of his alma mater's traditional music program, puts it best: "Liberal colleges think in terms of elite arts. The only thing I've got against liberal arts is that they aren't very liberal, they are very narrow. Doc Watson and Jean Ritchie are as fine as any artists anywhere."[11] Mike Clark, then director of the famed Highlander Center, echoes Jones' claim. Speaking at Berea in 1973, he claimed "Berea College was founded by missionaries who believed they had a divine purpose to bring enlightenment and education to this rugged land. But education in our society means control, not freedom. It means a way of transferring values from one group to another . . . by teaching students a new set of values, values based on the dominant middle class society."[12]

Though hired as a resident ethnomusicologist, Raymond K. once admitted to a writer penning a profile of the band that he wasn't entirely certain what that term meant. In the same interview, McLain went on to state that the job is "so exciting I can hardly stand it."[13] Juggling the McLain Family Band's performing schedule with his time in the classroom meant that McLain typically taught only one semester per academic year and only two courses per semester. From 1971 through 1979, he taught the following courses: The History of Popular Music, Introduction to Appalachian Studies, Appalachian Music, Materials of Music I and II, and Musical Experience in the Traditional Idiom. This last-named class was described in the Berea College catalog as "a practical course developing musical skills in the performance of folk and popular music." Its stated goals were to refine "the basic elements of musical communication" and inspire creativity "within simple musical forms."

Other courses were more theoretical in nature. Materials of Music I, for example, used the music of the Baroque and Classical periods to stress the analysis of harmony, sight singing, and keyboard skills. Materials of Music II tackled more advanced topics such as "non-harmonic tones, seventh chords, and modulation." While McLain's undergraduate and graduate coursework had prepared him for such formal subject matter, his love of the region to which he had moved made him well suited to teach classes more specific to Berea's mission. Appalachian Music, for instance, emphasized the "formative historic, geographic, and social factors" that shaped bluegrass and folk. Introduction to Appalachian Studies concentrated on other aspects of the region's culture and was "designed to give Appalachian students an opportunity to explore their own identity," while simultaneously gaining a deeper understanding of the values, attitudes, and strengths of those who lived in the district.

Despite these academic-sounding titles, McLain said that "what they are really about is getting together and jamming—playing, feeling, discussing and learning to appreciate folk and bluegrass and country music from a personal as well as an academic viewpoint."[14] Sometimes these courses were even held in the McLains' living room, with Betty providing refreshment for the students while Raymond K. spoke and encouraged his students to put aside their fears and try performing for their peers.

While Raymond K. was establishing himself as a teacher at Berea College, the family band continued to gain valuable experience on the road. Gigs at small local venues remained important, but eventually the group began performing out of state on a more regular basis. Signs of bigger things to come included appearances at the Metropolitan Museum of Art in New York and Chicago's famed Old Town School of Folk Music. In 1973, Bill Monroe invited the band to appear at the Bill Monroe Colorado Bluegrass Music Festival (known later as the Rocky Mountain Bluegrass Festival in Adams County, Colorado) and at his own festival, Bean Blossom. Founded in 1967 as a two-day event and held in Bean Blossom, Indiana, Monroe's festival had quickly become one of the most prestigious of its kind. An appearance there meant a band had made it and was recognized by its peers as belonging to the top echelon of the genre. The festival soon expanded to eight days, and today the venue hosts a number of other events, including a blues festival and a gospel event. The McLain Family Band's initial performance at this mecca was well received, and they began to appear regularly there.

Another indication of the band's growing profile was the publication of a feature article on the group in the October 1972 issue of *Bluegrass Unlimited*, the genre's most well respected journal. Many articles on the band at this time dwelt on their charm, and while the author of the 1972 piece, Chandler Davis, also mentions it, his praise extends far beyond their personalities. "What really makes their music such a delight," he writes, "is their attitude toward it. Music, to the McLains, is not a commodity, but a treasure which exists to be shared—a gift to be given unselfishly, for the pure joy of the giving."[15] Davis is also full of praise for Raymond W.'s banjo playing. He includes a quote from Don Reno, who describes Raymond W. as "one of the most talented young performers in this business. He's going to be up there with the greats one of these days, you mark my words."[16] Davis also recounts some remarkable stories about Ruth, then the youngest and, by his reckoning, toughest member of the band. After the index finger on her left hand was accidentally slammed in a car door, she simply bandaged it up for the next performance and carried on. A mishap with a school locker left her with a damaged little finger, this time shortly before she was due to demonstrate the mountain dulcimer at a church convention in Cincinnati. Undaunted, she kept the date, chording with her two middle fingers.

How Ruth came to play the dulcimer in the first place makes for another interesting story. Organizers for a White House Council on children's music contacted Raymond K., asking if he could provide them a young dulcimer player for the event. After a quick search bore no fruit, McLain simply began teaching Ruth how to play the traditional mountain instrument. Six weeks later she took the stage in the nation's capital on network television, and a picture of her playing the dulcimer graced the cover of the March 1971 issue of the *Music Educators Journal*.

If Monroe's imprimatur and the *Bluegrass Unlimited* article helped to establish the band as performers of note in the United States, their path to Europe started with the Italian composer Gian Carlo Menotti. In 1971, at a performance for the Music Council of the National Endowment for the Arts, Menotti heard the band perform at the Boone Tavern in Berea and was immediately intrigued. Having composed his first opera (*The Death of Pierrot*) at age eleven, Menotti was familiar with young musical prodigies. Born in Italy in 1911, Menotti accompanied his widowed mother to Philadelphia's Curtis Institute of Music at the age of seventeen. There he learned his craft, and before he reached forty Menotti had composed seven operas, including the celebrated Christmas piece, *Amahl and the Night Visitors* (1951). Two of his other works—*The Consul* (1950) and *The Saint of Bleeker Street* (1955)—were awarded the Pulitzer Prize for Music.

In 1958, Menotti founded the Festival dei Due Mondi (Festival of Two Worlds), an event designed to showcase European and American cultures. Enthralled by the McLain Family Band's Berea performance, Menotti approached Raymond K. and invited the band to perform at the music festival he had established in Spoleto, Italy. "I can't pay you much," Raymond W. remembers Menotti prophetically saying, "but it will change your lives."[17] Finances were, indeed, tight. In order to help cover his plane fare to Italy, Raymond W. sold two prized instruments, his RB 250 banjo and a Gibson hollow body electric guitar, for $250 apiece.[18]

The Festival of Two Worlds is held annually. In 1977, Charleston, South Carolina, began hosting the American leg of the festival, though this arrangement lasted only fifteen years due to personality disputes and artistic differences between Menotti and the American festival's directors. After Menotti's death in 2007, Spoleto and Charleston began negotiating to reunite the two cities, and this aim was accomplished in 2008.

In many ways, the McLains were already seasoned performers by the time they traveled to Spoleto in June 1972. The experiences they would have during this first foreign tour, however, confirmed the wisdom of Menotti's statement. They would, indeed, make a difference in their career and their lives. Accompanied by Betty and Bicky, an experienced international traveler, the band arrived on June 27 in order to get acclimated to their new surroundings before their first performance on July 1. Before their initial concert, Menotti met with the band at a nearby castle where he was staying. He had the band run through a few hours of material and then chose which numbers he thought they should perform at the festival. Though this might sound rather high handed, band members report that the famed composer treated them with great kindness and was quite approachable. Alice recalls that after Menotti selected what he considered their most interesting pieces, he asked if anyone had any questions. Raising her hand, Alice said that, yes, she did have one: "Where is the restroom?" Menotti smiled and took her over the marble inlaid floors and up a spiral staircase into a turret where the facilities were located. As if this hadn't been embarrassing enough for fifteen-year-old Alice, she then found she had locked herself in. "He also had to come find me and let me out."[19]

The McLains were billeted in a private home in Spoleto. Raymond W. has fond memories of his grandmother gracefully navigating cobblestone streets in her fashionable high heels. Bicky would get up early to go to the market, returning laden with eggs, tomatoes, cheese, and fresh basil, which became the ingredients for omelets. Alice remembers taking in the sights during this first trip abroad. "We were just kids from Kentucky. We didn't know anybody and were pretty wide eyed."[20] While excited and curious, the teenagers remained grounded and concentrated on staying in the moment. Between walks and sampling Italian fare (including gelato), the band made sure to get plenty of rest in preparation for their upcoming shows. Thoroughly professional from the start, band members knew the primary reason they were overseas. "We knew we had to do our job first,"[21] Alice recalled later. Doing their job brought certain challenges, of course. "Spoleto, Italy, was also the place where our dad taught us how to go to sleep immediately," Alice remembered. "We had a certain amount of time before show time, and he told us 'You *must* sleep.' When our dad told us to do something, we learned how to do it whatever it was."[22] Further describing the rigors of international touring, Alice recalls "getting good at eating when you're not hungry" and "finding a restroom when you don't need to go." In sum, she says, "Spoleto, Italy, taught us a lot of things."[23]

The Spoleto festival was designed to showcase all manner of musical entertainment, and it eventually expanded to include the visual arts and science. Besides the McLains, 1972's other acts included New York's Lar Lubovitch Dance Company and Princeton's Westminster Choir. Menotti's opera *The Consul* and Kurt Weill's *Aufstieg und Fall Der Stadt Mahagonny* were also featured. Dubbed "The McLain Bluegrass Singers," the group appeared on a double bill with Nuova Compagnia di Canto Popolare, a group from Naples that sang Italian folk music from centuries past. To their delight, the band formed an immediate bond with the Neapolitans. The McLains appeared every day from July 1 to July 9, and they were a big hit with the crowds, only 20 percent of whom were Americans. Many European listeners were undoubtedly hearing bluegrass music for the first time; the band's role as bluegrass ambassadors had begun.

Their Spoleto shows led to other appearances in Europe. A representative from America House, a government organization designed to foster understanding between nations, saw their performances in Italy and set about arranging dates in other parts of Europe. They played in five cities in Germany, gracing stages in Hanover, Hamburg, Stuttgart, Essen, and Nuremberg, where fourteen-year-old Ruth was the subject of a playful marriage proposal from a reporter. Her reply, taken from the old folk song "Frog Went A-Courting," was "without my Uncle Rat's consent, I would not marry the President." From Germany the band moved on to Belgium, having been invited to appear there by Josef Nuyens of Westmalle, an international stockbroker, car racer, and musician who had heard the band perform at a festival in Ottawa, Ohio, in 1971. Nuyens arranged for them to perform on Belgium National Radio and to appear at a number of concerts, including a festival of traditional arts in Ghent.

As they traveled from country to country, the band gained confidence in their abilities to meet logistical challenges and learned that one did not necessarily need to know the language to communicate with the locals. Their instruments and their voices bridged all such barriers, and the group began to look at their accomplishments in a new light. Speaking of their time abroad, Alice recalled that "it validated what we were doing. To be recognized as a group from Kentucky, a family group playing music from the Appalachian Mountains, made our dad especially proud."[24] Indeed, the McLain Family Band had come a long way, both literally and figuratively, in the four years they had been playing together. Raymond K. certainly felt deep satisfaction with the band's progress, but even bigger challenges and triumphs awaited the quartet.

CHAPTER 3

All in the Family

F amily acts have deep roots in bluegrass, old-time, and country music. Sharon and Cheryl White believe that harmony singing is a major reason such groups have enjoyed so much success over the years. "Family bands," claims Cheryl, "are notorious for having the closest harmonies because you have the same DNA." Sharon elaborates. "You can listen to any genre of music and hear families sing, and there's a sound, a certain something to it. Something about how their voices sound right together. I think in blending together, you're conscious of the other person singing, too. You try to match dynamically what the other one is doing."[1]

These dynamic harmonies constituted a notable component of many popular brother acts. Before founding his famous Blue Grass Boys, Bill Monroe performed with his sibling, Charlie, as the Monroe Brothers. Other important fraternal pairings include Alton and Rabon Delmore, Ira and Charlie Louvin, Jim and Jesse McReynolds, Ralph and Carter Stanley, Clarence, Roland, and Eric White, and Bobby and Sonny Osborne.

Beginning in the 1950s, a number of important family acts also began to appear in bluegrass circles. Among the most important of these were the Lewis, Cox, Stoneman, White, and Marshall families. Like the McLains, each of these groups featured significant roles for its female members. Though Little Roy Lewis was the undisputed star of the Lewis Family (active from 1951 to 2009), the lead singing and harmony of his sisters Miggie, Janis, and Polly were important in the group's success. Until the Lewises broke such new ground, it was considered damaging to a woman's reputation to be part of the rough and tumble world of bluegrass music. Mainly a gospel act, the Lewis family "grew up in a deeply religious environment where secular songs, especially if sung by women, would have been far too worldly." [2] Much like Betty McLain did later for her family, Mrs. Lewis worked behind the scenes, organizing performance dates, selling merchandise, and fashioning the group's wardrobe. In 2006 the Lewis Family capped their remarkable career by being named to the International Bluegrass Hall of Honor. The McLains enjoyed a close friendship with the Lewis Family over the years. Nancy Ann even wrote a high school term paper about their career, and Ruth composed "I'm Bound for Gloryland" with the Lewis Family in mind and was honored when they included it on their 1978 album, *Wrapped with Grace and Tied with Love*.

The Cox Family from Louisiana also concentrated on celebrating their faith in music and is renowned for its exceptional vocals. Daughter Evelyn plays guitar and is the lead singer, assisted by her sister Suzanne, who began to learn how to sing harmonies at the age of three. Their brother Sidney plays banjo, Dobro, and guitar. Founded in 1976, the group temporarily suspended their act in 2000 but reunited in 2015 to release a new album, *Gone Like the Cotton*.[3] In 1995 the group won a Grammy Award for Best Southern, Country, or Bluegrass Gospel album and received valuable exposure when their recording of "I Am Weary" was included on the best-selling *O Brother Where Art Thou* album.

Following the example set by the Lewis Family and the Cox Family, the Marshall Family also specialized in gospel music. Glen "Chester" Marshall first began playing music with his brother Mennis. Chester married a deeply religious woman, Angeline, and once the couple's children reached young adulthood, they began performing together at local churches as a group. Son David played banjo, and daughter Judy was the group's primary vocalist. A 1974 appearance at Ralph Stanley's Hills of Home Festival kick-started the group's professional career, which, while quite brief, was influential. Like the McLains, the Marshalls composed many of the songs they performed and lent infectious enthusiasm to their performances.

Ernest V. "Pop" Stoneman, originally from Carroll County, Virginia, enjoyed a distinguished career as an old-time musician before forming a family band in the early 1960s that helped to popularize old-time, bluegrass, and country music on the West Coast and included daughters Donna on mandolin and Veronica (Roni) on banjo. The Stonemans enjoyed a series of hits in the sixties, and the Country Music Association named them vocal group of the year in 1967.

The Whites, composed of father Buck White and daughters Sharon and Cheryl, straddled the worlds of bluegrass and country music and enjoyed a string of hits in the 1980s. Buck's wife Pat was originally part of the group as well but retired around the same time the family relocated to Nashville in the early 1970s. The Whites are perhaps best known for Buck's excellent mandolin work and the smooth harmonies his daughters crafted. All three members of the band befriended the McLains as they traveled the circuit together.

Following in the footsteps of these seminal groups are more recently formed family bands, including Cherryholmes and the Wells Family Band.[4] The six-member, Los Angeles–based Cherryholmes family featured mother Sandy Lee and daughters Cia Leigh and Molly Kate. One of the most commercially successful groups of its kind, Cherryholmes won the prestigious IBMA Entertainer of the Year Award in 2005. Less well known was the Wells family from Clayton, North Carolina, who performed together from 2003 to 2014. One of the few family bands to feature an entirely female lineup,[5] it is perhaps not surprising that the group points to the Whites, Alison Krauss, and Emmylou Harris as their major inspirations. Sara Wells identifies a family motto as a key to their success: "Our mom has always told us that to truly sing in harmony we must live in harmony."[6]

Members of family bands are quick to identify certain dynamics characteristic of such groups. Rhonda Vincent, who started her career playing with her family in a band called the Sally Mountain Show, notes that "when you're in a family, there's a protective element. Dad didn't go anywhere he couldn't take us. Back then, if you were with your parents you could go listen to the music in a club."[7] Vincent goes on to detail another strength of family bands: "Each person brings different dynamics to the sound. Even though it's a family group and there's this likeness, there's a uniqueness that each family member brings."[8] Sharon and Cheryl White also stress the sense of protection they enjoyed while touring with their father, Buck. Sharing close quarters and constantly being in each other's company can threaten even strong family relationships, of course. Sonny and Bobby Osborne found their own solution to this potential problem, one that wasn't always available to a family with younger members. "We looked at all the brother acts in the business at the time," Sonny recalled, "and knew that they fought like cats and dogs. We decided that the real reason they did that was because they were with each other all the time. When you're with somebody all the time, you learn too much about them. We decided that we would work together, but then when we were off, we wouldn't see each other. And we did that for fifty years, and it worked."[9]

The McLains genuinely enjoyed each other's company. Over the years, their friendships and professional respect for one another grew. They had a knack of bringing out the best in each other. Expanding on this thought, Raymond W. notes the importance of teamwork in the genre. "Bluegrass music is very busy. There's a lot going on all the time. But, of course, if you had just everybody just doing what they wanted to all the time it wouldn't sound like much. The trick of it is to make the other person sound good. My philosophy is to listen to the total sound all the time and add to it to make the total thing better."[10] Whether traveling the roads of rural America in a cramped Toyota Corolla or finding their way to a scheduled appearance on the winding roads of Spain, family members rallied around each other whenever one was down. Their job, they knew, was to present a united front and put on the best show they could, be it on the hallowed boards of Carnegie Hall or an improvised stage in the mountains of Bolivia.

In the 1970s, when the McLain Family Band was in full swing, "family bands were more prominent in bluegrass than ever before. Festival venues were a lot more conducive to family participation than the bars or the jamboree and show circuits, where earlier bands had begun their careers."[11] Most festivals had a rural setting, and many ran over entire weekends, offering enthusiastic fans a chance to camp on-site or nearby. Sunday morning shows that featured only gospel songs were typical and helped to reinforce the wholesome qualities of the gatherings.

The McLain Family Band performed not only at the usual bluegrass venues but also at more specialized events. A case in point is when the group appeared in the summer of 1977 at Kin & Communities, a symposium sponsored by the Smithsonian Institution. The purpose of the gathering was to "examine how American families are rooted in older civilizations, and to ask where kin and communities are heading in a changing world."[12] The event was altogether unusual: "Close to academic liturgy but more like a Pirandello play, the improvised ceremony showed our nation-state how to behave like an extended family at a reunion."[13] Former vice president Hubert Humphrey gave the main address at the event, and other speakers included Rosalynn Carter, author Alex Haley of *Roots* fame, and anthropologist Margaret Mead. The McLains performed "Stars and Stripes Forever" for the show and must have felt distinctly in their element throughout the proceedings.

Raymond K. obviously kept up on the literature surrounding the place of family in American life. An article entitled "The Family Out of Favor" appears in the McLain Family Band archives at Berea College and was likely closely read by the patriarch. The piece was written by Michael Novak, a professor of philosophy and religion and the author of more than twenty-five books, many about the theology of culture. His article's basic argument must have both alarmed and invigorated McLain. "We live in lucky times," Novak ironically notes. "So many, so varied, and so aggressive are the anti-family sentiments in our society that brave souls may now have (for the first time in centuries) the pleasure of discovering for themselves the importance of the family. Choosing to have a family used to be uninteresting. It is, today, an act of intelligence and courage. To love family life, to see in family life the most potent moral, intellectual, and political cell in the body politic is to be marked today as a heretic."[14] Raymond K.'s efforts to strengthen his own family and enrich the lives of others he entertained and later educated mark him as one of Novak's so-called heretics.

THE FAMILY BAND FESTIVAL

While hundreds of bluegrass festivals currently dot the landscape, their popularity is a relatively recent phenomenon. Fiddling contests had, of course, long been popular in the Appalachian region, but it wasn't until 1965 that the first major bluegrass festival was organized by Carlton Haney, when he arranged for bluegrass musicians and their fans to gather in Fincastle, Virginia. Haney (1928–2011) was a true character, both an intellectual and a "home-grown mystic" who was willing to gamble that "others shared his vision of [Bill] Monroe's importance and would pay to hear little else but bluegrass for several days running."[15] Thanks to the work of Haney and other promoters, by the mid-1970s bluegrass fans had a wealth of festival options from which to choose.

In the late 1970s, Raymond K. McLain was inspired to create a bluegrass festival designed to feature the talents of family bands. The McLains held their first family festival in 1977 in Kentucky's famed Renfro Valley. All subsequent festivals took place at Big Hill, a seventy-three-acre farm the family purchased for the purpose. "I had been thinking for years it would be nice to have a bluegrass festival each year featuring family groups exclusively," Raymond K. stated. "Then I found this farm with a marvelous hill forming a natural amphitheater. At the bottom of the hill is a grove of locust, wild plum and oak trees, a great backdrop for the stage. The rest is history."[16] McLain's explanation for staging the show was simple. "Historically, so many country music performers were family groups and there are still a lot of family groups out there. Since our group is one of them, I'm mighty interested in how other families work. It's fun to see how much they look alike or don't look alike, how they get along with one another."[17] Many of the groups mentioned above appeared at the festival over the years, including the Osborne Brothers, the Whites, and the Lewis Family.

Sharon White has fond memories of the first McLain Family Band Festival. A coterie of extended family members accompanied the Whites to Renfro Valley. "We wanted them to see the McLain

Family," she recalled. "Our grandmother loved to go to that festival. We have pictures of all of our grandparents there."[18] Besides the hosts, the Whites encountered folks from all over the world at the event. "We met people from Belgium, Japan, a bunch of different places."[19] Throughout the festival's long run, Cheryl White can remember missing only one—and that was for a good reason. She was due to give birth in September of that year, and her obstetrician deemed the festival's August date to be too near her delivery date. At home that year, Cheryl remembers feeling a keen sense of disappointment when she knew her sister and father were about to take the stage at Big Hill. "I literally was shopping with my mother and looked down at my watch and realized it was family showtime, and I started crying. The very next year my daughter wasn't a year old yet, but she was there."[20] Rhonda Vincent has fond memories of the festival as well. "It was the funnest festival. It was all family bands, so you felt this kindred spirit. We always looked forward to that and met lifelong friends there."[21]

Covering the event in 1987 for the *Los Angeles Times*, journalist Charles Hillinger noted that more than six thousand people were in attendance, some from as far away as France, England, Czechoslovakia, and Japan. A total of nineteen different bands appeared during three eleven-hour-long sessions that year. Among the performers was famed country singer Patsy Montaña. "I heard about the get-together of family bands last year and told my husband, let's go visit your kin in Knoxville and run up and take in that McLain thing,"[22] she told Hillinger. Backed by the McLains, Montana delighted the crowd by performing her hit, "I Want to Be a Cowboy's Sweetheart."

Besides Rhonda Vincent and the Whites, other notable performers who accepted Raymond K.'s invitation to perform at Big Hill include a veritable who's who of old-time and bluegrass music. Jim and Jesse McReynolds, with whom Raymond W. would play for ten years after the McLains stopped touring, appeared there on several occasions, as did the Osborne Brothers. Jean Ritchie had long been a friend of the family and regularly supported the event over the years. The famous luthier Homer Ledford made several instruments for McLain Family Band members and also performed onstage. Janette and Joe Carter lent their talents as well. *Hee Haw* star Grandpa Jones, together with his wife Ramona, was another big name that helped attract sizable crowds to the event. One of Raymond W.'s heroes, Don Reno, brought his band, the Tennessee Cutups, to exhibit his banjo wizardry for eager fans. Future Dixie Chicks member Martie Erwin and her sister Emily Strayer performed with the band Blue Night Express early in the festival's history. Ricky Skaggs demonstrated support for his fellow Kentuckians by gracing the stage. And the biggest name of all, Bill Monroe, brought his Blue Grass Boys to Big Hill one August.

If such stars helped draw crowds to the event, its heart and soul remained family bands. Big-name acts like the Lewis Family and the Marshall Family were joined by less heralded bands like the Foster Family String Band, the Outdoor Plumbing Company, the Anderson Family, the Earl Barnes Family, the Bayes Family, the Beaumont Family Band, the D'Epiro Family, the Ray Family, the Strong Family, Carol Urquhart and Family, and the Williams Family.

In an effort to expand the event and pay homage to the Scots-Irish roots of mountain music, the McLains also eventually decided to include some international acts in the festival lineup. The Irish trio Mick Moloney, Robby O'Connell, and Jimmy Keane, famous for their song "There Were Roses," appeared in 1988, as did Scotland's Tannahill Weavers. Also flying over for the event that year was the French band, Bluegrass 43. Besides these European acts, the Far East was also well represented at the 1988 festival. The famous Japanese bluegrass band, Appleseed, lent their brilliant musicianship and natural charm to the Big Hill stage, while Gao and Chen (Gao Yang and Chen Guang) from China showcased their virtuosity on the *erhu* (a two-string violin) and the *yangqin* (a Chinese hammered dulcimer) for the audience. Looking over the range of nations represented throughout the years, it is easy to understand why the McLains included in their festival program Bill Monroe's paraphrase of John Wilson's famous statement: "The sun never sets on bluegrass music."[23]

Festival attendees were treated to much more than just great music at Big Hill. Dance music remained important to the McLains their entire career. Groups like the Green Grass Cloggers and Rhythm in Shoes, under the direction of former Cloggers member Sharon Leahy, delighted the crowds with both traditional mountain dancing and displays of inventive choreography. Nancy Ann McLain's crowd-pleasing displays of clogging were also a regular feature at the gatherings. The McLains even occasionally invited nonmusical acts to Big Hill. Among those lending variety to the proceedings were the Puppetry Caravan, and the Cherelaine Mime Troupe.

The McLains' family festival usually began on Friday and concluded on Sunday. On Thursday evenings, the McLains hosted a watermelon party for bands that had arrived early. The hosts performed up to five shows lasting thirty to forty-five minutes over the course of the weekend. Most other acts would take the stage two, three, or four times, while headliners like the Osborne Brothers might perform only once to accommodate their busy touring schedules. An open stage, sometimes managed by Raymond K.'s sister Rosemary, was held on each of the three days in order to provide a space for new bands to perform. Raymond K.'s mother Bicky staffed the Hostess Tent on occasion and held workshops on folk songs and folk dancing.

Besides offering world-class entertainment, the festival provided an annual boost to the local economy. Indeed, the growing popularity of bluegrass and old-time music has had a significant economic impact on many parts of the Appalachian region. In an honors thesis written in 2011 for East Tennessee State University, Kevin Anderson Lane examines the economic impact of a bluegrass festival held in Stone Mountain, Georgia.[24] The most obvious benefit of any kind of festival, he finds, is its ability to attract patrons from other communities. While local businesses—especially restaurants, motels, and gas stations—benefit from such tourism, Lane points out that other organizations also can take advantage of increased exposure. Local artisans and service groups often see a surge of interest at such gatherings. According to John Crompton and Stacey McKay, in addition to hearing the music they love, those attending bluegrass concerts are "likely to be seeking cultural enrichment, education, novelty, and socialization."[25]

The festival Lane studied was held on a single day and was still in its infancy, having been inaugurated only the previous year. Lane surveyed attendees, tracking demographic data and how much money they spent on the day of the festival. By administering a short survey,

Lane was able to determine that 88 percent of the festival patrons were visitors to the area, and that more than 90 percent of them would not have traveled to Stone Mountain except to attend the festival. The fifty-nine survey respondents spent more than $3,000 inside the village of Stone Mountain on the day of the festival and a further $1,900 in the immediate vicinity. For such a small community, such spending represents a significant boost to the local economy.

While no such study was conducted for the McLain Family Band Festival, it brought thousands of visitors to an area of the state that they would not otherwise have visited. The event's programs were filled with ads for local businesses, ranging from restaurants, garages, and hotels to specialty shops featuring quilts and crafts, and they sometimes included favorite McLain Family recipes like Alice's pecan-oatmeal muffins or Raymond K.'s lima bean casserole. Nearby Berea College also figured prominently among the sponsors listed in the program.

Michael Johnathon, host of the *Woodsongs Old-Time Radio Hour*, was never able to attend the McLains' festival, but it had long been familiar to him before he moved to Kentucky. "I would hear stories about it—'Oh, you should have been around when the McLains had their festival.' Raymond Sr. was an extremely adventurous entrepreneur. The McLain Festival was Merle Fest before there was a Merle Fest. As I was absorbing the musical culture of the Appalachian region, I kept finding that the McLain Family Band was very prominent."[26]

The fact that the McLains were able to hold their festival twelve consecutive years indicates how successful it was. Putting on the event did involve a staggering amount of work, however, and might be categorized more as a labor of love than a moneymaker. While financial figures for all years of the festival are incomplete, enough data exist to draw some valid conclusions. Over its twelve-year run, the festival's annual revenue (ticket sales, concessions, and merchandise income) varied from a low of $33,076 in 1980 to a high of $47,723 in 1985. In 1979, the net loss was $8,623. That year proved exceptional, though. In 1981 a profit of $7,426 was realized, and most other years the festival broke even. Attendances ranged from a high of 6,632 in 1982 to a low of 4,673 in 1980.[27] As expected, the gate on Saturdays was

generally much higher than totals for either Fridays or Sundays. As
Neil Rosenberg observes, however, "a festival's commercial dimension
is downplayed," and Raymond K.'s purpose was never monetary gain
but rather the same sort of "cultural and artistic goals"[28] that Carlton
Haney had stressed in his pioneering work. By founding his festival,
McLain hoped to celebrate families who played music together, and
in this respect his efforts were certainly rewarded.

The final Family Band festival was held in 1988. Several reasons
combined to spell the event's demise. The band was reducing its performing and recording schedule, and a dangerous storm at the 1988
festival raised new concerns. Lightning hit a flagpole on the grounds
that year, sending it crashing down near a row of campers. This incident brought with it new worries about insurance coverage, and the
family reluctantly decided it was time to bring down the curtain on
the event. A major part of the McLains' legacy, the festival stands as
a testament to their belief in the importance of the family and their
willingness and ability to publicly promote it.

CHAPTER 4

Going Classical

B esides impressing Menotti at the Boone Tavern appearance in 1971, the McLains caught the attention of another composer, Phillip Rhodes. The group's "elegant and complex vocal arrangements"[1] made an immediate impression on him and set in motion a chain of events that would lead Rhodes to compose a bluegrass concerto specifically for the band. Born in Forest City, North Carolina, in 1940, Rhodes completed his BA at Duke in 1962 and his MA at Yale in 1966. In 1969, Rhodes took a job in Louisville as a professional in residence, working mainly with the Louisville Symphony Orchestra. Part of his job was to write music for anyone who asked him to. In this capacity he had already worked with the Kentucky Ballet Theater, the Louisville Youth Orchestra, the Louisville Bach Society, and many other musical organizations in the area before meeting the McLains. "It kept me busy, but it was great fun!" he recalls.[2]

Even though Rhodes grew up in the Blue Ridge foothills of North Carolina, he was not terribly familiar with bluegrass music before meeting the McLains. As a youth, Rhodes listened to the so-called Nashville sound on radio and then later was exposed to Elvis Presley and early rock and roll. Neither country, pop, nor rock made much of an impression on him, however. That the McLains were able to make a bluegrass convert of Rhodes says a great deal about their talent and charm.

In 1973, Rhodes was sent to Berea by the Kentucky Arts Commission on a short-term residency. While there he sat in on Raymond K.'s Appalachian Music class. The two men quickly became good friends and discovered they shared a philosophy that playing music was mainly about communicating with the audience. That same year, the Cincinnati Pops Orchestra invited the McLains to accompany them on a summer tour of Ohio, Indiana, and Kentucky. The tour was designed to re-create "old-time" rural events. Following a friendly softball game between members of the orchestra and local citizens, a picnic dinner was served. An open-air concert would conclude the day's festivities. Once the McLains decided which tunes they wanted to play with the orchestra, the job of creating orchestral arrangements fell to Rhodes. Crafting these arrangements paved the way for his later work on the concerto. Among the songs Rhodes worked on were "You Sing for Me," "Silver Creek," "Back Up and Push," "On the Road," "I'm Bound for Gloryland," "Movin' on to Higher Ground," "Take One Step at a Time," "High Hopes," "Raymond's Breakdown," and "Live it Up, Honey."

The McLains' initial performances of these pieces were enjoyable for the band and well received by others. In fact, Louisville Symphony Orchestra conductor Jorge Mester called the September 21, 1973, concert with the band "the most exciting event we've ever played in Louisville."[3] Reviewer William Mootz was equally enthusiastic, describing the McLains as "a marvelous group, smoothly professional and bursting with talent."[4] Praising Raymond W.'s banjo work, he unknowingly anticipated the future by stating, "If I didn't think it might curb his free-flowing style, I'd wish for some shrewd composer to write a concerto for him."[5]

During the summer they performed together, a mutual admiration society of sorts was formed between the McLains and orchestra members. In a letter to the band in October 1973, John Gidwitz made his feelings clear. "This is just my own personal fan letter to tell you how much I enjoyed your singing and playing throughout the summer. I feel rather sure that if a big nationwide public success is something you're interested in, you could catch on with a very wide public. But as far as I'm concerned, I will be delighted if you just keep doing what you're doing. It takes a rare symphony musical quality to keep musicians interested and enthusiastic through several weeks of repeated performances, and there's no question that that is what you did. It's remarkable how infectious and satisfying your wonderful music is."[6]

Performing with the orchestra made Raymond K. realize that bluegrass and classical music were not as dissimilar as he and many others had previously thought. "We and the symphony found that our music was more formal than they had perhaps thought, and their music was more informal than we had perhaps thought. There really wasn't a whole lot of difference in the spirit."[7] In between rehearsals and performances, Raymond W., Ruth, and Alice shared licks with the symphony players and vice versa. Years later, one of the orchestra's bass players even gave Ruth a new instrument.

Though Rhodes believes the genesis of the bluegrass concerto originated with Raymond K. and James Edgy, executive director of the Kentucky Arts Commission, the task of actually composing the music fell to him. The original aim was to create a piece eighteen to twenty minutes long in traditional concerto form—a composition in three movements (fast, slow, fast) that features one or more solo instruments accompanied by a full orchestra. As Abraham Veinus has observed, the word "concerto" has "manifestly changed in its meaning from one century to another."[8] In its most basic and original connotation, "concerto" simply means to play together, in concert. If composers came to regard the form in slightly different ways, some common traits are generally present. "The most important part is the contrast of sound achieved by dividing the performance group into two parts, normally the orchestra and soloist or group of soloists."[9] As Western music progressed, concertos became known as a form where composers could write solo parts for virtuosos on any number of instruments. In classical music, famous concertos have been written for piano, violin, cello, clarinet, trumpet, and, in Vivaldi's case, mandolin. Rhodes's desire was to give Raymond W. and other members of the family band a showcase where they could display their solo skills amongst the sounds of a full string orchestra.

In the spring of 1974, a formal commission for the composition of the *Bluegrass Concerto* was drafted, with funding coming from both the National Endowment for the Arts and the Kentucky Arts Commission. Though Rhodes took a new job at Carleton College in Northfield, Minnesota, as Andrew W. Mellon Professor of Humanities and composer-in-residence that same year, work on the concerto continued. Once it was complete, the composer's wife, Jane Rhodes, sent Raymond K. a piano version of the full orchestral score so that he could teach it to the band members. The band tried out some parts and sent the results via reel-to-reel tapes to Rhodes in Minnesota. He would listen and send back suggestions. In turn, Raymond W. would send Rhodes tapes of what he wanted to play on the banjo for the concerto, and Rhodes would create the notation. At one point Rhodes arranged to live with the family to help simplify the process. "He stayed with us for a month," remembers Raymond W. "He said for me to play all the kinds of licks you can do on the banjo."[10] There were still obstacles to overcome, of course. The fact that none of the children read music complicated the task but did not render it impossible. Rhodes was amazed at the McLains' ability to remember what they heard and then replicate it in performance. "I have always been envious of this ability and I wish I could do it myself," he noted, "but I am tied to having to write it down so I can remember it."[11]

When the concerto was finally ready for rehearsal, the band again worked with the Louisville Orchestra and its conductor, Mester. Rhodes describes the process:

> After introductions and niceties were exchanged, the McLains went about spreading on the floor a number of large poster boards which, I began to realize, represented an alternative version of the notated score. They had cleverly invented a "story line" for each of the three movements and attached rehearsal numbers at the appropriate places. (The corresponding rehearsal numbers were printed on the orchestra score the conductor was using.) And so the rehearsal began "from the top" as they say. After a couple of minutes, the conductor stopped the orchestra to make adjustments or corrections

and proceeded by saying: "Okay, start four measures before rehearsal number 2." The McLains would huddle around a particular poster board, confer briefly, and confirm where they were supposed to play. When the conductor gave the downbeat, they played in exactly the right place! I have to say I was astounded. And so was the conductor. Clearly, the McLains knew the piece . . . including the orchestra parts . . . so thoroughly that they had little difficulty keeping up with where they were in the score. The rehearsal went well and everybody seemed delighted with the result.[12]

The first performance of Rhodes's *Concerto for Bluegrass Band and Orchestra* was held on December 21, 1974, in Freedom Hall in Louisville. Reviewing the premier for the *Courier-Journal & Times*, Nelson Keyes dubbed it "a real joint effort of soloists and orchestra."[13] While he feels Rhodes's goal of expanding the bluegrass into symphonic form is not fully achieved, Keyes notes that "all four McLains are infectious players, healthy and exuberant." He concludes his short article by hoping the band takes the piece "far and wide, for it deserves many exposures, and it is a vehicle ideal for symphonic pops programs."[14]

On the 1981 recording of the concerto, the first movement, "Breakdown," is just over four and a half minutes long and is designed to showcase Raymond W.'s banjo skills. The previously orchestrated piece, "Raymond's Breakdown," was used for the beginning of the movement. Numerous quotations from the traditional tune "Cripple Creek" are included, and a cadenza occurs three minutes into the piece. Raymond W. displays his flexibility throughout, mixing three-finger style with traditional clawhammer picking. A brief vocal passage ("Sun so hot and I'm so dry / Going up to Cripple Creek 'fore I die") is heard near the end of the movement.

The slow second movement, "Ballad," features Alice, occasionally joined by Ruth, singing "My Dear Companion," an original Rhodes composition designed to emulate a traditional mountain ballad. A quiet, stately passage serves as an introduction to Alice's plaintive vocals. Raymond W.'s banjo cleverly mimics the singer's tears and is heard midway through the piece and then again at its conclusion. Though Rhodes's score challenges Alice's range, her soulful performance is beautifully poignant. Rhodes was aiming for the "high, lonesome" sound of bluegrass singing here, and Alice delivers the goods.

While Raymond W.'s banjo is also heard in the third movement, "Variations," the cadenza is played on the fiddle. Remarkably, Raymond had taken up the instrument only about a year before the piece premiered. "Phil wanted to include a fiddle solo," he recalls. "Well, I had always wanted to play the fiddle ever since I was small. It's an instrument that communicates well."[15] Almost eight minutes long, the final movement is nearly double the length of the first two. Rhodes adroitly inserts fragments of Beethoven's Symphony No. 6 throughout the piece. Nicknamed "Pastoral," that symphony, of course, includes elements of folk music and is thus quite in keeping with the tone of the concerto. In his lecture on his concerto, Rhodes notes the similarities between the trio section of the symphony's scherzo and the folk song, "Sally Goodin," which provides the other major theme of the work. Vocal snippets from that song pop up throughout the piece and display how well folk and classical music can complement each other.

Rhodes had three goals in writing the piece: (1) to expand the bluegrass idiom into a concerto format; (2) to display the virtuosity of the players; and (3) to have fun.[16] He succeeds on all three counts. Though other bluegrass artists—most notably the Osborne Brothers, Mark O'Connor, and John McEuen—performed with symphonies, *The Concerto for Bluegrass Band and Orchestra* is the most fully developed composition devoted to the genre. The concerto doubtless served as an introduction to bluegrass for many fans of classical music and helped underline its legitimacy as an art form to any who might have doubted it.

The McLains performed the concerto more than two hundred times over the years with orchestras in Cleveland, St. Louis, Houston, Atlanta, Baltimore, Louisville, Milwaukee, Cincinnati, Rochester, Phoenix, Anchorage, and Flagstaff, among others. Reviews were largely positive. Becky Ball's description of a 1982 performance of the concerto is typical. "The piece has an interesting interplay between the country and symphonic idioms. It also has a strong identity. It makes concise, catchy, and original statements with showy banjo and fiddle virtuoso spots and it mellows beautifully before taking off again in full orchestration of harmonies and singing melodies."[17] Stephen Wigler found the piece "every bit as exciting and original as the fusion between jazz and symphonic music in Gershwin's 'Rhapsody in Blue.' Don't miss it."[18]

Rhodes' concerto was not the only time the McLain Family Band ventured into classical music. On numerous occasions, the band also performed the third movement of Bach's *Brandenburg Concerto No. 2.* So comfortable were they performing symphonic music, in fact, that in 1984 the McLains commissioned Peter Schickele, aka P.D.Q. Bach, to write another orchestral piece for them. Best known for his comical adaptations of classical pieces, Schickele composed the music for the McLains under his true name and not that of his alter ego. This is perhaps an indication of how seriously he took the assignment. With the exception of the hymn "I Will Arise and Go to Jesus," the tunes employed are all original compositions by Schickele. Titled "Far Away from Here," the piece premiered in December 1984 with the Baltimore Symphony. Reviewing the five-movement composition for the *Baltimore Sun*, Karen Monson wrote that it "has not an ounce of pretension" and is "well-crafted and wholly congenial."[19]

Washington Post writer Joseph McLellan also responded positively to "Far Away from Here." "The orchestra is expertly used, with a sound that underlines the American roots, the Smoky Mountain flavor of the music. It gives a firm foundation and colorful background to the fiddle, banjos, mandolins, double bass and singing voices of the five soloists (one of whom also does a little dance after handing off her double bass to her sister). But in this *concerto grosso*, the concertino is clearly the star; the orchestra's massive power is kept on a tight rein when the soloists are in the spotlight, which is most of the time."[20] Though most critics applauded the McLains' work with orchestras, there were some dissenters. Writing for the *Cincinnati Enquirer*, for example, Ray Cooklis noted that "their music is strong enough to stand on its own. It's too bad several of their numbers were saddled with superfluous orchestral scores which did little except clutter up their sonic background."[21]

In 1989, the McLains made another foray into the world of classical music. Raymond W. conceived a piece called "The Fast Lane," which was arranged by the well-known American conductor and composer Newton Wayland (1940–2013). The suite consisted of six movements: "Mountain Parkway," "As Soon as You Give Me Your Love," "Life in the Fast Lane/The Morning After Ragtime Blues," "Solitude," "I Loved You Most of All," and "Straight Ahead and Rolling." Michael McLain helped with "As Soon as You Give Me Your Love," and Fred de Rosset was cocomposer of "I Loved You Most of All." The suite tells the familiar story of a young man who leaves his country home for the city but becomes disenchanted with the change and decides to return home.

The McLains' willingness to experiment was not lost on their peers. Sharon White comments on what the band's performances with orchestras did for the genre. "It raised the level of the spectrum of bluegrass," she says. "And they were the perfect band to take that because they were a showy band."[22] Perhaps inspired by the example of the McLain Family Band, a handful of bluegrass performers began to play with symphony orchestras. Among these were Dan Crary, Spontaneous Combustion, John McEuen of the Nitty Gritty Dirt Band, and fiddler Mark O'Connor.[23]

One group that certainly benefited directly from the groundbreaking work the McLain Family Band did with orchestras was the famed Osborne Brothers, perhaps best known for their 1967 hit, "Rocky Top." In a career that spanned nearly fifty years and culminated in their being elected to the International Bluegrass Music Association's Hall of Honor, the Osbornes recorded seventeen albums and placed eighteen singles on the country charts. Always curious to learn new ways to approach bluegrass music, Sonny Osborne had heard about the McLains playing with orchestras and decided to see for himself. "It intrigued me because they were different," said Osborne. "It absolutely amazed me how they did that. I got to thinking, 'I wonder if I can do that.' I don't know if they read music, but I sure couldn't. So we got an agent and told him what we wanted to do, and he said, 'Okay, I'll set that up.' I called Raymond (the boy, Raymond) and told him what we were going to do and I asked him if we could meet up at their house and ask them all a thousand questions."[24]

The Osbornes eventually went on to play with both the Bismark/ Mandan Symphony in North Dakota and the San Antonio Symphony. One of their band members who understood notation would write out the music for these pieces so that the orchestra knew what to play. The process was far from orderly, mirroring in some ways the process the McLains and Rhodes employed. "I had certain things I would do on the banjo that would lead up to when my brother was supposed to sing. You should have seen the paper I had written out," Sonny recounts, describing his own system of noting cues. "Nobody on God's earth could understand what I had written on it."[25] Osborne notes that while the McLains seemed still in their comfort zone while working with orchestras, he and his brother felt far less at home. "I was amazed at how they pulled it off. They all had a good time."[26] Recalling his performances with trained musicians, Osborne says, "We were never that comfortable playing with an orchestra. They [the McLains] were comfortable doing this because they knew what they were doing."[27]

In 1979, the Osborne Brothers released an all-instrumental LP titled *Bluegrass Concerto*. While not in formal concerto form, the four-and-a-half-minute title track does vary in some ways from typical bluegrass instrumentals. Mainly an extended banjo workout augmented by fiddle and mandolin breaks, the piece includes a number of unexpected tempo changes, specifically one minute into the performance, where a stately fiddle passage arrests the listener's attention, and then again, more briefly, at the 3:10 mark. The fact that the Osbornes named the album after the piece and included it on their *Essential Osborne Brothers Collection* of 2001 demonstrates the affection they have for the number.

The Osborne Brothers' orchestral collaborations and their own *Bluegrass Concerto* furnish ample proof of the influence the McLain Family Band had on other performers in the genre and are a good example of the group's innovation and their desire and ability to stretch the boundaries of bluegrass. These forays into classical music speak to their musicianship and willingness to constantly challenge themselves as players. Raymond K. noted some additional advantages of performing such pieces. "It's good to broaden audiences and always get more kinds of people interested in the music. It's good for employment, too.

We don't have to rely on festivals all the time. It's fun to travel around to different kinds of audiences." [28] Raymond K.'s background certainly helped make such ventures possible. It's not every bluegrass group, after all, that has a musicologist among its members to thus expand its repertoire. Their expansiveness sets the McLains apart from most of their contemporaries and demonstrates how they endeavored to establish a place for themselves outside of the confines of traditional bluegrass music.

CHAPTER 5

In the Studio

etween 1972 and 1986, the McLain Family Band recorded fourteen albums: twelve in the studio, one featuring their performance of Phillip Rhodes' *Bluegrass Concerto*, and, finally, a live recording of their 1982 performance at Carnegie Hall. The band's general pattern was to enter the studio annually in order to have new material available to sell at concerts and via mail order. Altogether, the McLains produced more than four hundred minutes of music. A good majority of their tracks are quite brief: of the 147 tracks they recorded on their original twelve studio albums, 39 are less than two minutes long, 84 are between two and three minutes in length, and only 24 are three minutes or longer. Albums vary in length from 22:29 (*On the Road*) to 41:58 (*Country Dance Album*), usually running between 26 and 34 minutes. On nearly every song, the lead vocalist is joined by one of his or her siblings, showcasing the group ethos that Raymond K. always stressed. On tracks that feature a lead vocalist, Raymond W. steps to the fore most often, followed by Ruth, then Alice.

The band's recorded repertoire can be grouped into three categories: (1) McLain Family originals (those composed by Rosemary, Raymond K., Raymond W., or Ruth); (2) songs written by twentieth-century bluegrass, folk, and country artists; and (3) traditional numbers. The group shows their reverence for the Carter family by committing seven of their songs to disk. They cover three Jean Ritchie songs and two each from Bill Monroe and Don Reno. That they also include two marches (one by John Philip Sousa, the other by Josef Wagner) among their thirty-six recorded instrumentals shows their diverse tastes and that they weren't afraid to occasionally risk incurring the wrath of bluegrass music purists.

According to Raymond W., choosing which songs to record for the albums resembled the process of an author outlining a book. The band members asked themselves what they wanted to say with their selections, who their audience was, and which pieces fit well together. "All art is unity and variety," Raymond W. stated in 2016. "You have to decide what goes together to make the statement or feeling you want to make."[1] Every time the group entered the studio, it had grown in some way and was different from the year before. As the years passed, a number of personnel changes took place. Raymond K., Raymond W., and Ruth were core members featured on every album. Alice played on nine albums, Nancy Ann and Michael on six.

The band's entire recorded output appeared on their own label, Country Life Records. At first, this decision was made not by choice but by necessity. In 1972, the band was not yet well known enough to merit interest from major bluegrass recording companies. Since Raymond K. felt confident in his ability to help with the album's production, manufacturing, and distribution, he decided the group should found its own label. The fact that this allowed them to be their own bosses suited their desire to record what they wanted when they wanted. They were not beholden to anyone who didn't share their vision. Such autonomy also allowed them to utilize Raymond F.'s woodcuts to supplement their cover art, and his distinctive lettering style lent the records an appropriately rustic look. Describing the McLains' approach, Sharon White notes another way the group innovated: "It was all in-house: album cover, artwork, graphics. And Mrs. McLain became their booking agent, their manager, if you will. It was a family business in every way. They took that up a notch, too. Back in the day bluegrass was not considered a business that was conducted in a very businesslike way. What was different about the McLains was that they carved out their own niche."[2]

The McLain Family Band's eponymous first LP was recorded at the Mississippi Recording Company's Malaco Studios in Jackson, Mississippi, and mixed by Jerry Puckett, who had previously worked with Rosemary McLain on her solo album. As an experiment, the band recorded their second album, *Country Ham*, at Rite Records Studio in Cincinnati, Ohio. They were not entirely happy with the results, however, and returned to the Mississippi Recording Company for all subsequent studio ventures. The Country Life albums were manufactured by Rite Record Productions, Inc., also based in Cincinnati, and engineered by Lan Ackley. The McLains produced their own albums, and if this entailed hours of effort, the control the group retained over their sound made it worth the time.

Once the band had established themselves as a major act, representatives from other companies did knock on Raymond K.'s door, but he was happy with the status quo and saw no reason to change what he considered a successful model. The fact that the group established their own label is another example of the band's drive and innovation. While it is common today, in the early 1970s this practice was still unusual, if not unheard of.[3]

EARLY ALBUMS

The group's first album (titled simply *The McLain Family Band*) is in some ways typical of those that would follow, though its nine original compositions are the most the band would ever include. Two instrumentals and three gospel songs appear, following a practice employed by many bluegrass groups. Nearly twenty-nine minutes in length, the eponymous debut paints a portrait of a family band in its nascent stages. At the time it was recorded in 1972, Raymond W. was only eighteen, his sisters Alice and Ruth sixteen and fourteen respectively. In some ways, then, it is a developmental effort, but it is certainly full of high spirits, fine musicianship, and joyful singing. The black-and-white album cover photo shows the band in matching striped outfits, made by their mother Betty. Raymond W. looks delighted as he plays his banjo, and Ruth is regarding him with admiration as she plucks the bass. Mandolin cradled in her arms, Alice is singing, eyes closed in concentration. Raymond K.'s calm demeanor masks the great pride he must feel in the family's accomplishment.

Country Ham (1974) includes six original compositions by Rosemary, one instrumental, and one near-instrumental, the title track. Its twelve selections run to just more than twenty-six minutes. The color album cover shows the family once again in matching outfits, this time burgundy in theme. They are outside, standing in front of trees denuded by winter. Father and son frame Alice and Ruth, whose faces are turned towards their brother, as he sings to his banjo accompaniment.

MIDDLE ALBUMS

The six albums the McLain Family Band recorded between 1975 and 1980 show them at their best. Compared to their debut and *Country Ham*, these albums demonstrate a new maturity. The vocals are surer, and the instrumental accompaniment is even more solid than before. Raymond W.'s prowess on the banjo, mandolin, and guitar continually impresses the listener. Perhaps most vital to the success of these recordings, however, is the original material they include. Ruth finds her voice as a writer, contributing "Bound for Gloryland" and "Come On Out Tonight." Rosemary adds three of her most beautiful compositions, "Always," "Sail Away," and "Our Song." But it is Raymond K.'s songs that stand out most in this period. "Can't We Get Together Once Again?" "Kentucky Wind," "My Name's Music," and "You Sing for Me" are numbers that will forever be associated with the group.

Country Life (1975) sounds considerably fuller and more polished than the group's first two albums. Half of the tracks are McLain family originals, with Rosemary contributing three strong songs. Its two instrumentals are striking, and the group's harmony singing reaches new levels of precision. Algie Brun took the cover portrait of the band relaxing in the haymow of a faded blue barn, overgrown with creepers but still solid in foundation.

At just 22:29 in length, *On the Road* (1976) is the shortest album the band recorded. Reflecting its title, the album is fast paced, frenetic, and full of humor. One of the McLains' strengths is their remarkable energy, and it is on full display here. The album is a coming-out party for Ruth in some ways, as she sings lead on five numbers, and her bass is increasingly featured. Raymond K.'s contributions to the album are also substantial. Four of the original compositions on the recording are his, making up for the fact that his sister Rosemary contributed only one piece. The album cover was photographed by Betty McLain and shows the group in new stage outfits rehearsing for an appearance on NBC's popular morning TV program, *The Today Show*. Both sisters look to Raymond W. as he concentrates on his banjo. The family dedicated the album to Raymond F., whose woodcuts again adorn the cover.

Kentucky Wind (1977) leans more towards old-time and country music than straight bluegrass. Raymond K. and his sister Rosemary contribute seven songs between them, and they are among the best and most enduring pieces either composed. A peak performance in many ways, *Kentucky Wind* certainly ranks among the best recordings the band ever made. Its cover is similarly excellent. Shot by Betty, it shows the group, more casually dressed than on previous shots, assembled at A. P. Carter's birthplace in Maces Springs, Virginia. Trees in the background are leafless; the earth they stand on is uneven and brown. Smiling, the band members look into the distance. The McLains had long enjoyed a close relationship with Janette and Joe Carter, and they are obviously pleased and honored to be photographed at such a sacred spot. The family dedicated the album to Betty, who, according to the liner notes, "happily conducts most of our business."

Their longest album to date at 33:27, the *Family Album* (1978) introduces Al White to the group's growing following and features a wide variety of musical styles. Al and Alice had met at the Grand Ole Opry in 1975 when he was playing with the Bluegrass Alliance. While Al and Alice performed with the McLain Family Band in 1977 and 1978, they eventually decided to move to New Mexico and strike out on their own. "It was really hard for us to be a married couple and have our own identity and at the same time to be in the family band with my dad being such a strong leader," Alice recalled years later. "We needed some time away from the family band to become a stronger unit within our own marriage."[4] Al's influence is felt throughout the recording as he lends his considerable musical chops on guitar and mandolin to bluegrass and old-time numbers and takes the band on a few excursions into the music of his native Southwest. The album cover shows the group performing during the Kentucky Educational Television series, *Bluegrass, Bluegrass*.

A number of factors led to the band's *7th Album* (1979) being unusual. First of all, it was recorded during a major flood in Mississippi. "Downtown where the recording studio was, they were expecting the dam to break," Raymond W. recalled years later.[5] Parts of the city were closed off, but the band gained permission from city officials to try to complete their work. This they did, but under pressure and in much less time than they had been granted for previous LPs. The album was basically recorded one day and mixed the next. Perhaps also indicative of the rush with which the album was produced is the fact that no liner notes were written. It is also the first album that didn't include Alice, who had moved west with her husband Al White. Nancy Ann McLain stepped in to fill the void, taking over the bass on many of the tracks. Though she was only fourteen at the time, she acquits herself quite well. This is perhaps not surprising given the emotional support lent to her by her siblings and the gentle guidance of her father. "Daddy never made us feel that we were young," says Raymond W. "He made us feel that we were musicians."[6]

For the first time, the band also brought in a nonfamily member, Tim Owen, to help with the recording. An excellent banjo player, Owen had played with the group on occasion at festivals, and the family found that his style suited theirs. Owen's presence freed up Raymond W. to contribute a good deal of excellent fiddling to the album. Finally, *7th Album* is the band's first recording that does not feature a song composed by Rosemary. Nor is there a new number written by any other member of the family. The cover shot shows the group seated in a pasture on their farm, Big Hill, near Berea. Their smiles shine nearly as brightly as the sun. Tim Owen sits dead center, perhaps indicating how much at home he felt in the band.

1980's *Big Hill* is a big album. Its fifteen tracks constitute a new record for the group, and it is also their longest LP to date at 35:32.

Five of the numbers are instrumentals, the most on any recording at this point in their career. *Big Hill* is also the first recording to feature the talents of Michael McLain, only thirteen at the time the band entered the studio. Though he would later become known for his banjo and guitar work, on his debut Michael plays mandolin and tambourine. Raymond W.'s first wife, Beverly Buchanan, also plays banjo on the album. Both new members of the band are shown on the album cover, as the ensemble, now six strong, advances across a meadow at the family's farm, for which the recording is named. The hills of Kentucky are seen in the distance, and if one looks closely, the barn used on the cover of *Country Life* is visible in the background. On the back of the album, Raymond W. is shown solo, playing his fiddle. Raymond's ability on the instrument was growing as the months went by; it now featured as often as his banjo on the band's recordings.

LATER ALBUMS

The five albums the McLain Family Band recorded before going on studio hiatus represent a wide range of approaches. *All Natural Ingredients* and *Troublesome Creek* resemble their previous efforts in scope, but the gospel recording *Sunday Singing* and 1986's all-instrumental *Country Dance* album are more specialized departures. Finally, their Carnegie Hall LP represents the band's lone live recording. Ruth's first husband, Michael Riopel, contributes guitar and harmonica to these LPs, while Al and Alice return to the fold for the instrumental album. Though varied in nature, each recording in this final phase features the same characteristics that marked the band's earlier efforts: fine original material, exquisite playing, and strong singing.

The McLain Family Band in Concert at Carnegie Hall (1982)

Born in 1949, Phyllis George was named Miss Texas in 1970 and Miss America a year later. In 1975, she gained further acclaim when she joined the all-male cast of the popular show on CBS Sports, *The NFL Today*. Four years later, George married future Kentucky governor John Y. Brown Jr. As first lady of the Commonwealth from 1979 to 1983, George made it her mission to promote Kentucky culture and the artists who promulgated it. She befriended the McLains and arranged for them to play at events like store openings for firms such as Bloomingdales in New York and Neiman-Marcus in Beverly Hills. Charles Hamlen and Edna Landau of IMG Artists were representing the McLain Family Band at the time, and in the spring of 1982, George worked with them to book the group at Carnegie Hall.[7] The world-famous venue's schedule did, in fact, have one opening at the time, but the band did not learn they would be performing on that renowned stage until the night before the show.

The McLains were playing in Morehead, Minnesota, the evening they heard the news. Ashland Oil offered to fly them from nearby Fargo, North Dakota, to New York shortly after their performance so that they could keep the date. Fresh from the red-eye special, the McLains were greeted by NBC limousines in New York ready to take them to record a spot on *The Today Show*. Upon arriving at the studio, however, the family learned that the Falkland War had broken out and that their appearance would thus be taped for later broadcast. The band was not well known in New York at the time, and because the concert had been so hastily arranged, they feared attendance might suffer. Raymond K. thus asked Doug Tuckman, president of the New York Bluegrass Club, to help with some last-minute promotion for the event. Their efforts bore fruit. When the curtain rose, a good crowd filled the seats, and Phyllis George took the stage to introduce the band.

While planning for the event, the McLains and Phyllis George decided that the program should honor their home state: every selection should be written by a Kentuckian or should be about Kentucky in some way. In the dressing room, Raymond W. felt "nervous as a cat."[8] A list of performers who had trod these boards before him filled his head and threatened to overwhelm him. "Jascha Heifetz had performed here. Flatt and Scruggs. Merle Travis. I remember thinking, 'My job right now is to tie this necktie.' "[9] While their brother calmed his nerves, Ruth, Alice, and Nancy Ann ironed the dresses designed by Laura Ashley that Phyllis George had arranged for them to wear during this special performance.

In the album's liner notes, Raymond K. described the buildup to the show. "We've kissed mother Betty just in from Berea, grandmother Bicky in from Tuscaloosa, and sister Alice with Al White and daughters in from Albuquerque, all six to join us later on the stage. We've slept too briefly, taped for the TODAY SHOW, ogled our posters on Manhattan street corners, checked out the sound system, the lighting, and made the dry runs necessary for this live album." Seasoned performers that they were, the band delivered a rousing show that was well captured by the hall's sound system. Ruth assisted Ken Keith with the album's cover, a black-and-white photo based on a poster made for the show.

All Natural Ingredients (1983)

In his liner notes, Raymond K. indicates that the album's title "means whatever you think! This music is down to earth. One regular serving contains most basic elements needed to sustain and enhance life!" Though it features only two original compositions, *All Natural Ingredients* is one of the band's longest at nearly thirty-six minutes and is perhaps best characterized as a tribute to folk, country, and bluegrass giants. Songs by Hank Williams, Fred Rose, the Delmore Brothers, and Bill Monroe dominate the LP. The cover shot shows the sextet gathered in an appropriately natural setting. For the first time, the liner notes list which band member performs on which instrument for each particular track.

Sunday Singing (1984)

The McLain Family Band had generally included at least one song with a religious theme on each of their previous recordings. Here they reflect the deep faith that informs their lives by devoting an entire album to what Ralph Stanley has called "mountain gospel soul." The album cover (shot by Peter Schaaf) was designed by Ruth and shows a bearded Raymond K. in the midst of the same lineup featured on *All Natural Ingredients*. Nancy Ann supports her bass at her father's side, while the band's other instruments lie at rest before them.

Troublesome Creek (1985)

Featuring five outstanding original compositions, *Troublesome Creek* is one of the band's best and most balanced albums. The title track and "Cherry Road" are two of the group's finest instrumentals; Raymond K.'s contributions ("You're Why I Try" and "Show Me That You Know Me") are similarly strong. Paired with these new numbers are excellent covers from contemporary songwriters (Don Reno's "Emotions" and Tom T. Hall's "Shoeshine Man") and pieces from the past ("In the Pines" and "You Are My Flower"). With a running time of over thirty-seven minutes, the album is also one of their longest. As the group's career progressed, they gradually began to include longer numbers, a sign of artistic maturity. The cover shot shows the band bathed in sunlight while taking a break in the woods.

McLain Family Band Country Dance Album (1986)

The band's final recording before embarking on a thirty-one-year break from the studio in this configuration found them returning to their country dance band roots. The McLains dedicated the album to Ethel Capps, who led the Country Dancers at Berea College from 1958 to 1974. Under her leadership, the dancers performed all over America and in several foreign countries. John Ramsay succeeded Capps and asked the McLains if they would be willing to record this themed album. Ramsay had requested the McLains to select tunes to fit specific dances or dance styles. The tracks are played with great precision to match the tempo indications listed under each tune on the album's sleeve.

Unusually, the group employed a click track for this project to ensure a consistent tempo. The album was recorded and mixed at Track 16 studios in Lexington, another departure from past practice. Also noteworthy is the fact that this is the first album the group recorded that was issued as both an LP and a CD. Alice and Al rejoined the band to work on the project. Alice plays mandolin, while Al showcases his versatility, picking guitar, four-string mandolin, and clawhammer banjo. Michael McLain provides banjo parts, while Ruth plays bass. On this recording, Raymond W. concentrates on fiddle but also contributes sock guitar, high-strung guitar, and mandolin on "Sugarfoot Rag." "Yesterday's Waltz" is the only track on which he plays banjo. With Al and Raymond W. playing guitar, Raymond K. is here free to concentrate on his first love, piano. Though obviously recorded with dancing in mind, the album also makes for pleasurable listening. As an indication that the pieces, not the performers, are the focus, for the first time the band is not shown on the album cover. Instead, a yellow and red folk art design shows dancers and instruments joined in a circle. The subtitle of the album is "Dances from Appalachia #3," referencing the fact that two other albums in the series had previously appeared, one of which the McLain Family Band had recorded with Donna and Lewis Lamb.

REVIEWS

With few exceptions, the critics were kind to the McLain Family Band. Walter Saunders reviewed three of their albums for *Bluegrass Unlimited* in the 1970s. In his write-up of *Country Ham*, Saunders notes the band's diverse sound and considerable ability. "It's difficult to categorize the McLain's music, for while the instrumentation is bluegrass, their singing combines elements of traditional, folk, pop and country, giving them a sound unlike anyone else in the business." Saunders concludes by noting that the album "reveals talent all over the place."[10] He calls their next album, *Country Life*, their best so far. "The girls' voices have matured, improving the quality of their vocals (especially Alice who has developed a strong, beautiful lead voice), and their harmonies seem closer than ever." He describes "Joe Clark's Dream" as a little offbeat but otherwise praises the group's originality. "The McLains continue to demonstrate an uncanny ability to come up with fresh, unusual material and imaginative arrangements, in a style that is distinctively all their own." Furthermore, he acknowledges the group's work outside the studio, hailing them as "America's bluegrass ambassadors to the world."[11] Reviewing *Kentucky Wind*, the critic returns to the theme of the band's place in the genre. "I have never been able to properly define the McLain's approach to bluegrass because it doesn't neatly fit into any of the usual categories," he writes. Concerning the band's performance, however, he feels no such confusion. "As usual the singing and instrumentation is without fault." He closes by citing the band's strengths. "They play happy, sunlit bluegrass, even when they do a sad song. Since so much bluegrass is tragic and soul-searching, it's kind of nice to have some folks like the McLain Family Band around to buoy us up when we need it. I hope they never change."[12]

Reviewing *On the Road* for *Bluegrass Unlimited*, James Griffith also struggles to define the band's approach. "Perhaps 'cheery,' 'light,' and 'wholesome' come as close as any words can, but that doesn't quite say it all," he writes, before noting what some saw as a failing in the band's sound: "Even 'Sad and Lonesome Day,' magnificent bluesy fiddle and all, though it is certainly sincere, doesn't *hurt*. Mind you, this isn't a fault, it's a difference." Griffith also believes the songs the band selected to record for the album rely too greatly on their stage show. As an example, he cites "Jump Josie." Songs like this, he believes, "lend themselves to visual presentation and may lose a bit as purely aural experiences." Such apparent flaws noted, he closes the review positively, stating "Nevertheless, a fine job."[13]

Jim Hatlo begins his review of *Big Hill* for *Frets* by admitting his previous unfamiliarity with the group. He then goes on to praise a number of their performances on the record. " 'I Will Arise and Go to Jesus' and 'Light in the Stable' feature gorgeous blends of voices and instruments. 'Bugle Call Rag' is rendered as a dynamic banjo duet that could have been synchronized by Longines, and 'Pig in a Pen' is presented as a headlong dash in the bluegrass fast lane. 'Under the Double Eagle' is highlighted by—get this—a spunky slap-bass solo with clog-dancing percussion." Hatlo concludes his review with what amounts to gushing admiration. "Reviewers are supposed to remain aloof and objective, but 'Our Song' melted away my last vestiges of objectivity, so I'd better shut up before I say something gauche like 'Oh wow!' "[14]

Reviewing the Carnegie Hall concert for the *New York Times*, critic Robert Palmer notes that while "their playing and singing weren't virtuosic," the band "performed an attractive mixture of old favorites and originals, and their instrumental and especially their vocal arrangements were consistently fresh."[15] John Roemer reviewed the same album for *Bluegrass Unlimited* and lauds their singing on the LP as "smoother and stronger than on some of their previous efforts." He singles out "I Don't Want to Go" as boasting "a warm, layered, building vocal chorus." He concludes by stating, "If you've liked the McLains' mixture of pop, folk, and downhome picking at festivals, this album captures them at their best."[16]

Berea College music professor William Tallmadge reviewed *All Natural Ingredients* for the *Berea Citizen*. Tallmadge hails the album as "a superb example of material, style, performance, and arrangement." He notes how the band's sound has matured, writing, "These days Raymond's solos no longer cause one to think of his remarkable facility; rather one thinks only of the beautiful music being played and how right it all sounds." Tallmadge feels the group's new lineup works well together, calling the band "a company of artistic equals. Each member carries his or her weight and makes his own unique contribution to the excellence of the total ensemble." As an example, he lauds Nancy Ann's "rock steady" rhythms on bass. Finally, he describes Raymond K.'s piano on "Blue Ridge Mountains of Virginia" as "purposely square and imitative of certain jazz stomps of the 1920s and 1930s."[17]

Bluegrass Unlimited reviewer John Hartley Fox calls *Sunday Singing* his favorite McLain Family Band album. "I think the main reason I like the McLains more than other bands who work the same turf," he writes, "is that the McLains are wholesome (comes with the territory), but never self-righteously pious and almost never too 'sweet.'" Though few who were aware of the band's previous output would be unfamiliar with their chops, Fox nonetheless ends the review by addressing skeptics, who, he writes, "will be surprised by just how hot these folks can get when they want to."[18]

In their reviews of McLain Family Band albums, *Bluegrass Unlimited* writers continually raise the issue of how the group's sound doesn't always match traditional bluegrass. In his review of *Troublesome Creek*, the journal's Richard Spottswood follows suit, noting that the band's vocal style "owes as much to the Coon Creek Girls and Chuck Wagon Gang as it does to bluegrass." And, as has so often been the case, the writer feels compelled to raise the "cheerfulness" issue. "In the past I've been one of those who has felt a mild bias against the McLains' music, feeling it to be a mite too cheerful and wholesome. And, you might just say, 'What on earth is wrong with that? In a musical age of Twisted Sisters and Dead Kennedys, a little cheerful wholesomeness is just what's needed.' To which I'd now have to say amen, especially when confronted with an LP that's as smooth, professional and enjoyable as this one." [19]

Raymond K.'s musical life was greatly influenced by his parents and sister, pictured here near Tuscaloosa, Alabama. *From left to right*: Raymond F., Rosemary, Beatrice Kane, Raymond K. (Courtesy of the McLain Family collections.)

Bill Monroe introduced the McLain Family Band to the Grand Ole Opry, where they performed many times. Here they are sharing the stage with Bill Monroe and the Blue Grass Boys. *From left to right*: Kenny Baker, Bob Black, Raymond W., Bill Monroe, Ruth, Alice, Randy Davis, James Monroe, Raymond K. (Courtesy of the McLain Family collections.)

The McLain Family Band graced the cover of *Bluegrass Unlimited* magazine in October 1972, following their first overseas tour. *From left to right*: Alice, Raymond W., Raymond K., Ruth. (Courtesy of the McLain Family collections.)

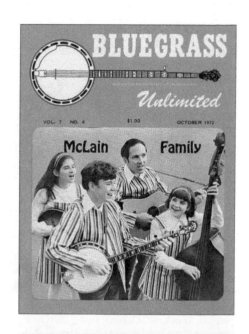

Betty McLain was the band's office manager, handling the booking and correspondence, writing newsletters, sewing performing outfits, and producing the McLain's Big Hill Festival. (Courtesy of the McLain Family collections.)

The Kentucky Arts & Crafts
Foundation and Ashland Oil Inc.
Present
THE McLAIN FAMILY BAND
in concert at Carnegie Hall
Monday, April 26, 1982
8:00 p.m.

The Bluegrass family
that plays "down home" style music

Concerts at Carnegie Hall in 1982 and 1985 were career highlights for the McLain Family Band, though Raymond K. often said that whatever concert you are doing at the time is the most important one! (Courtesy of the McLain Family collections.)

As music director for the Berea College Country Dancers, Raymond K. toured in Central and South America and was honored to meet President John F. Kennedy after the band's performance for First Lady Jacqueline Kennedy's Musical Programs for Youth by Youth on the White House lawn on April 22, 1963. (Courtesy of the McLain Family collections.)

The McLain Family Band's Family Festival at Big Hill, Kentucky, brought thousands of musicians and fans together for a fun weekend of music each August from the mid-1970s to the late 1980s. *From left to right*: Michael, Raymond K., Alice, Ruth, Nancy Ann, Raymond W., and Al White. (Courtesy of the McLain Family collections.)

The McLains became great friends with the other performers, including the "Father of Bluegrass" himself, Bill Monroe. Pictured with Monroe are Raymond (20) and Ruth (16) at the Monroe Festival in Rosine, Kentucky, 1974. (Courtesy of the McLain Family collections.)

The McLain Family Band has given more than two hundred concerts with orchestras nationally and internationally. In 1973 the McLain Family Band first toured with the Cincinnati Symphony Orchestra's summer minifestivals in Ohio, Indiana, and Kentucky. The band and orchestra are pictured here with their friend, conductor and music director Carmon DeLeone. (Courtesy of the McLain Family collections.)

Gian Carlo Menotti invited the McLain Family Band to perform at his Festival of Two Worlds in Spoleto, Italy, June 20–July 9, 1972. This photo shows the McLains along with the Italian band, Nuova Compagnia di Canto Popolare, in the Piazza del Duomo. (Courtesy of the McLain Family collections.)

International tours took the McLain Family Band members to perform in more than seventy countries, often as musical ambassadors through a branch of the U.S. State Department. They are pictured here in Germany, 1972. (Courtesy of the McLain Family collections.)

While the band was on tour in Alaska, an iceberg at the Portage Glacier became the location for a photo shoot for the cover of *Pickin'* magazine, July 1977. (Courtesy of Rick Goodfellow.)

All of the McLain Family Band's worldwide tours brought opportunities to share experiences with local musicians. Here, Raymond K. appreciates a young musician playing his homemade flute in Haiti, 1976. (Courtesy of McLain Family collections.)

There has been a great connection and respect for generations between the McLain Family and the Carter Family. In addition to decades of annual performances since the beginning of the Carter Family Fold in Hiltons, Virginia, Raymond K. and Raymond W. were each on the board of directors and served as the artistic director at the Fold. *From left to right*: Michael, Jennifer Banks McLain, Ruth, Raymond W., Nancy Ann, Alice, and Al White, January 2017. (Courtesy of Emma White.)

Besides her role in the McLain Family Band, Ruth has filled in on bass with many of the early bluegrass legends. Her passion for the future of the music shows through her teaching at the Kentucky Center for Traditional Music at Morehead State University and as a board member of the International Bluegrass Music Association Foundation. (Courtesy of Terry Vaught.)

Thoughtful practice and attention to musical detail help make the McLains' sound unique. Raymond K. said that practice was the most exciting part for him! Raymond W. is shown here working out a new banjo lick. (Courtesy of the McLain Family collections.)

The McLain Family Band keeps a positive attitude, respect for the business, care for each other, and appreciation for the lifelong friends along the way. *From left to right*: Al White, Alice, Raymond K., Michael, Ruth, Raymond W., Berea, Kentucky, 1985. (Courtesy of Peter Taylor.)

There's nothing like family harmony! Ruth and Alice are pictured singing at their annual Al, Alice, and Ruth Holiday Music concert in Berea, Kentucky, December 2015. (Courtesy of Rachael White.)

Michael and his wife, Jennifer, tour nationwide as "Michael & Jennifer McLain and the Banjocats" from the Nashville, Tennessee, area. (Courtesy of Peter Nash.)

In 2018, the McLain Family Band celebrated its fiftieth anniversary. This photo was used for their CD *Celebrate Life*, their picture book *The McLain Family Band—50 Years of Music: A Pictorial History*, and for their fiftieth anniversary tours. *From left to right*: Daxson Lewis, Alice, Raymond W., Ruth, Al White. (Courtesy of Frederick Park, Apalache Professional Imaging.)

CHAPTER 6

Rosemary's Songs

The twenty-two songs Raymond K.'s sister Rosemary wrote for the band to perform and record represent some of their finest material. The joy she found in living is apparent in both her lyrics and her melodies, and it is this joie de vivre that is such a trademark of the McLain Family Band's sound. In some ways, Rosemary's songs provide the foundation upon which much of the band's later work was based. Whether or not this was her intention, she certainly found delight in the group's success and remained close to her brother, nieces, and nephews her entire life.

Rosemary's solo album, titled simply *Rosemary*, was the first recording for the Country Life label and appeared in 1971. The cover shows a smiling Rosemary, guitar slung over her shoulder, advancing through a field in yellow slacks and vest. The "R" and "m" in the woodcut her father used as lettering for the album cover are colored yellow to complement both her outfit and the wildflowers that adorn the field. Thirteen of her own compositions comprise the album. On each track, Rosemary accompanies herself on guitar. Raymond W. adds lead guitar to seven of them and plays banjo on one ("Live It Up, Honey").

Rosemary's voice is sweet, expressive, and generally well suited to her songs. In the album's liner notes, she writes, "In presenting you with these songs, I feel shy to share so much of myself with you, for

95

many of them express feelings and moods of which I seldom speak." Those listeners already acquainted with her songs the family band covered will find much that is familiar here. Most are sunny and breezy, but the collection also includes four songs more serious in nature. "All I Ever Wanted" and "It's My Turn to Cry" are genuinely sad songs, and "Plastic Party" offers commentary on superficial members of society. "The Loved and the Unloved" pays tribute to those with no voice in the community, members of the animal kingdom among them. While some pieces lean towards country, others have an easy-listening feel to them. Four songs included here were later recorded by the McLains: "Let Time Walk By," "Hikin' Down the Interstate," "Live It Up, Honey," and "Sweet Tomorrow."

While she recorded a number of compositions for her own purposes, certain pieces were written expressly for her nieces and nephews to perform. This was especially true of the band's early albums, where nearly all the original compositions came from her pen. Rosemary's songs span a range of topics and emotions. She writes of jubilation and sorrow, the reassurance that comes with faith, and the peaks and valleys that accompany love. Asked to characterize his aunt's music, Raymond W. describes it as being "about love, life, situations. They're just good songs. Not just good bluegrass songs. A good song is a good song. Some are funny, some are love songs."[1]

The sense of humor her nephew notes is most apparent in "Bubblegum Baby" and "Live It Up, Honey" which feature on *The McLain Family Band* and *Country Ham* respectively. Early in the band's career, Raymond K. worried about finding appropriate content for his children to perform. With "Bubble Gum Baby," his sister provides a lighthearted look at adolescent romance for her nieces to sing. Surely this is the only time in bluegrass music where bubble gum is employed and exploited to such remarkable romantic effect, literally uniting the two teenagers by its adhesive qualities. Rosemary's repeated use of internal rhyming is indicative of both her playfulness and her songwriting skills. Musically rousing and verbally inviting, it is not difficult to see why this engaging piece was popular with audiences. In their performance, Alice and Ruth lend the right amount of silliness to the lyrics, and Raymond's Dixieland banjo shows his emerging versatility on the instrument.

Rosemary's high-spirited side is again on full display in "Live It Up, Honey." The petty jealousies displayed in the song sound entirely appropriate when sung by high school girls. The short, spoken exchange by Alice and Ruth is quite endearing, and the nature of the performance fits the tone of the piece. The composer's predilection for word play is again in evidence, and the listener can't help but smile both at the song's endearing goofiness and the exuberance of the band's performance.

In complete contrast to these humorous numbers are the five gospel songs Rosemary contributed to the band's recorded repertoire. "Gather Together" (*The McLain Family Band*) was arranged while the band drove to a gig through the Pennsylvania snow. The word "together" from the title is picked up nicely by the fact that the song is largely sung in unison by Alice and Ruth. A call and response technique also features in the latter half of the piece, with Alice taking the higher register. The lyrics' message to follow God's call is typical for the genre and echoes the entire family's deep sense of faith. Raymond's banjo nicely glides above the vocal line in the last verse.

Raymond K. begins his sister's gospel song, "Moving On to Higher Ground" (*Country Ham*), with an a cappella vocal. This device nicely matches one of the piece's themes: that we begin alone but are strengthened when joined by the power of our creator. Rosemary's song sounds straight from the tradition, a true compliment to her ability as a songwriter. The call and response between the mandolin and banjo is handled well, and Raymond K.'s guitar provides a strong underpinning to the vocals. The song's conclusion features tight harmonies, a trait that is featured with increasing regularity on future recordings.

"Straightaway to Jesus," Rosemary's first contribution to 1975's *Country Life* album, compares faith to music. The narrator wants to join her savior in the ultimate angel band, one where she is happy to simply be part of the chorus. The band again shows its gentle touch by slightly muting its accompaniment during the last verse before building it back up in time for a joyous final chorus. Alice's lead vocals are sure and strong, but the lasting impression one gets from the song is how newly powerful the group's harmonies have become.

"Take One Step at a Time" is the standout piece on *The McLain Family Band*. Anthemic in nature, it has surefire appeal to anyone and everyone who's ever felt down or overwhelmed. While it is essentially another gospel number, the song also boasts secular appeal. Raymond W.'s lead vocal carries the theme well, and his banjo seems to affirm that anything is possible if you have the right attitude and a firm faith. Featuring an irresistible chorus, it is no wonder that the song quickly became one of the band's most requested numbers and delights fans of many musical genres. In his liner notes, Raymond K. recalls how fun it is "to think of everyone with whom we've 'taken one step'. Bill Monroe backstage at Beanblossom especially comes to mind."

"Sweet Tomorrow" (*The McLain Family Band*) was often used as an encore in the group's European performances. Again, the McLains lend some interesting twists to the arrangement, beginning the piece with infectious clapping, designed, no doubt, to invite the audience to join in. Like "Take One Step" and "Gather Together," this song celebrates how faith can help us negotiate life's rocky paths and emerge unharmed. Alice and Ruth's shared vocals beautifully complement the song's theme of support. That the band chose to include "Sweet Tomorrow" in their Carnegie Hall set list in 1982 indicates how much they continued to value it as the years passed.

Related in theme to these gospel songs are "Christmas on the Farm" (*The McLain Family Band*) and "Follow the Light" (*Sunday Singing*). The former is a gentle and touching song Rosemary wrote for her first husband, Jim. The sentiment of enduring love expressed in the lyric is again quite universal. One of the hallmarks of Rosemary's songs is her unabashed openness about expressing her emotions. Much more reserved in person, she often used art to explore her more intimate side. "Follow the Light" is slightly reminiscent of the popular Christmas carol "The Little Drummer Boy" in that a young child tells the story of meeting the Christ child and coaxing a smile out of him with his music.

More difficult to classify than her other compositions are two tracks from *Country Ham*: "I Got High Hopes" and "Hikin' Down the Interstate." The former may owe something to the famous Van Heusen and Cahn composition recorded by Frank Sinatra and dozens of others. The uncertainty of life cataloged in each of the three verses is countered by the optimism of the song's chorus. "Hikin' Down the Interstate" features husky vocals by Raymond W. The fact that hitch-hiking is now considered dangerous and is illegal in many states makes this number rather a period piece. The joys of the open road captured in the lyrics are now sadly unavailable to contemporary travelers. In the performance on *Rosemary*, an additional verse was included, and Raymond W.'s guitar evoked rock and roll, lending the piece an entirely different sound. Here the band's performance is straightforward bluegrass, and the number lasts scarcely more than a minute and a half.

Ten of the songs Rosemary wrote for the band can be classified as love songs. Again, they vary greatly in theme and treatment. It's appropriate that our introduction to the McLains on vinyl is "My Very Sunshine," a number that radiates innocence and also served as the theme song for the band's weekly TV series in Hazard. Alice and Ruth introduce the song with unaccompanied singing before Raymond W.'s banjo sparkles into action, sounding remarkably assured and mature for a player of his tender years. "My Very Sunshine" can be viewed as a tribute to the narrator's love interest, someone who eases her burdens and lights her way through life. The song concludes with a fadeout, one of the few occasions the group would employ this device.

"Please, Mr. Sunshine" picks up on the solar imagery Rosemary often employed in her work. After an upbeat introduction, the song quickly changes pace, morphing into a more relaxed tempo. This technique is then repeated at intervals throughout the remainder of the piece. The song's theme is well suited for performance by youthful musicians, a bright and innocent plea to the sun to continue to shine down on the narrator. Ruth has lead vocal duties here, supplemented by her siblings on harmonies, and Raymond W. contributes a bluesy banjo break. The "hey, hey" in the chorus and the phrasing of "every morning" indicate a pop tendency often found in Rosemary's early compositions.

Rosemary contributed three songs to 1975's *Country Life* album. While they all bear her distinctive mark, each is quite different in subject, tone, and character. "Let Time Walk By and Lose Me" is one of Rosemary's most tender and beautiful compositions. Raymond W.'s moving lead vocal expertly captures the thrill of early love, a time when no one else matters. His banjo fills emulate a tender stroke of the cheek, and his solo is similarly evocative, rising with the passion of new love before resolving gently after its fulfillment. As the liner notes state, "the best of music often has the quality of stopping time." A companion piece of sorts to its immediate predecessor, Rosemary's "Love, Love, Love" features repeated internal rhyming and a newly mature lead vocal from Ruth. This isn't the teenage love of "Bubblegum Baby." Raymond W.'s second banjo solo is quite inventive, and the group once more demonstrates its new prowess by ending its best album to date with a sustained and stirring chorus.

Ruth sings lead on "Always," from *Kentucky Wind*. Her phrasing of "always" is imploring and fits the message of the song perfectly. Here the composer returns to her earlier "stand by your man" stance and includes some of the good humor that typified the songs her nieces and nephews performed on previous LPs. In some ways, the composition is a secular version of "Sweet Tomorrow." Both pieces share the message that it is difficult to go it alone in life. Faith in both God and loving companionship is celebrated in the two songs. As if the band's crisp execution of the composition was not enough, Raymond K. playfully points out in his liner notes that the angel band makes a cameo in the third verse with otherworldly "aaaahhs." "Always" is a lovely way to end one of the band's finest albums.

The honor of closing the band's next recording (*Family Album*, 1978) also fell to Rosemary. "Today is Gone" is a song of parting that lends the proper sentiments to its place on the disk, and its lyrics are sadly appropriate to the lifestyle any traveling band experiences. Genuinely friendly people who took time to speak with members of their audience after shows, the McLains here sing from personal experience and from the heart. In typically positive fashion, however, the narrator stresses the fact that while parting is difficult, a reunion is both desired and possible. In some ways, then, the song is similar to Raymond K.'s "Can't We Get Together Once Again?" recorded in 1976.

With the release of their fourth album, *On the Road* (1976), Raymond K. began to find his own voice as a composer, and the band no longer relied on Rosemary to provide so many of its original songs. "Brown Eyed Baby" is Rosemary's single contribution to an album filled with many short tracks. At just more than three minutes in length, it is the longest and most developed song on the album, but it is not entirely typical of Rosemary's compositions. Here she writes more from imagination than experience. The tender composition sounds as if it could have been a hit for Crystal Gayle of "Don't It Make My Brown Eyes Blue" fame or any number of other country performers. Ruth's vocals are tender and precise. Her phrasing is inventive throughout, especially on "ra-di-o." This quiet love song offers a change of pace from the numerous upbeat numbers on the album and was recorded by the Foster Family String Band on their album, *Bluegrass Old and New*. In her novel, *Pinkhoneysuckle*, Barbara Everett Heintz's narrator mentions hearing the McLains perform this song and notes how universal its sentiments are.[2]

At 4:25, Rosemary's "Bad News Blues" (*Country Ham*) is one of the longest tracks the band ever recorded and has a pleasant, easy-listening feel to it. As is so often the case in songs composed by family members, music is seen here as a tonic for what ails the narrator. Raymond W. adds some typically inventive banjo to the piece, his notes darting up and down the scale to complement the sentiments of the composition.

"Sail Away" (*Kentucky Wind*) is one of Rosemary's finest efforts. Over the years, some reviewers had applauded the band's talent but taken them to task for not being "deep" enough. The brilliance of this song, both in composition and performance, helps to refute this claim. There is tremendous depth of feeling here in Alice's vocals. The song displays both a strong statement of independence and a desperately sad feeling of resignation and regret. If her other songs often display adherence to traditional female roles, "Sail Away" sees Rosemary planting her feet squarely in the 1970s, when NOW (the National Organization for Women) and the ERA (Equal Rights Amendment) were so often in the news and women all over the country were reexamining their relationships with men and their place in contemporary society. It is a sad fact that songs about personal turmoil are often the most lasting and important. While her lighthearted songs are excellent in their own way, this composition showcases Rosemary's true talents as an artist.

After *Kentucky Wind*, Rosemary's songs began to appear with much less frequency on the McLain's recordings. None of her songs feature on the *7th Album* (1979), and 1980's *Big Hill* features only one of her compositions. But if McLain Family Band fans had been forced to wait some time to hear another composition from Rosemary, the beautiful "Our Song" more than rewards their patience. Though written as a tribute to her cancer-stricken father, the composition is as universal as its title. Every family can relate to the piece's tender theme. "You can enjoy this song on a lot of different levels," states Raymond W. "It speaks to me on a very basic level. We have sung it at practically every family wedding or funeral. It's comforting and speaks to life."[3] The song is quite long by the group's standard, and this lends added depth to its sentiments. Like the love mentioned in the lyrics, "Our Song" is a bright star in the night. This is the McLain Family Band at its best. The song originates with them and displays their vocal and instrumental talents as well as their considerable artistry.

In 1982, the band performed two of Rosemary's previously recorded songs on their *In Concert at Carnegie Hall* album. Their spirited play on "Sweet Tomorrow" elicited a strong reaction from the crowd, and verses from "Today is Gone" augmented the number with which they chose to close the show, "I Don't Want to Go." "Blow the Candle Out" appears on 1983's *All Natural Ingredients*. Not to be confused with the traditional English folk song, "Blow the Candles Out," this composition conveys a message of reassurance from the narrator to her sweetheart. Ruth's intimate vocals convey just the right feel to this touching number.

The McLains rerecorded Rosemary's "Take One Step at a Time," "Follow the Light," and "Straightaway to Jesus" on their 1984 album of gospel songs, *Sunday Singing*. The fact that her work sounds on a par with the canonical numbers also included on the album is testament to Rosemary's compositional capabilities. On these and the other songs discussed above, Rosemary's faith, love for life, and optimism are consistently apparent. If a songwriter's mission is to distill life's many challenges and joys into short pieces of art, then Rosemary McLain truly earned that designation.

CHAPTER 7

On the Road

D uring the McLain Family Band's busiest years, they played in all fifty states, both as festival participants and as featured concert performers. While Raymond K. taught at Berea College and his children attended classes there, the family split their time between academics and music, spending one semester concentrating on school, and the other as professional performers.[1] That they were able to excel in both arenas is testament to the family's ability to focus on the task at hand. If their domestic schedule was considerable during these split years, it picked up in the early to mid-eighties, reaching a high of 287 shows in 1983.[2]

It is their time abroad, however, that distinguishes the McLains from their peers. Between 1972 and 1980, the McLain Family Band performed in sixty-two foreign nations, establishing themselves as the most widely traveled bluegrass ambassadors.[3] While this role of promoting bluegrass internationally is one of the band's most significant accomplishments, the McLains were not the first artists to bring the music to foreign shores. Before their experiences abroad, Bill Clifton had established a reputation as a kind of bluegrass envoy.[4] Besides performing his own infectious brand of music, Clifton helped to pave the way for Bill Monroe and other bluegrass artists to follow in his footsteps. A few months after Clifton performed at London's Royal Albert Hall in 1966, for example, Monroe packed the same venue and began to gain a taste for bringing his music to foreign shores. The father of bluegrass would eventually visit a number of countries, including Japan, Israel, Ireland, Germany, Switzerland, and the Bahamas.[5] Still, it is important to note that no other bluegrass performers approached the extent of the McLain Family Band's international presence.

Their appetites whetted from their first experiences overseas in Italy, Germany, and Belgium in 1972, the McLain Family Band was able to return to Europe in 1974, touring England, Romania, Hungary, Spain, Sweden, Norway, Finland, and Iceland. Unbeknownst to other members of the family, Alice had begun to write to various European embassies to gauge their interest in sponsoring appearances by the band. As Raymond W. aptly points out, "a seventeen-year-old person doesn't know what she cannot do."[6] Alice was an avid reader and spent lots of time in the Berea College library. There she found the addresses of cultural attaché officers in U.S. embassies, and she would offer the band's services, painstakingly employing her best penmanship and noting that all they needed in terms of finance were travel costs, a per diem, and a modest honorarium (usually in the range of $400 for a three-day stay). In her letter dated December 26, 1973, to C. Robert Dickerman, public affairs officer for the U.S. Information Service, for example, Alice writes, "We do not consider our tour to be a 'money-gaining job'—we love to perform, and are only interested in coming out even, or a little ahead."[7] She would include a copy of the band's first LP with her letter to give the representatives a taste of what the group had to offer. Once responses began arriving in Kentucky and after the U.S. State Department had called with an offer to help with arrangements, Alice finally revealed what she'd been doing to the rest of the surprised but delighted family. Eventually Betty would take over most of the band's business arrangements, and Beverly Gerstein, from the Office of International Arts Affairs, Department of State, became the point of contact for many of the group's international engagements. Lexington travel agent Martha Pulley was also a key member of the team, charged with the complex task of booking flights for many of the band's early foreign tours.

Betty McLain's role in the success of the band's international tours cannot be overstated. She wrote and responded to mountains of correspondence, all the while juggling availability dates and making last-minute changes to previously established itineraries. Nancy Ann and Michael were still quite young while the family was abroad, and Betty's letters to the travelers were full of details of their daily life back home. In a 1974 letter to Alice, she obliquely notes how much she misses them all. "I think I will start with Weight Watchers, though. I seem to be eating for companionship and that's no good." She then passes on news from the youngest member of the family: "Michael says 'I miss you. Yesterday and the day after that, too.' "[8] While on the road, her children also regularly asked Betty to schedule dentist and doctor appointments for them upon their return to Berea.

Ruth and Alice wrote home frequently, often with their younger siblings in mind. "Michael, do you remember the planets?" Ruth writes in April 1976, before passing on advice to Nancy Ann about which shampoo to use to make her hair appear more shiny.[9] Other letters from Ruth touch on schoolgirl concerns. On March 3, 1974, she notes that she sent "a card to Mrs. Davis—my school counselor—to tell her that I'm not doing *exactly* like we had planned—writing about architecture or a building or something like that, but writing down EVERYTHING."[10]

As the McLains traveled from country to country, the U.S. Information Service posted regular reviews of the group. Local newspapers often wrote enthusiastic reviews of the band as well. The *Independent Helsinki Daily*, for example, was impressed with the band's musicianship, writing, "The indisputable star and absolute master of the band is Raymond W., 20, whose virtuosity and finger acrobatics in playing the banjo were followed with breathless attention."[11] Ruth, too, came in for praise. "The most joyful moments of the concert were offered by the youngest performer of the group. Her bass solos were delightful in their freshness and stylistic genuineness."[12]

The McLain Family Band's tour of England in 1974 included appearances on BBC radio and BBC television, as well as numerous visits to folk music clubs, then very popular in the country. Bicky accompanied them on this trip and opened a great many doors. She had been a member of the International Folk Music Council for years and was friends with a number of important figures in the English

Folk Dance and Song Society, including Maud Karpeles (1885–1976) and Peter Kennedy (1922–2006). Another key contact in England was Sibyl Clark, a regional organizer for the English Folk Dance and Song Society. The frequency of Clark's correspondence with Betty indicates how vital she was to the success of the McLains' appearances in the Birmingham area. Club crowds reacted enthusiastically to the family band, though sometimes Alice and Ruth were subjected to unwelcome attention from young Brits who had imbibed too freely. "It's just that they're overly friendly," Alice diplomatically notes in a letter of February 12. "But we're getting quite good at handling that."[13]

The band's performance at the Grand Old Opry of Newmarket left a vivid impression on attendee Pete Sayers. In a letter written more than three years later, he recalls the band's performance as "one of the most memorable nights we have ever enjoyed in the Opry's lifetime" and goes on to note that "since your appearance we've booked Bill Monroe, Bill Keith and Jim Rooney, Bill Clifton and Red Rector, plus John D. Lowdermilk [sic] and George Hamilton IV."[14]

On tours put together with the cooperation of the U.S. State Department, cultural affairs officers helped ensure that the group's travels were successful by briefing band members about cultural dos and don'ts. In 1974 in Hungary, for example, the McLains were greatly aided by the efforts of cultural affairs officer Stephen Dachi. Dachi was intent on strengthening cultural ties between the United States and Hungary, where he had grown up. Raymond W. notes that "We were the first group to play in Hungary since the Second World War with the official permission of our government."[15] Dachi stressed that appearances by groups like the McLains must be seen as cultural, not political or as a form of Western propaganda. Conscious that an informal appearance might be the best way to present the band, Dachi hosted a large house concert that featured the McLains and included among its attendees music critics, local musicians, and impresarios. "We didn't want to be perceived as trying to draw a crowd," Raymond W. remembers.[16] The band impressed and were invited to return in 1976 to perform as part of a large traveling variety show that also featured popular Hungarian singers, vaudeville acts, comics, dancers, a fashion show, and even a rock band.

THE ALASKAN TOUR OF 1975

To many Americans, traveling to Alaska is like visiting a foreign country. During their 1975 visit to America's Last Frontier, the McLains certainly found much that was surprising. They arrived in Anchorage from Lexington, Kentucky, on February 1, greeted by Alaska State Arts Council liaison Molly Jones. From Anchorage they headed to small towns including Ketchikan, Craig, Skagway, Haines, Wrangell, Petersburg, and Sitka before spending three days in Juneau. From Juneau they returned to Anchorage before driving nearly nine hours to Fairbanks. The band visited the villages of Delta Junction, Glennallen, Valdez, Seward, Kenai, Homer, Kodiak, Bethel, Kotzebue, Noorvik, Noatak, and Kivalina before returning to Anchorage in order to fly to Japan on April 1.

Leaving family members at home when a tour began was always difficult. On this occasion, Betty, Michael, and Nancy Ann were able to join the group in Alaska on February 21 and stayed until March 18. At the moment of parting, when a separation was again necessary, Alice noted in her diary that "the younger ones, especially, didn't want to see us leave. They still don't really understand." [17]

The family quickly learned that navigating the largest state in the union involved numerous modes of transportation. At various points in their journey, they flew on small planes—mainly "goose" pontoon planes but also "beavers" and "golden nuggets." Snow machines (how Alaskans refer to snowmobiles) were sometimes used for shorter journeys. When necessary, the group rented cars. These experiences were among their most troublesome. On March 1, for example, their rental broke down in Delta Junction. A few days later, near Anchorage, their reserved car wasn't ready on time, and when it was it developed engine trouble. To further complicate matters, Raymond K.'s back began to trouble him. Things grew serious enough that he had to occasionally use a wooden board while traveling by car to ease his pain. A visit to a chiropractor helped somewhat, but the discomfort remained for much of the tour.

In the small Alaskan villages, band members would often board with local hosts. The quality of these accommodations varied greatly. Many times, the lodgings were comfortable and the host families gracious; sometimes, however, they performed such duties with obvious reluctance. The food that the families provided varied greatly in quality and portions as well. At times, band members were not provided with the food they had been promised and even occasionally missed meals altogether. Seafood (chiefly salmon, crab, and clam chowder) became their staple diet, though Alice notes in her tour diary that none of them ever developed much of an appetite for the raw, smoked fish highly prized by the natives. And luckily, her fears of having to eat seal blubber were never realized.

Molly Jones became pregnant during the tour, but her replacement, Rick Goodfellow, proved to be a godsend. A staff member at the University of Alaska and later performing arts director for the Alaska State Council on the Arts, Goodfellow lived up to his name by providing a variety of services during the band's stay in Alaska. He acquainted them with local customs, drove them to some gigs, developed photos they shot during the trip, and served as general liaison.

Though the group entertained at a correctional institution in Juneau, an armed forces base in Fort Richardson, and a pipeline camp near Glennallen, schools were their most frequent venues. Shows there usually lasted between thirty and sixty minutes. Attendees usually numbered between 150 and 300, but there were sometimes as many as 600. Concerts performed after normal school hours drew varied audiences. "The auditorium was really full of all kinds of people," Alice notes in her entry from February 13. "Fishermen, high school and grade school kids, housewives, white collar workers, and blue collar workers, everyone from everywhere."[18] It was not unusual for the band to perform multiple shows a day. In fact, on March 23 they established a record with seven separate performances in Kotzebue. Frequently the PA system employed was primitive, and the group often performed without one.

At nearly every school appearance, the group delighted children in the audience with their performance of the "seven jumps dance game." The dance, which originated in Denmark, doesn't include any actual jumps but involves participants holding hands while walking in a circle. At different times in the dance, members balance on one foot, kneel on the floor, bow, or touch their head to the ground. The

bond the McLains were able to establish with the children by means
of this game is typical of how the group always found a way to connect
with their audience, no matter its composition.

While any traveling act will tell you there is no such thing as a
"typical day" on the road, Alice's diary entry for February 9 can be
considered representative.

Haines.

We saw the northern lights tonight. Not very colorful, but exciting to see. This morning we left Skagway on another "goose." It
landed and took off on the ground, although I had some doubts
that we would. The reason I had doubts was that the wind was
extremely fierce. I (and the rest of us) was very sure that we were
going to land on the side of the mountain, on a glacier, on the
bottom of the ocean, or on the broken ice covering the water.
We were trying to turn a curve in a valley with no room, with
one wing up and the other down. The lady beside me was so
frightened that she had her eyes tightly shut the whole trip. It
was enough to make even a healthy person feel queasy in the
stomach. The pilot was very rigid and tense as he sat in his chair
gripping tight to the steering wheel pulling knobs and jerking
levers. Daddy sat in the co-pilot seat, feeling much the same
about the journey. We were relieved to arrive in Haines about
7 minutes after takeoff in Skagway. We took our baggage to
Norman Smith's house where we are spending the night. Ruth's
knees turned purple as the dramatic winds swept across them
during the walk Daddy, Ruth, and I took following our arrival.
She was wearing a dress because she and I were "looking different" today. We stopped at a grocery store, picked up some flying
magazines, chocolate (for our chocolate lovers), raisin crackers,
and dry-roasted pecans, then went to a small restaurant for chili
and tea. We all have decided that at least Raymond (W.), and
possibly all of us, should learn to fly. After returning from our
walk, we spent the rest of the afternoon in bed, getting up at
5 for pizza, giving our evening concert at 8. After the concert
we came back to the house to a party the Smiths were giving in

our honor. (It's now ten minutes after 2 and we're finally getting relaxed to get to sleep. As a matter of fact we're very relaxed.) We gave another small concert for the party by request. There is a possibility that we'll be coming back to Alaska in the future.[19]

Promotion of the group's Alaskan gigs varied greatly. Sometimes performances were well advertised, but on occasion the band found little had been done to alert the local population that they were coming. In these situations, the band sometimes gave impromptu performances earlier in the day before an evening concert to spread the news. On February 28, for example, they played in the cafeteria during lunchtime at the University of Alaska–Fairbanks to drum up a crowd for a performance later that day. On other occasions, however, the band's reputation preceded them. Crowds showed that they were already acquainted with the group by singing along with certain numbers and asking band members to sign albums they had brought with them to the concert. Many audience members created lasting memories by taping the concerts for themselves on cassette recorders.

Alice notes with understandable satisfaction how well they were received by audiences throughout their Alaskan tour. Locals often informed her that the band's show attracted larger crowds than other touring acts. They were given standing ovations and asked for encores at every performance until near the end of the tour (March 18), when the crowd at Bethel failed to rise to its feet. Certain songs went over especially well in Alaska. "Bubble Gum Baby" and "Me and My Gal Sal" were notable hits with youngsters and adults alike. Older Eskimo ladies favored gospel numbers like "I'll Fly Away" and "Amazing Grace." While Alice noted that in general the Eskimos were "very reserved and unemotional," she did often detect "a very quick grin flashing through the crowd."[20]

The tour's schedule was quite demanding, granting the McLains only one true "day off" during their two-month run up north. Any downtime was spent sightseeing or practicing. A rendition of "Big River Blues" was worked up early on in the tour, for example, with Ruth fashioning a break in a new three-finger style on the bass.

Raymond K. wrote "Heavenly Song" (recorded the following year for the *On the Road* LP) during an Easter celebration near the end of the trip.

Performing in the arctic climate was not without its challenges. Band members learned to breathe through their noses whenever possible and found the best way to stay warm was to avoid working up a sweat. Raymond W. lost his voice near the end of the tour in Fort Richardson, forcing the band to give five programs without his vocal contributions. Last-minute changes to the set list were made to accommodate the misfortune. The band's instruments also suffered in the dry air. Raymond W. broke three banjo strings in a single performance in Fairbanks and found the fiddle nearly impossible to tune due to shrinking tuning pegs. Despite such hardships, the McLains enjoyed their time in Alaska, returning there the following three years, and then again in 1980, 1981, and 1984.

JAPAN AND THE FAR EAST

After two months in Alaska, the band flew directly to Tokyo. Again, this part of the tour was made possible by Alice's initiative. She felt that since they were already so far from home in Alaska, they might as well expand their trip to include the Far East. Her attitude illustrates the group's nearly boundless confidence and optimistic outlook. "It seemed as if we could do anything," Alice recalls. Ruth echoes her sister, adding "that's something that Daddy empowered us to feel."[21] Also instrumental to the group's successful tour of Japan were the friendships the family had cultivated earlier in their career. In the early 1970s, for example, the McLains had become familiar with the music of Bluegrass 45, a Japanese bluegrass band founded in 1968 by brothers Saburo (Sab) and Toshio Inoue (Watanabe). Bluegrass 45 quickly established themselves as one of the first major international bluegrass acts, winning over crowds with their musicianship and gaining an invitation to appear at the Bean Blossom festival in 1971. Sab and Raymond W. struck up a friendship, and Sab invited the McLain Family Band to perform in the Land of the Rising Sun as his guests, following in the footsteps of artists like Bill Monroe, the Country Gentlemen, and Bill Clifton. Still,

Sab's invitation was different in nature. While the previous acts had been lured over to perform by wealthy patrons such as Robert Tanaka, Sab's offer came from a more grassroots level. At the time, the Japanese bluegrass scene was beginning to flourish, with more than a hundred bands in existence. This passion for the American-born music spread to audiences as well. During his time in Japan, Raymond K. frequently noted how knowledgeable many members of their Japanese audiences were about bluegrass music.

Sab Inoue greeted the McLains in Tokyo before they began a 250-mile journey to Osaka via monorail. The group was astonished that the lengthy trip took only three hours, half the time it would have taken them to make the journey by car. After months spent in the arctic, they were struck by views of Japan's lush greenery as they made their way south. Fatigued and disoriented from near constant travel, the McLains nonetheless looked forward to meeting bluegrass fans in this Eastern land that had so taken to their form of music. Once they reached their destination, the first order of business was an outdoor afternoon workshop, held in a parking lot. Alice led a two-hour mandolin session, made challenging by the shy nature of the participants and language difficulties. A concert that evening featured three other bands, including one that boasted three female performers. When the McLains launched into "Take One Step," they were surprised to see more than a dozen audience members join them on stage for an impromptu can-can. A long autograph session followed the show. As usual, Alice and Ruth received a good deal of attention from admiring male fans. "One fellow got my autograph," Alice writes in her diary, "said 'I love you' and ran off."[22] Ruth also experienced a memorable encounter. At dinner, where the family employed proper chopstick technique as taught to them earlier by Rick Goodfellow, she asked what kind of fish was featured in the dish they enjoyed. After a long pause, the server answered, "Chicken of the Sea."

The following day the band returned to Tokyo to give two forty-five-minute concerts. Their sightseeing included observing a Buddhist service that Alice describes as simultaneously mysterious and exciting. Just as they were becoming properly acclimated to Japan, it was time to move on to their next port of call, in this case the Republic of China (Taiwan). A U.S. Embassy representative met them at the airport and introduced the band to their sponsor from Far Eastern Artists Management, Adam Cang. The group quickly discovered that advance publicity for their performances had been handled with meticulous professionalism. As they began to look forward to their first appearances, however, they received disappointing news. Radio broadcasts announced that Chiang Kai-Shek, the Republic of China's beloved leader since 1928, had died. During the mourning period, they learned, all forms of entertainment were to be canceled. A hasty meeting with the band's representation and U.S. Embassy staff confirmed that their hands were tied. Before moving on to the Philippines, however, the McLains were asked to tape a previously arranged television show. Alice notes in her diary that the Taiwanese studio was set up to resemble an American town from the Old West and featured haystacks and wagon wheels. Though the TV appearance paid $300, the loss of revenue from canceled shows in Taiwan amounted to more than $700. Alice's diary entry for April 7 voices the band's disappointment. "People recognize us when we go walking, people in stores, and even the guards, that seem to be all over. The magazine with our picture on the front is in most newsstands. It's a shame we can't perform here. Everything is so well set up."[23]

The temperature in Manila was 96 degrees on April 8 when the McLains arrived. After some sightseeing, the band met up with the McNeil family, friends from Berea. On April 10, they played three shows at the International School. As was so often the case on their travels, the group experienced problems with a bass borrowed for the occasion. Even though the instrument's bridge fell off five times during the program, the student audience remained patient and quite appreciative, asking the band for numerous encores. Later that evening, after enduring a typical Manila traffic jam, they relaxed by watching Charlie Chaplin's *The Great Dictator*. Between performances, Alice continued to record local customs in her diary. "There are no street lights at intersections," Alice writes in her entry for April 10. "The most aggressive driver goes first, and if you follow close enough behind, you can go, too. That is, unless the driver going the other direction is even more aggressive. Although there are all these problems, no one loses his temper. Everyone honks their horn and smiles."[24]

While out with the McNeils the next day, Ruth and Alice observed native dancers and, in turn, showed the locals how to clog in best Appalachian style. Sporting sunburns, the band then performed at the University of the East. Though the program was delayed by an hour, it went well, and the institution's founder presented the band with a beautiful plaque to commemorate the occasion. "Our name was misspelled," Alice writes, "but in such a way that it looks like Old English and contributes to the plaque's charm."[25] Their eventful day ended with dinner at the McNeils and a jam session that featured Mrs. McNeil performing on dulcimer.

April 12 was highlighted by a visit to Taal Lake, a unique attraction that features a volcano with a lake inside it. On the drive out with the Cooper family (friends of the McNeils), the group passed numerous fruit markets filled with bananas, papayas, and pineapples. That evening's concert was at the Thomas Jefferson Cultural Center. At the reception afterwards, Alice received a marriage proposal, the suitor noting that Americans looked healthier than Filipinos. An appearance followed on what Alice describes as the "Ed Sullivan Show" of the Philippines.

The Quirino Grandstand at Rizal Park was the site of their next concert appearance. There, "many people wanted to know the purpose of our coming," Alice notes. "They couldn't understand that we don't have any particular message, except to make people happy, and that we play music because we love it."[26] For once the PA system worked well, and as the band's music was heard across the grounds of the park, the crowd began to swell. Afterwards the group was again swarmed by fans and well-wishers.

On April 14, the band left the Philippines for their next destination: Jakarta, Indonesia. A representative, Flemming Nyrop, met them at the airport and briefed them on local customs, which Alice noted in her diary. "Don't take, pass, or gesture with your left hand—as it is considered unclean. Don't cross your legs or point the sole of your foot at anyone—it is a deep insult. Don't touch the back of anyone, if you must be familiar with someone, a light touch on the elbow is greatly appreciated. Don't pat anyone on the head, even small children, for that is where your soul lies."[27] Acting on Nyrop's advice was not always easy. Family members found eating without using their left hand to be a challenge, and the water was unsafe for them to drink. They settled for pear juice and enjoyed the spicy food typical of the region.

The band's Indonesian shows were very well promoted, many of them selling out days in advance. Beautiful posters of the group seemed to be everywhere, and huge banners advertising their performances were spread over the streets. If the concerts were well promoted, local conditions sometimes made performing difficult. The show at the Public Attorney's Office, for example, found the group coping with swarms of mosquitoes. Such discomfort was offset by their discovery of a Berea College graduate in the audience. A concert at the Youth Center helped to celebrate its tenth anniversary, and the McLains were tickled to learn that Queen Elizabeth had appeared in the same building a year previously. As was often the case, local musicians played for them before the show. The McLains particularly enjoyed hearing the *anglungs* (an instrument made up of two or sometimes four bamboo tubes attached to a frame), and eventually ordered a pair for themselves to be shipped back home to Kentucky.

On April 18, Raymond K. celebrated his forty-seventh birthday. His family played that day for children (about half of whom were American) at the embassy school before flying on to Bangkok in the evening. The band was overnighting there, en route to Laos the next day, and had not previously arranged for accommodations. They asked a local taxi driver for a recommendation, and he took them to a hotel to spend the night. There the band was dismayed to find their rooms teeming with hundreds of insects. "Bugs! Everywhere you look there's another kind of bug!" Alice notes in her diary entry.[28] The band quickly moved on to Luang Prabang, the royal capital of Laos. There an interpreter taught Ruth some phrases in Lao, including "thank you" and "we're glad to be here." When she practiced the phrase on their driver for the day, however, he was so confused (or impressed) that he immediately stopped the car in an effort to regain his composure. At the theater where they performed that night, the band was delighted to see themselves depicted on a larger-than-life sign painted especially for the occasion.

The political situation in Laos was very volatile during the McLain's time there, a coalition government trying to keep the nation together in a period of civil war. At one performance in Luang Prabang, Alice recalls that there were "soldiers from one side with their machine guns over on one side, and soldiers from the other side also in the audience, complete with weapons."[29] Much to their relief and satisfaction, the band saw that they could—at least for a moment—make a difference during such difficult times. "It was our mission to connect," Alice recalled, "to draw people together. During our shows we'd see them sharing cigarettes with each other, talking with each other. I don't know if that was because of us, but our goal was to connect people. The audience seemed to be drawing together in a very visible way even with the military present."[30] Mere weeks after the band left the country, the communist Pathet Lao organization assumed power in Laos.

The group's next destination was Burma. "We are being sponsored by the Burmese government while we are here," Alice notes in her diary. "We're the second group ever sponsored on a cultural exchange. Martha Graham's dance troupe was the first. It seems we are following her all over the country."[31] The McLains were always looking for ways to connect with their foreign audiences. In Burma they were provided with words and music to a Burmese folk song that organizers hoped they would perform in concerts. Ruth was chosen as the band member to learn the song, which she did admirably. The task proved difficult since she had only two days to memorize the piece and its musical scale was so different from Western traditions.

Alice's diary entry for their April 25 stay in Rangoon details another busy day and shows the difficulty the band had learning the popular Burmese song.

> Slept late.
> 10:00. Worried about Burmese song, practiced on it some.
>   Ruth particularly concerned. Rehearsing all the time.
> 11:00. Met with Minister of Culture, hosts, and Mr. Coward,

US Ambassador for dinner. Very nice, starting with
Burmese orchestra containing a harp—in the shape
of a cradle, a kind of a cross between an oboe and a
recorder, a bamboo xylophone, drums (tuned with
rice and ash peso) and a wood block and cymbal. 3
girl singers. They played for approx. 45 min. Received
presents from the Home Minister.

2:30.   Went to USIS to learn song.
4:30.   Back to Hotel to rest. Daddy to Airport to meet
        Grandmother.
6:00   Left for open air theatre—Grandma arrived.
7:30.   Rehearsed Burmese song.
10:30. Party. With Rock Bands playing all the time.[32]

OTHER PORTS OF CALL

After Burma, the band moved on to Nepal, India, Afghanistan, Iran,
Egypt, Lebanon, and Tunisia before finishing their exhausting year
with performances in Austria, Romania, Hungary, Czechoslovakia,
and Poland. In the years that followed, the McLain Family Band
continued to spread the gospel of bluegrass around the world. In
1977, 1978, and 1980 the band toured Africa, visiting Algeria,
Benin, Burundi, Cameroon, Chad, the Central African Republic,
Congo, Liberia, Mauritius, Rwanda, Zaire, and Zambia. During
these visits they were assisted by Ms. Gail Gulliksen, whose lengthy
title was program officer, Africa Regional Services, International
Communication Agency. Ms. Gulliksen's pretour letters to Betty
are full of detailed instructions for inoculations, as well as various
forms of documentation the group would need. Eager to help, Dr.
Charles Harris, director of the Berea College Health Center, provided letters stating that the family members were in good health
and bore no communicable diseases. Nor, according to the Berea
Police Department, were they likely to create civil unrest. For an
earlier visit to Brazil in 1976, the same organization had described
the McLains as "fine, upright, loyal citizens of Berea, Kentucky, the

United States of America, whose conduct is above reproach. We do not expect that they ever will cause any trouble."[33]

While the McLains kept up their customary good spirits throughout their foreign tours, they did, of course, encounter numerous hardships and adversity. Staying in good health was always a challenge; each band member lost his or her voice on more than one occasion. Homesickness was also common. In a letter to her mother, for example, Alice writes, "I want so much to be home in Berea. I don't want to travel anymore. Touring is a constant strain on the nerves—trying to keep everything smooth and trying not to do the wrong thing."[34] An earlier letter home from Ruth expresses similar emotions but ends with the characteristic McLain optimism. "I kind of feel like I'm missing out on so much at school and w/all my friends—but just think what I'm doing and where I am and where I'm going and how many people never get to do this!"[35] Again, in 1975, Ruth writes home from Cairo, noting that "we're homesick. We're ready to come home. Here we are with some days that we're not giving shows and all we can think about is how we'd like to be home!"[36]

While abroad, financial concerns often surfaced, sometimes due to enforced changes in their schedule. In 1974, for example, the band arrived in Madrid only to find that their appearance needed to be delayed for a week. Besides affecting upcoming dates in Sweden, this unforeseen complication forced them to find less expensive accommodations outside Madrid and tested Raymond K.'s schoolboy Spanish. A year later, while in Lebanon, the band received only one day's per diem, even though they were scheduled to be in the city for five days. This Middle Eastern visit was rife with complications, in fact. In a letter home, Ruth expresses fear that their concert won't be well attended "especially with all the trouble here now. There's hardly anyone walking along the streets, particularly at night." She rather ominously notes that she can hear planes landing and taking off often, before moving on to more concrete details. "We just watched a man, from our balcony, who had a gun and shot 4 shots. Nobody killed. Maybe he was shooting birds?"[37] Years later, Alice recalled: "Sometimes we would be told: 'It would be better if you stayed in your rooms.' The most important thing was the connection, though. If you let the fear overcome that, then the fear has won."[38] Despite the exposure to such tensions, however, group members managed to keep their cool, following the example Raymond F. had set during the Suez Canal crisis.

Mixed in with such periods of stress were moments of real magic, including a workshop in Lebanon that Raymond W. will never forget. "About 50 to 60 people came," he recalled years later. "Some with band instruments like tubas, and some who were voice majors at the university. They all came to learn how to play bluegrass music, and none of them spoke much English. Daddy thought, well, almost everybody can *count* in English. So he wrote a counting song right there on the spot, made up entirely of numbers. Within minutes, he had everyone singing along, having a great time."[39]

As paterfamilias, Raymond K. bore considerable pressure on the group's foreign tours. To help plan for possible complications, he prepared as best he could before trips abroad began. One year, for example, the band landed in Paris, only to find that Raymond K.'s Martin D-35 guitar was missing. Leaving nothing to chance, Raymond K. had earlier written his name and Berea address in the instrument's sound hole. While the rest of the family set out to view a performance by the famous mime, Marcel Marceau, Raymond K. stayed behind in the hotel room to await news of the instrument's whereabouts. Sure enough, a call soon came through from Betty reporting that the guitar had been found and that she had directed that it be sent on to Paris. All band members carried extra passport photos as well. This came in handy when Al White's passport was confiscated for unknown reasons by government officials in Mauritius in 1977.

Despite occasional complications, however, most trips presented few major difficulties, and the McLains were always greeted enthusiastically by foreign audiences. A letter from James D. Burns, deputy cultural attaché in Chile, provides a typical example of the impression the band made. "Based on Chile, you all have a lot to be proud of because of the friends you made for yourselves, your music, and our country. I have been impressed by the unanimity of Chilean comments from North to South about you. After they exhaust their supply of adjectives describing you as warm and friendly people they can relate to almost instantly, they rave about how they dig your bluegrass music and hope you return very soon."⁴⁰

An American Embassy report from Algeria in December 1978 is similar in tone. "It's a long way from Kentucky to Algiers, but the McLain Family Band bridged the miles, the barriers of language and culture and totally different musical traditions to bowl over the Algerians with their homespun Kentucky spontaneity, consummate musicianship, and finger lickin' good sounds from Appalachia." The embassy official goes on to mention that the audience was mainly university students and faculty and that the concert was taped for nationwide broadcast. "While programs of American regional music are not a high post priority, perhaps no American artists to perform here in recent memory had so much personal contact with so many members of their audiences and did so much to popularize the American folk music tradition. The McLains' easy informality proved particularly effective in demonstrating to Algerians that Americans are warm, approachable, and concerned about their fellow men."⁴¹

Jack Perry, chargé d'affaires ad interim for the U.S. Embassy in Czechoslovakia, was equally enthusiastic in his praise and notes the group's wide appeal:

I feel too strong about the kind of music you do to write diplomatic notes on it. I grew up on that kind of music, and I love it. And I loved you. The interesting thing is, though, that everybody loved you, not only Southerners but also Yankees and even (among others I noticed in the crowd) a gaggle of ambassadors from Bulgaria, Britain, Afghanistan, Burma and such-like places; a Prussian count; a Czech lady who graduated from Vassar in the twenties; Embassy gardeners and laundresses and also Ministry of Foreign Affairs functionaries; Czechoslovak doctors, businessmen, officials, and especially Czechoslovak young people—in short, everybody. For us at the Embassy, contact with the people of this country is not easy, especially with the young people. Your music reached right out and brought them in, and that is wonderful for us. We think you are splendid emissaries and we hope you will come back for sure next year. Thanks for uplifting us.⁴²

In fact, some members of the Czech audience were so moved by one of the band's performances that they came up to the band with tears in their eyes and touched their faces.

While the McLains genuinely enjoyed every stop on their travels, some countries seem to have stood out as favorites. Writing home in 1976, Ruth notes her love of Afghanistan and Laos (visited in 1975) but states that Bolivia "goes top of my list." Her description paints a vivid picture of life there. "So much vigor with all the open markets, mostly lit by little fires, Indian women rushing around, dressed in many layers of clothing, topped off with large shawls—then really topped off with a Derby hat."[43] In order to help adjust to the altitude there (thirteen thousand feet), Ruth notes that at the airport, band members were given a welcome kit that included pills to accommodate the change. She also mentions her father's fascination with the large number of old cars still being driven there. On another stop on the same tour, Ruth writes about the devastation wrought by a recent earthquake in Guatemala. "We were told that our shows were the first times they've seen some of these people smile since the earthquake."[44]

Everywhere they went, in fact, the McLains bonded with their audiences. Early on, Raymond K. had instilled in his family the importance of connecting with concert attendees, and his lesson was not lost on Alice. "The audience is just as much of a performer as the performer is himself. If an audience is very passive, if they don't react to the performer, the performer cannot give as much himself because he's not helped. An audience needs to help a performer just as much as a performer needs to give something to the audience."[45] During their U.S. tours, the band had already experienced the different ways audiences might react to their music. Eastern Kentucky crowds, for example, were quite reserved, but their staid demeanor masked the fact that they were often deeply moved by the music. "They might not be outwardly showing any response at all," Alice recalled, "but after the show in talking with them you'd find that this was the most meaningful thing in their life."[46] Thus when audiences in the Far East failed to applaud at the conclusion of their numbers, the band was not unduly fazed. "You have to understand the audience you're playing for," Raymond K. said years later. "In Burma, we didn't hear much applause and that worried us a lot until someone explained to us that there is a religious thing about not killing organisms that might be in the air between your hands as you're clapping, so people were clapping out of kindness to us but they were doing it very gingerly so they wouldn't hurt anything either."[47]

The nuances, not to mention the basic storyline of a song, were, of course, often lost on foreign audiences. Happily, this did not prevent them from enjoying the energy of the band's performance, and the McLains masterfully communicated the spirit and general thrust of a song even to those who might not understand precisely what was being revealed to them. "Language doesn't seem to make too much difference in this kind of music," Raymond K. later noted. "It seems to come through just fine. I think it's because we like the music so much."[48] The band also quickly learned that the between-song patter and introductions they used for American audiences needed to be curtailed or eliminated altogether when performing abroad. Occasionally an interpreter would brief the crowd on the lyrical content of a number, but generally it was left to the vocalist to convey the meaning of a song.

One of the most difficult emotional challenges of touring was leaving behind friendships that had been established. "When we go to a country there's often someone put in charge of us," Alice recalled. "Someone who takes care of us, and just as soon as we begin to feel that we know them or can have any kind of a friendly relationship with them, we leave them immediately. That's the hardest thing for me."[49] Ruth's letter home conveys similar thoughts. "The people have been just marvelous, but what is hard is making all these nice friends and then leaving them. You get kind of so you don't want to make good friends, because you know you'll have to say goodbye right away."[50]

Bidding farewell to fans was equally difficult, of course. Upon returning home to Berea, the band was gratified to find plenty of fan mail in their PO box, often written in broken English (reproduced here). Akila Bellahouel from Algeria wrote to Alice in 1978: "Perhaps you have forgotten me but I don't." She asks for photos of the band and what they thought of her home country. "Let me tell you that you were fantastique and I passed two hours of my life very nice in admiring you. I wish to enjoy you again but I don't know if it's possible then I'm sad."[51] Another fan wrote, "I'm be in love with your record, it's really, very, but very good. When I listen it, I remember your wonderful show, and I cry, because I long for it. When I received it, I jumped of gladness. I listen it every day, and, now, I'm listening it, because I love it very much. Could you send me the letters of your music? I want to know it, because I want to sing, and know the significations of it."[52]

Peter Kandler saw the band perform in Stuttgart. His letter of September 16, 1972, to Raymond K. shows that some of the group's fans were already quite familiar with other bluegrass artists.

> I have a great collection of original bluegrass-records from the U.S.A. (Flatt & Scruggs, Reno & Smiley, Bill Monroe, Stanley Bros, Country Gentlemen, Jim & Jesse, Earl Taylor, Jimmy Martin, Red Allen and many others) and all my great joy is bluegrass. This was the greatest true bluegrass-feeling of a group and it makes me so happy to hear the beautiful voices of the girls in her perfect harmony and the masterful five-string-action of your son. Your songs and sounds make me searching to see and visit the land of your home and your people. The sound of five string and harmony singing of your group is in fact the best bluegrass that I have ever heard. I hope I can find the right words to tell you what I mean. My English is not so good. Your group give me so much devotion that I can only say: that evening was the biggest evening in music for me.[53]

A letter from admirer Carlen Kreutzer includes a lovely turn of phrase that well summarizes the impact the family band had on its audiences. "It has been nearly a week since your concert at the Cairo American College and my soul is still singing. . . . People are smiling because of your presence—we hope you are too!"[54]

There were some destinations the family hoped to visit but were not able to due to scheduling complications or for financial reasons. These included Argentina, Bangladesh, Cyprus, the Dominican Republic, Greece, Jamaica, South Korea, New Zealand, Paraguay, Portugal, South Africa, Sri Lanka, Togo, and Yugoslavia. In 1982, the group was invited to perform in the Soviet Union. Leland Cross, cultural attaché at the U.S. Embassy there, had held a similar position earlier in his career in Mexico and Guatemala and had worked with the McLains. "We are presently trying to put together a mini-cultural festival for the week preceding the Fourth of July—an expression of some of the best of several facets of American culture—and, remembering your wonderful work as musical representatives of the U.S., I thought I would sound you out as to the possibility of us bringing you here for some concerts during the June 27–July 4 period. The performances would be for invited Soviet audiences and the American embassy community."[55] The McLains accepted the offer only to learn a month later that the opportunity had been mooted due to lack of financial support from the embassy.

On their foreign sojourns, the band members gained a new perspective on their identity as Americans. "One of the things we were aware of even when we were very young is that we were representing the United States," Alice said years later. "We were representing families. We really felt the weight—in a good way—of being cultural ambassadors. We were making a connection that our governments might not be making. All we were was a family. We were genuinely connecting to the people we were playing for and with. That connection is what's so important. I think that often when people met us they realized that maybe they had a misunderstanding of what the United States was."[56] Indeed, many who saw the McLain Family Band perform were familiar only with the image of Americans as portrayed by Hollywood films. The fact that the group was a rural, family act definitely appealed to audiences all over the world. In modern parlance, foreign audiences felt they could relate to the band. After performances, patrons would often chat with group members and share stories from their own lives.

Raymond K. nicely summarizes the impact touring overseas had on him and the value of international travel. "It means a lot to play for foreign audiences," he noted, "because it's a matter of pride in our nation really. I didn't realize how terribly American we are until I was overseas. I think it would do us all good in this country if we could step away and look at ourselves a little better and realize just how we are. We're very pleased to try to show some of the better aspects of our country."[57]

Reflecting on what she learned overseas, Ruth succinctly states why music is known as the international language: "All cultures in the world have the same basic things. They all have some kind of vocal music, usually some kind of percussive music, some kind of string music. We all have the same basic needs and interests."[58] Thanks to their infectious good spirits, toe-tapping music, and a genuine willingness to make new friends, the McLain Family Band were ideally suited to play the role of bluegrass ambassadors. It is hard to imagine how families, America, or bluegrass music could have been better represented.

CHAPTER 8

"My Name's Music"

The thirty-two original tracks the McLain Family Band recorded between 1973 and 1986 represent some of their finest and most lasting work. The fourteen instrumentals display their virtuosity and melodic gifts, while the eighteen songs demonstrate both their originality and the valuable lessons they learned from their peers and those who came before them. These works constitute an integral part of the group's enduring legacy.

INSTRUMENTALS

Raymond W. wrote all but three of the group's original instrumentals. According to his father's liner notes, "Raymond's Breakdown" from the band's debut album was dedicated to Don Reno. An early demonstration of Raymond W.'s virtuosity, the piece is nicely augmented by the driving rhythm of his father's guitar, and we also hear Ruth's first short bass solo midway through the track, a slow interlude that lends a nice contrast to the rest of the performance. Raymond W.'s affection for the composition is reflected by the fact that he would record it again twenty years later on his solo album, *A Place of My Own*.

Describing Raymond W.'s banjo technique can be difficult. In an article originally written in 1975 and then republished in 1983, Wayne

Shrubsall acknowledges this challenge. "Pinning the McLain style down is impossible," he states, "since he apparently approaches each song with no set banjo 'attack' in mind. Such a method allows the artist a great deal of flexibility; it promises the listener a pleasurable and dynamic listening experience."[1] Shrubsall contends that when listening to McLain play the banjo, one never knows just what to expect. Raymond W. has "created a banjo style synthesizing various banjo techniques with his own prodigious ideas about how a banjo should be played. . . . Frequently McLain will employ a melodic-chromatic approach. But never will the style he'll use on any one song be predictable. This eclectic tendency assists in making his banjo work both enjoyable and exciting."[2]

The title of "Silver Creek," another of Raymond W.'s originals that appears on the band's first album, stems from a long tradition in bluegrass and old-time music of naming pieces after bodies of water. Shrubsall included the banjo tab for the number in the article cited above, though the author is quick to admit that "space will not permit all the variations McLain plays."[3] In his essay, Shrubsall, a player of considerable talent himself, provides a detailed analysis of the complex piece that is addressed to fellow banjo players. For our purposes, it is important to simply note that McLain's melody and his execution of the composition "push aside limitations of banjo technique within a Blue Grass format."[4]

Mostly an instrumental, with a few lines added by Rosemary near the end to provide spice to the number, "Country Ham," the title track of the band's second album, was written by Raymond W. to glorify southern cooking. According to the liner notes, the piece also captures in music how the entire family feels about performing. "Communicating through music is more than a satisfaction for us. It is a kind of urgent responsibility. The feeling is difficult to describe in words. It's easier in sound. 'Bon appétit!' " Ruth is given another chance to solo on bass, while her brother's banjo conjures a tasty stew bubbling in the pot.

The title track of the band's fourth album, "On the Road" clocks in at just over a minute in length. Some listeners may not be sure if Raymond W. is playing the banjo or whether it has taken him over and he is merely channeling its dynamic energy. Obviously a favorite of the composer, Raymond W. rerecorded it on *A Place of My Own*. While it can be difficult to concentrate on anything but the lead instrument in this number, Ruth's bass wonderfully underpins her brother's efforts throughout. She also contributes a short bass solo near the end of *Country Life*'s "Blue Licks Breakdown," a piece that somehow manages to sound simultaneously relaxed and insistent.

An easygoing fiddle piece named for the family farm, "Big Hill" provides the title track for the band's eighth album and recalls western swing. The band revisited the composition on their *Country Dance* recording, pairing it (as "Big Hill/Fiddle-a-Little") with a tune Raymond W. wrote to accompany his KET program of the same title, which aired in the 1980s. In 1983, Raymond W. worked with Dr. John Forbes to produce a spiral-bound book to accompany the series. Subtitled *A 'Start from Scratch Guide to Fiddling,'* it includes both standard notation and fiddle tabs to help students learn some basic tunes. In this short work, Raymond describes a fiddle player as "someone who learns to play by watching and imitating others."[5] Based on the performance on display here, listeners would do well to use Raymond W. as a model. "Yesterday's Waltz" is a gentle piece from the same album that, like "The Bells of St. Mary's," is contemplative in nature. The McLains recorded three waltzes throughout their career, indicating their love of the form that many have called both sad and uplifting.

"Skaggs' Rag" (*All Natural Ingredients*) is a stately instrumental Raymond W. wrote to honor his friend, country music star turned bluegrass revivalist Ricky Skaggs. In 1982, when Skaggs was still topping the country charts, Raymond W. interviewed him for KET's *Bywords* series. "One of the questions I asked him was, 'Why are we not competitive?' We've always been friends, the same age, doing the same sorts of things. His answer was, 'Because we don't have to be.'"[6] This refreshing exchange wonderfully characterizes the personalities of both men. "Skaggs' Rag" opens with Raymond W. on fiddle, and it also features Michael Riopel's guitar and Ruth's bass solo. The fiddle finale concludes the performance in fine style and is a fitting tribute to a fellow Kentuckian.

On the liner notes for the band's first album, Raymond K. wrote the following in regard to "Silver Creek": "Raymond wrote this 'creek' instrumental to describe the stream that runs through Berea. He should have done one back in Knott County where he was raised. How would 'Troublesome Creek' sound?" More than a dozen years later, Raymond W. took his father's advice and wrote "Troublesome Creek." This instrumental is one of his best compositions and is still performed regularly by the band during concerts. Its provenance is fascinating. While on tour in Benin, Africa, Raymond W. observed numerous villages built on or near water and began to ruminate on his own experiences with rivers, streams, and creeks. The composition thus began to grow in his subconscious, and he added the second half of the piece when he returned home. "Growing up in Eastern Kentucky, you're conscious of the way the water flows," Raymond recalled in an interview. "People give directions that way."[7] A banjo lick from friend Craig Wales influenced the tune's harmony section, and both Michael and Ruth collaborated with their brother to complete it. The brothers' conversant banjos emulate the flow of the creek and take the listener on a bouncing ride downriver. Ruth's mandolin work on the piece is also noteworthy. Her solo is skillfully played, and her aggressive chording in the middle of the piece adds a new level of energy as the performance gains momentum. A short bass tag concludes what has become one of the band's signature tunes.

Raymond W.'s "Cherry Road" nicely bookends the *Troublesome Creek* album. Both the piece itself and its recording are unusual. Raymond W. describes "Cherry Road" as the only composition he wrote in this particular style, and the band used overdubs in the studio to lay it down, a practice quite rare for them. This is as close to a rock sound that the group ever got. Throughout the number, the banjo and the guitar seem to swap roles and complement each other as they separate and ultimately reunite. The mandolin included near the conclusion of the piece adds a nice touch to an engaging performance.

Ruth and Michael also contributed original instrumentals to the band's oeuvre. "Dickenson County" is the fifth and final instrumental on *Big Hill* and was written by Ruth at Ralph Stanley's festival as a tribute to him and his brother. Raymond's fiddle is heard to good effect throughout the piece, but it is Ruth's mandolin that drives the number. Her "October Rose" was recorded for the *Country Dance* album. It is a sprightly tune that reflects its composer's engaging personality and was written to elicit the nature of a country outing during Indian summer. "Quicksand," one of Michael McLain's earliest compositions, is shorthand for Kentucky's Quicksand Creek, the inspiration for this banjo tune that was recorded at Carnegie Hall. The mandolin drives the piece and is joined by Raymond W.'s fiddle, which ornaments the melody. Parts of this interesting composition contain elements that hint at music from the Far East and indicate the youngest McLain's emerging talent.

SONGS WRITTEN BY MCLAIN FAMILY BAND MEMBERS

On "Bound for Gloryland" from *The Family Album*, Ruth tries her hand at writing a gospel tune and succeeds admirably. Composed on her birthday with some help from her father while the band was on tour in Zambia, "Bound for Gloryland" was recorded by the Lewis Family before its appearance here and was later covered by Rhonda Vincent in 1994 when she was a member of the Sally Mountain Show. While the McLains would often open shows with this number, Vincent recalls that she liked to employ it as a finale.[8] The "angel band" mentioned in the chorus is a concept the McLains continually returned to. The group recorded "Angel Band" for the *Family Album*, Rosemary makes indirect reference to the celestial music makers in "Straightaway to Jesus," and Raymond K. uses the phrase in "Back Up and Push." On that composition, recorded for *Kentucky Wind*, Raymond K. faced a difficult task: take a well-loved and established instrumental and provide it with lyrics that are as good as the tune. Such challenges have been met before, of course. Pee Wee King set lyrics to "Bonaparte's Retreat," and Bob Wills's "San Antonio Rose" began life as an instrumental before it was turned into a song. In any case, here Raymond K. succeeds magnificently. After hearing the band perform the number on the Grand Ole Opry, no less a figure than Roy Acuff, the king of country music, told Raymond W. how much he liked the lyrics. As he does in so many of his compositions, Raymond K. addresses the listener directly in this song ("Did you ever wonder about the riddle?") and also uses a conditional phrase

("If you let the devil, play on your senses") to set up a proposition for the listener. One of the band's most popular and requested numbers, they often opened shows with it. Raymond W.'s singing is flawless on this recording. He hits all the high notes and pauses in all the right places. To top off his performance, he answers the riddle of the fiddle with some inspired bowing.

In "Back Up and Push," Raymond K. successfully instilled humor into the rather serious business of eternal salvation. His predilection for taking a lighter approach to life is also evident on several of his other compositions. "Old Maid Song" (*On the Road*) shows off his considerable songwriting chops on this amusing and original look at an oft-treated topic. The melody is catchy, and the lyrics are well executed. While "Old Maid Song" and the band's earlier recording of the traditional "Married Me a Wife" at first glance display an old-fashioned mountain attitude towards courtship and marriage, the humor lent to both pieces helps soften the message. The proud father composed the song in jest for Ruth's seventeenth birthday during the group's 1975 Far East tour. Band members display their sense of humor as they echo Ruth's lead vocal line, stating, "I guess she'll never share her apple pie!" The short (1:38) song features a rare guitar break and a fine mandolin solo.

"Believe Me" (*On the Road*) is another brief (1:24) diversion Raymond K. wrote for the band. Apparently a good many additional verses not included here were composed and improvised for various occasions, including one dedicated to their friend Janette Carter: "Although it may be cold and wet, / We're glad to see our friend Janette." On the recorded version of the piece, the McLains ruminate on two basics of the human experience: "No matter if it's fried or stewed, nothing tastes as good as food. / Another lesson mighty plain, nothing hurts as much as pain." Raymond W.'s fiddle is nicely answered near the end of the song by Ruth's bass interjection.

"Wild Honey" was Raymond K.'s first original composition to be recorded by the band and serves as a fitting beginning to the bucolic *Country Life* album. The lyrics detail the risk/reward proposition of attaining the product of foraging bees, as the composer again uses a conditional phrase ("But if you want the best") to make his point. Like many of the band's arrangements, this one was perfected on the road, bouncing along in a little Fiat in Spain. Ruth beats up on the bass at the end of every verse, and Alice supplies a nice mandolin break before the last stanza. Raymond's vocals sound suitably playful, and his sisters provide lovely backup singing. Surely it is the only bluegrass song ever recorded that features a grinning bear.

Equally playful is "Alaska Airlines," cowritten by Raymond K. and Raymond W. for *Big Hill*. The McLains toured Alaska quite frequently, and this very brief (1:00) jingle serves as their tribute to the airline that flew them up to the Last Frontier. The melody certainly had legs. When Thelma Stovall (1919–1994) ran for governor of Kentucky, she adapted the piece as her campaign song. Years later it also served as the basis for Morehead State's recruiting song when Raymond W. became director of the Traditional Music Center there.

"Down Home Waltz" (*Family Album*) shows that the apple doesn't fall far from the tree. Just as his father did with "Back Up and Push," here Raymond W. pens appropriate words to accompany the lovely waltz written by family friend Buck White. The gentle mandolin introduction suitably prepares the listener for the soothing, heartfelt lyrics that follow. The notion of looking back on "old dusty albums of faded photographs" with a sense of longing for the past is universal. Unabashedly sentimental, the song recalls Rosemary's sensibilities. Featuring a lovely guitar break and first-class singing, this recording ranks among the family's best work. In concert the group sometimes paired the piece with "Suwanee River" and "Old Kentucky Home." Such is its quality that it does not sound out of place in such esteemed company.

In 1976, while on tour in Brazil, Raymond W. and his father worked together to create another excellent song, the lovely and timeless "Kentucky Wind." Father and son were suffering from a bout of homesickness when Raymond K. noted that the breeze blowing across their faces in South America was the same one they had felt so often in Kentucky. Like so many of the group's arrangements, this one begins with unaccompanied vocals. The rapid strumming of the mandolin nicely evokes the zephyrs of the title. If nature is depicted as mysterious early in the song ("it's not in our experience to know"), its constant presence is also reassuring ("It brings back now and then an old-time feeling / Left over from its never-ending race"). This uncertainty is reflected in the rather unresolved nature of the song's ending, where another conditional ("If I could only see things as the wind does") hints at the possibility of true understanding. The rerecording of "Kentucky Wind" nine years later for *Troublesome Creek* was prompted by KET producer Russ Farmer's suggestion that during a video shoot, Raymond W. could add some bluesy banjo licks to simulate the gentle breeze mentioned in the song.[9] Raymond W. rose to the challenge but believed he wouldn't be able to sing the piece sufficiently well with this additional instrumental responsibility. Lead vocals thus fell to Ruth, whose artful ornamentations lend a different feel to the new recording.

"Show Me That You Know Me" (*Troublesome Creek*) was written by Raymond K. much closer to home, on the way to a band performance at the Carter Fold in Hiltons, Virginia. Remarkably, the group performed the number on stage that same night. The lyrics include playful use of parallel structure ("Show me that you know me, and I'll show you") and yet another conditional ("If you've got the feeling, let's get on with the healing"). Like Raymond K.'s other compositions, the song stresses that in order to find happiness, it is often necessary to take chances. The piece is also interesting musically, as Raymond W. employs a six-string banjo given to him by Sonny Osborne to accommodate the additional range the song required.

"You're Why I Try" (*Troublesome Creek*) celebrates the power of friendship. Though written for band managers Charles Hamlen and Edna Landau, its sentiments are universal and serve as an appreciation of any of those wonderful intimates who raise our spirits and inspire us to carry on. The narrator contrasts his life before he met his friend ("Once upon a time I didn't care") with how things currently stand ("So now I've said hello, let's get on with the show"), again demonstrating Raymond K.'s belief that contentment can only be obtained by taking positive action. Raymond W. sings lead on the song, which also features one of his signature fiddle breaks. Together with the album's title track and "Kentucky Wind," the song was often performed by the band with orchestras as the "Troublesome Creek Suite."

The infectious "Can't We Get Together Once Again?" closes *On the Road* and was often performed near the end of concerts or as an encore. Raymond K. wrote it as a gift of sorts to the group's growing fan base, and the song's theme is certainly one that every touring band can relate to. His direct question to the "you" in the song (equally effective here as a reference to either an individual or the band's audience) is a technique he employed regularly. Raymond W. has also spoken about how the song evokes the joy of a family reunion. Berea College faculty member Fred de Rosset translated the song into Spanish for performances abroad, and Ruth once heard it played in this language on a Delta Airlines flight. Musically reminiscent of "The Girl I Left Behind Me," the song features call and response vocals and a typically riveting banjo solo.

SONGS THAT CELEBRATE THE POWER OF MUSIC

As we have seen in earlier chapters, Raymond K. continually extolled the powers of music. The following five songs wonderfully illustrate this universal language and rank among the band's most important and lasting compositions. Perhaps taking inspiration from the 1975 winner of the Kentucky Derby, Raymond K. wrote "Foolish Pleasure" (*Family Album*) for Raymond W.'s birthday. Here the composer reveals that he is completely willing to abandon himself to the art that has provided such delight throughout his life: "If this is what you're calling foolish pleasure, / You're looking at an ever-ready fool!" Perhaps the key phrase to the song, though, is repeated twice for emphasis: "I tell you bringing folks together is my mission, / Especially such folks like you and me." This statement would remain central to the band's mission throughout its career. Whether they were playing in their own country or abroad, what motivated the McLains most was their ability to connect with an audience and find common ground through music. Alice's lead vocal is well suited to the number, and the honored birthday boy contributes banjo and fiddle to the mix.

"My Name's Music" (*Kentucky Wind*) is another birthday present, this time presented to Ruth by her proud father. If music provides temptation in "Back Up and Push," here it is portrayed as seductive:

"Enter if you dare, this sensuous affair." The line "My heart's beating out a rhythm for you" is reminiscent of Gershwin's "I Got Rhythm." Raymond K.'s use of insistent questions ("Don't you feel it? Can't you feel it? Don't you know it?") drives the song and recalls the gentle coaxing of courtship, and surely every listener can endorse the notion of a lifetime spent living in harmony. Ruth's sly bass intro is wonderfully playful, and some very effective mandolin also features in the piece.

"You Sing for Me" (also from *Kentucky Wind*) has a similar provenance, having been written for Alice's twentieth birthday by her father. Here Raymond K. succinctly captures music's ability to "keep those lonesome blues away." In the liner notes he asks, "How many times have we all looked forward to meeting with friends, only to get there and not know what to say? Making music is the answer." Another important message the song endorses is how humans need to support each other, how we should strive to join both our spirits and our voices together to enjoy life to its fullest. So universal is the song's appeal that it is included (in the section for Grade 6, alongside the likes of "Barbara Allen" and "Wayfaring Stranger") in McGraw-Hill's "Spotlight on Music" interactive music curriculum.[10] The "doot doot doots" of the chorus recall Rosemary's style and lend a cheerful tone to the recording. The band employs call and response vocals throughout, and the song features a false ending, after which another chorus is sung.

If the selections above overtly mention music and the power of song, Ruth's "Come On Out Tonight" (*Family Album*) serves to illustrate the concept. Upbeat and catchy, the song is instantly memorable. One can easily imagine audiences clapping hands, tapping toes, and dancing to it upon first hearing the number. Describing Ruth's songwriting style, Raymond W. notes that "some people's songs tend to sound alike, but hers are individual. She has lots of variety in her writing style."[11] Listening to this composition, it's easy to see why Ruth went on to teach a songwriting class at Morehead State University. It is generally simple in melody and lyric, but as Pete Seeger is purported to have said, "Any darn fool can make something complex; it takes a genius to make something simple." Raymond W.'s lead vocal is joyous, and Al supplies an excellent guitar solo, but Ruth appropriately inserts the final word in her composition by providing a short bass break at the song's conclusion.

The McLain Family Band's original compositions stand out recognizably on their studio recordings. They sparkle with wit and vitality, feature lovely melodies and original sentiments, and serve as a wonderful advertisement for the power of music. Though they represent a relatively small percentage of the group's oeuvre, these thirty-two tracks are among the most memorable the McLains recorded.

CHAPTER 9

In the Classroom: The McLains as Educators

s we have seen, the McLain family had deep roots in the world of education. Raymond F. McLain became president of three universities, and Raymond K. established some of the first courses on bluegrass music at the college level. It is not surprising, then, that all five McLain children (plus Al White) entered the classroom after the group ceased touring on a regular basis. Alice gained certification and began teaching first grade at Silver Creek Elementary School in Berea, where she stayed for twenty-six years before retiring in 2018. Raymond W. already had some experience as a teacher via his work with the Fiddle-a-Little program, and while living in Nashville he began teaching at Belmont University, leading the Bluegrass Ensemble and giving individual lessons on a number of instruments. In 2000, he became the assistant director of the Bluegrass and Country Music Program at East Tennessee State University (ETSU). Located in Johnson City, Tennessee, ETSU is a public university that was founded in 1911 and falls under the auspices of the state's board of regents. Its urban campus is home to more than fourteen thousand students.

Jack Tottle established the bluegrass program at ETSU in 1982. An experienced and talented musician himself, Tottle felt the university should offer instruction in regional music to address what he deemed a vital need. He contacted the new chair of the university's music department, Dr. Richard Compton, and offered his services. Compton shared Tottle's enthusiasm for the idea and embraced it wholeheartedly. Tottle began by offering instruction on guitar and mandolin, as well as teaching a course on the history of country and bluegrass music and establishing a bluegrass ensemble. Tottle admits that at first "there was no master plan involved. It was more like planting a new kind of tree in an unfamiliar environment."[1]

The program did experience some growing pains. "During the 1980s I heard comments from a few folks in the region to the effect that 'Our kids have heard that old bluegrass stuff all their lives—we don't need it in our schools.' One radio station executive said, 'I wouldn't insult our listeners by playing that stuff for them.'" The project remained a labor of love. Tottle was still only a part-time adjunct at the university and did pretty much everything on his own, describing himself as the "sole administrator, music director, spokesperson, publicist and events coordinator for the program."[2]

A turning point of sorts came in 1988 when Tottle produced a well-received album called *East Tennessee* that included compositions written by ETSU bluegrass band members Tim Stafford, Adam Steffey, and Barry Bales. Stafford went on to perform with Blue Highway, while both Steffey and Bales joined Alison Krauss and Union Station. The recording brought the program new recognition and resulted in increased enrollments, including future country superstar Kenny Chesney.

The university was suitably impressed with Tottle's efforts, and he became a full-time member of its faculty in 1993. The program eventually moved out of the music department and into the institution's Appalachian studies division. Along with the original offerings, students soon were able to take courses in music theory, recording, and sound technology. The number of ensembles expanded as well, adding old-time, Celtic, and country to the original bluegrass group.

When Raymond W. joined the faculty at ETSU, the program had established itself as the best in the nation. Students came from all over the world to further their skills there. McLain was enthusiastic from the start. "I think great things are happening," he said. "I don't mean just the splashy events; those are nice things that happen sometimes, but I like even the daily improvement. I like to see the progress not only by the accomplished players, but by beginning players as well. Learning is such a positive experience because you're always getting better."[3]

Tottle knew that McLain could bring considerable attributes to his rapidly expanding program. "Raymond may well be the most widely traveled bluegrass musician alive," he stated in 2000. "He loves to work with his music students, as well as to perform for concert audiences, and he brings a great deal of warmth and energy to whatever he undertakes."[4] In a tribute to McLain written in 2014, Tottle noted how he "facilitated a new dynamism both in the growth of the program and in the ever-increasing numbers of highly motivated and remarkably talented students who enrolled."[5] McLain returned the compliment: "I'm impressed with the energy, enthusiasm, commitment, and abilities of everyone involved in the program from the students and faculty to the administration."[6]

If the program's head knew what he was getting in landing McLain, ETSU students were also well aware of his credentials and full of praise for him. "He really knows what he's talking about and goes out of his way to help us," said Marsha Bowman, a banjo and guitar player from Ararat, Virginia.[7] Another student, Abe Spear from North Carolina, described McLain as a mentor. "If we need any special help on a tune or with a harmony, he'll meet with us outside of class—and we all know how busy his schedule is! But no matter how busy he gets, Raymond is always willing to make time to jam with us, and that really says something about him, not only as a teacher, but as a person."[8]

Though his students were now enrolled in a formal course of music study, McLain was always quick to remind them of the roots of their passion and of the power of music. "I want them to remember why they wanted to play in the first place; they need to remember what it was about music that excited them. I guarantee it was that 'feeling,' a feeling that moves time and space, that changes our environment, how people get along and, ultimately, our lives. It's not about who can play the fanciest licks, it's not about who can play the most difficult thing, and it's definitely not about who's better than who. It's all about that 'feeling' and the ability to play together and make one another sound good. I want my students playing music to have a good time and to share the pleasure."[9]

The location of the program certainly played a part in its success. "They can jam somewhere almost every night of the week," McLain noted, "because so many within the community play."[10] His statement from an article written in 2000 to announce his arrival proved prophetic: "I think we will begin to see more and more musical opportunities opening up in the Tri-Cities region. We already have the strong bluegrass program here at ETSU. Bristol was recently declared the Birthplace of Country Music. We have such a rich musical heritage in this area with gems such as the Carter Family Fold in Hiltons, Va., and the Down Home in Johnson City. This is the place to be!"[11]

In 2006 Tottle retired, turning over leadership to Raymond W. Under McLain, the program continued to thrive. Over a ten-year period, the number of students in the program grew from 123 to nearly 450. The faculty experienced a similar expansion, growing to nineteen, a mix of full-time and adjunct positions. In 2010, however, McLain felt the need to move on and accepted a position as director of the Traditional Music Center at Morehead State University. While he relished a new challenge, personal reasons also compelled McLain to make the move back to Kentucky. His mother Betty was suffering from Alzheimer's disease, and he had learned he was soon to become a grandfather.

A public university located in Morehead, Kentucky, Morehead State is slightly smaller than ETSU, with an enrollment of approximately ten thousand students. The mission of the institution's Kentucky Center for Traditional Music (KCTM) is made up of four components: (1) provide a nationally accredited, quality education in Traditional Music styles; (2) preserve, develop, and celebrate the area's cultural heritage; (3) collect, maintain, and provide access to culturally significant materials to foster better understanding of traditional music; and (4) represent the area's cultural heritage through performance, educational outreach, and interaction.[12]

Don Rigsby, a bluegrass musician who directed the KCTM in the early 2000s, offers a more concise description of the program: "Our motto is to educate, preserve, and entertain."[13] Rigsby was able to pull in some big names to add to the Friends of KCTM board. These included songwriter and musician Ronnie Reno, guitarist and promoter Melvin Goins, and singer-songwriter Larry Cordle. The fact that Dr. Wayne Andrews, past president of Morehead State University, took banjo lessons from Raymond W. also played a role in the program's success. Referring to Andrews, Raymond W. notes, "he understands what we're about—the importance of stewardship and not forgetting our roots."[14]

Nathan Kiser, operations manager of the Kentucky Center for Traditional Music at Morehead State, entered the institution as a freshman in 1998 and later received a master's degree there. He works with Morehead students in a number of ways and sees networking as one of the most valuable skills they learn there. "That experience outside the classroom prepares them for other things that come along with being a musician. Being able to just stand and talk to an audience, learning to connect with an audience. Remember that you're there to entertain them. And to also get used to meeting people, talking to people who may be from different cultures or background. Those experiences are what really help out students more than anything."[15]

Students come to Morehead State with a wide range of experience. Some enroll as established musicians, but other Morehead students have no aspirations or expectations to play music professionally. High school students, for example, take classes as part of the institution's early college program, and retirees enroll free of charge simply to learn the rudiments of an instrument. Sometimes the two groups intersect and benefit greatly from the experience.

In his time at Morehead, Kiser has worked closely with Raymond W. and has nothing but praise for him:

Raymond is really interested in helping people learn how to live their lives as artists. He mentions people like Elvis Presley or

Hank Williams who had extremely successful careers, but they weren't exactly happy people. If you look at Raymond and his family, they've traveled all over the world, they have played in some of the most prestigious places that you can think of. But at the same time they're very humble people, very approachable, and they seem to be extremely happy. I feel that's what his teaching style is about. It's not about teaching someone to play perfectly necessarily. It's more about people taking what they can learn in music and using it in a way to make themselves happy. To do with it what they feel they're called to do with it. Raymond could very well have continued being just a performer, but he made the choice to go into education because he felt that was what he needed to do. People who have taken lessons with Raymond will probably never forget the time that they've spent with hm. Not only does he have the expert musical knowledge, but he has stories he can tell you forever about his experiences about being on the road. I think those things really mean a lot to our students. They like to sit and talk with him. They ask him to tell them about Bill Monroe, Earl Scruggs, Jim and Jesse, and all these people that Raymond knew personally. Students can ask him questions that aren't necessarily about technique. It's more about the lifestyle of being a musician.[16]

The personal touch Raymond W. brings to his interactions with his students is well illustrated by his work with Samantha Cunningham. After learning her mother's heart problems had worsened, Cunningham decided to learn one of her favorite fiddle tunes, Dale Potter's "Fiddle Patch," to play in her honor. Sadly, her mother died before she had mastered the composition, but Cunningham persevered. Though a talented and experienced fiddler, she enlisted McLain to help her learn the piece because of its difficulty. Together, McLain and Cunningham watched a performance of "Fiddle Patch" on YouTube and began trying to master its triple stops and difficult rhythms. Every twenty seconds of the composition took her twenty minutes to learn. Finally, two months after her mother passed,

Cunningham felt ready to play the song on stage. McLain joined her, acting both as guitar accompanist and emotional supporter. After the triumphant performance, McLain spoke admiringly of his pupil's tenacity, determination, and motivation: "Going through this process has been inspiring to me to watch her do this for her momma," he said.[17]

Ruth joined her brother at Morehead State as an adjunct instructor in 2012, teaching classes on bass, singing, and traditional music history. Kiser notes that her expertise filled a gap in the Morehead team. "In a lot of ways, she's doing us a great favor by teaching here. One of the things we were lacking was someone to teach bass, and she's one of the greatest that there is around. Her teaching is very personal and friendly."[18] Ruth believes that instruction is about much more than merely providing information. "Teaching includes listening, caring, and realizing what is wanted or needed. In addition to covering course material, we may be sharing tips about how to practice or study, how to work better with others, how to focus, or balance time and energy, or where to find inspiration. We may be giving students much needed reassurance or nurturing a great attitude. I appreciate every student, their gifts and their potential. It is inspiring to help bring out the best in them and discover things that will help them have a happy and productive life."[19]

Two distinguished recent graduates of the Kentucky Center for Traditional Music are the Price Sisters: mandolinist Lauren and her twin sister, fiddler Leanna. In 2018, Rebel Records released their first full-length album, *A Heart Never Knows*, to critical acclaim. Each sister has benefited from the instruction of the McLain siblings. "I can't say enough about how much Raymond McLain's fifty years of experience in music helps the program thrive,"[20] says Lauren. "Raymond knows so much about how to work together as a band, to achieve the best sound as a whole, as well as working to help each player achieve their own goals and potential as an individual artist."[21] Leanna's fiddling improved markedly under Raymond W.'s tutelage. "I can tell a big difference in both my playing and level of confidence when performing," she notes. Her singing ability also progressed at KCTM. "Ruth has helped me learn better ways to care for my voice, and sing with more projection and control."[22]

Michael McLain has also carried on the family tradition of teaching, working at Belmont University in Nashville, Tennessee, from 2000 to 2014. A private Christian institution, Belmont was founded in 1890 and enrolls nearly six thousand students. The campus boasts three professional-grade recording studios, where the likes of Sheryl Crow and Dave Matthews have worked. Belmont's School of Music plays a vital role in the school's success. Its location near Music Row makes it an ideal place for students to hone their art. The school's mission statement stresses "excellence in scholarship, performance, and practice" while also encouraging "creativity, innovation, and stylistic diversity."[23] More than forty ensembles are part of its curriculum, including a bluegrass ensemble.

Michael's background as a graduate of Belmont's guitar program and his experiences as a successful professional musician helped form the basis of his approach to teaching others. His Commercial Applied Guitar course syllabus included the following objectives: "Students will develop their instrumental skills and musicianship through the study of repertoire and technique. The student will gain proficiency at reading music notation and instrument tablature. Accompaniment ability will be developed through the interpretation of rhythm charts. Lead playing will be developed through the study of soloing approaches and transcribed solos. Technical exercises will include scales as well as open and closed position chords. The student will demonstrate understanding of concepts by applying them to tunes."[24]

The motto of the course as listed in its syllabus stressed active learning: "What you hear, you forget. What you see, you remember. What you do, you understand." In the "Practice" section of the syllabus, Michael makes clear some of his philosophies. "Each student should practice a minimum of six (6) hours per week. It is infinitely more productive to practice regularly for 6 days during the week than for hours in one day. Roger Siminoff says, 'Practice brings us closer to perfection and stimulates our joy of playing, which, in turn stimulates the desire to practice.' I think the best fruits of your practice show up about 3 days later. I also think it's best to do your most serious practicing 2 days before you want to be at your peak (i.e. for an audition or performance). Having that day of rest to let your muscles strengthen and let the material really soak in is very valuable." Students in Michael's classes were graded on their "quality preparation and conduct, technical development, quantity of concepts mastered, and ability to demonstrate mastered material with proficiency."[25]

Besides the obvious and purely musical aspects of training musicians, Michael focused on practical but often overlooked or underemphasized aspects of the craft, such as the students' ability to deliver interesting and informative introductions to songs, an art that must be practiced. He encourages an upbeat, storytelling style that strikes a balance between information and conversation and touches on the piece's composer, its subject, and message. Michael also instilled in his students the importance of a balanced set list, including how to open a performance, how to vary keys from piece to piece, and how to ensure variety by spacing songs with different feels, structures, and tempos.

In order to gather material for the bluegrass ensemble he led, Michael asked each student to compile four CDs of possible songs and instrumentals to showcase. The four categories of CDs were broken down as follows: contemporary bluegrass (Rhonda Vincent, Grascals), second-generation bluegrass (Ricky Skaggs, Del McCoury), Americana bluegrass (Alison Krauss, Tim O'Brien), progressive bluegrass (Sam Bush, David Grisman), gospel (Cox Family, Doyle Lawson), instrumental icons (Chris Thile, Bela Fleck), and, finally, traditional bluegrass (Bill Monroe, Flatt and Scruggs). McLain required that each song on the CD be charted to include its title, original key, tempo, chord structure, arrangement details, and instrumental fills. Lyric sheets should also be provided with verses, choruses, and possible harmony parts indicated.

Noting that performers are often asked about their instrument, Michael developed an assignment that required his students to give a short (five-to-seven-minute) talk about it. Elements of this presentation included explaining why they chose the particular instrument, how it is similar to or different from others, and how its sound is produced. The remainder of the talk should be devoted to demonstrating rhythm, backup, and soloing techniques. As with all of his assignments, Michael stressed professionalism. Students should practice the talk and always remember to stay upbeat, adjust their talk to the nature of their audience, and strike the right balance between information and conversation.

The ability to improvise is, of course, a major component of becoming an accomplished bluegrass musician. Michael's graduate work at Belmont included the development of an approach to improvisation that can be applied to country, bluegrass, and folk music. It incorporates a blend of concepts such as paraphrasing a melody, developing musical ideas, and using licks that fit together in various ways. This approach influenced his own musicianship and inspired his work with advanced students. Michael drew from a variety of sources, including Hal Crook's *How to Improvise: An Approach to Practicing Improvisation* to stress certain aspects of the art. Among the topics Michael covered is the nature of the solo. Are the notes adjacent or separated? Where does a solo reach its peak? Is the melodic range wide or narrow? Is the phrasing dense or sparse? Are the ideas similar or contrasting? Michael also goes into the finer points of soloing and improvisation, such as responding to musical impulses, surrounding ideas with rests to give them shape and definition, and the importance of ensuring that solos be neither too predictable nor so complex as to be ineffective.

Michael's teaching techniques found great favor with his students. Amanda Combs, for example, studied banjo at Belmont and was a member of the Bluegrass Ensemble. She found Michael had a "keen ear for details in our music preparation. Somehow, without ever raising his voice, he commanded the room and made us want to do our best. At the same time he created families out of each of his groups. Laughter at our own mistakes kept us from negative perfectionism. Even so, the groups he put together were so talented, we each were challenged to be our best by simply working with each other."[26] Another student, Maggie White, offers additional qualities that make Michael an effective instructor. "It is rare to find a teacher that both teaches and inspires. Somehow, though he was our teacher, I never felt that student-teacher divide. He seemed to think of us, not so much as students, but as fellow musicians."[27]

While Michael was still at Belmont, Alice's husband, Al White, eventually picked up the baton from his father-in-law to revive the tradition of teaching bluegrass music at Berea College. When Kentucky native Joseph Dinwiddie returned home to attend Berea in 1996, he hoped to be able to pursue study of Appalachian music and improve his proficiency on the banjo. Much to his surprise, however, he found that such opportunities were not open to him. In a 1998 article entitled "Where Have All the Fiddles Gone?" he acknowledges Raymond K.'s work at Berea but laments the fact that since his departure, the music department had reverted to its previous philosophy of concentrating on Western classical music. Courses on African-American and Appalachian music were still being offered, but Dinwiddie noted with surprise that the 1997–1999 Berea catalog suggested that instead of choosing these options, music majors should take courses in French or German to "satisfy the Cultural Area Requirement."[28]

Dinwiddie concludes his article by noting that he and another music major have coauthored "a formal proposal asking that the college include regional music instruction in its applied music lessons."[29] He also notes that he has begun taking clawhammer banjo lessons with Al White. "Like most Berea students," he writes, "I didn't have disposable cash for music lessons, and Al graciously allowed me to barter my gardening skills for lessons."[30]

Dinwiddie's proposal bore fruit. Berea hired Al White in 1999 to begin working in their music department. At first Al worked part-time and was charged with establishing a bluegrass ensemble. Currently, he offers instruction on folk guitar, banjo, and fiddle while also leading the Berea College Bluegrass Ensemble and the Mariachi Ensemble. Consisting of up to six members, the bluegrass ensemble performs both regionally and internationally. Al took his students to Ireland in 2004, 2007, 2010, 2012, 2013, and 2017 and to Japan in 2005, 2008, and 2013. "I just found that to be really exciting," White says. "It's real meaningful and terrifically educational to get this kind of worldview. It's an education individually for us band members. And you know it is a good way to promote the college. It's been a great meeting ground for us all. It brings a group together like nothing else I know."[31]

A former member of White's ensemble, Sam Gleaves, has gone on to a successful career in music, releasing a highly regarded CD, *Ain't We Brothers?* in 2015. In 2014, while still at Berea, Gleaves interviewed White as part of a school project designed to explore the history of the Mountain Folk Festival. In the interview, White mentions a number of people who were instrumental in his own musical instruction and whose techniques helped form the foundation of his own teaching philosophy.

White's life in music began when he took up the mandolin at age eleven. A key figure in his development was Lynn Wooldridge, who taught him Travis-picking guitar in Hobbs, New Mexico, for two years during high school. By the time he began playing with bands, Al had learned flatpicking and was performing on mandolin, bass, and guitar. After marrying Alice in 1977, he enrolled at Berea. His required labor position at the college was helping Loyal Jones index recordings in the college archives. There, Al discovered the music of Buell Kazee (1900–1976) and began to learn his banjo style from one of Kazee's former disciples, Karen Collins.

Speaking with Gleaves, White describes the working relationship he enjoys with his ensemble students. "You know, it's kind of democratic in the group. You bring in songs, I bring in songs, we all bring in songs and arrangements. Somebody's got to be responsible ultimately, which I guess I am, but I think it helps people learn what it's like to be in a group, a real group and the dynamics of putting together songs and arrangements and taking it on the road. We travel a lot, we play a lot. I think it's a great experience for everyone concerned. It seems to work pretty well."[32] Members of the ensemble often come to the group with varying levels of experience. While Gleaves was already an experienced performer by the time he joined, White recalls another singer he recruited for the group. "She'd never hardly even heard bluegrass but was a great singer. She thought she was auditioning for the jazz band and not the bluegrass band, but she was quite amazed that I wanted her to sing bluegrass. People come together from various places, and they form groups based on common musical interests."[33]

Gleaves describes White's leadership of the bluegrass ensemble as democratic. "He would ask us which material we wanted to perform as a band,"[34] Gleaves says. "He wasn't overbearing as a teacher at all." Gleaves notes that White is a friend, bandmate, mentor, and teacher. White instilled in his charges a sense of professionalism, stressing how the band should dress, how to work with a single microphone when the situation so demanded, and how to create harmonies. "He's such a good listener and has such a good ear," Gleaves states. Gleaves also notes Al's tremendous work ethic. "He would lose sleep over problems in the band,"[35] he says.

Rehearsals were sometimes held at the White family home, so Gleaves also got to know Alice. "She was like a band mother," he remembers. "It was always comforting to see Alice's face in the audience. She was always smiling. If she was smiling, that was good enough for everybody." Gleaves also has fond memories of listening to Al and Alice perform duets, noting that he could tell how much they love each other. "What a unit they are!"[36]

Al's work with the country dance ensembles has its roots in his experiences at Berea in the mid-1970s. "I kind of fell into the music and dance music world when I came to Berea and started playing Christmas Country Dance School events with my in-laws starting in '76. I felt that that was an interesting thing to do with music that I'd really never done before." While recognizing the difference between such work and more conventional performing, White notes how enjoyable it can be. "You're there for the dancers and the dance is upfront, and you're helping to propel the dance, but you're not performing a show as a musician. It's a very distinct and different role and you've got to be comfortable with that and appreciate the dance."[37]

It is not only college students who have benefited from the McLains' personal touch in the classroom. Ruth and Nancy Ann found work that benefits children, becoming services representatives and senior directors with Usborne Books & More. Founded in 1973, Usborne Publishing is the brainchild of Englishman Peter Usborne and has a strong international presence. Specializing in fiction and nonfiction titles for children, Usborne is highly respected in the industry and has won numerous awards, including being named the Independent Publisher of the Year and International Children's Publisher of the Year in 2014. In the United States, Usborne Books & More is a division of Educational Development Corporation, which distributes Usborne and Kane Miller titles via a network of independent consultants. The company's mission statement stresses its commitment to education: "The future of our world depends on the education of our children. We deliver educational excellence one book at a time. We provide economic opportunity while fostering strong family values. We touch the lives of children for a lifetime."[38]

After touring as a full-time member of the McLain Family Band from 1978 to 1985, Nancy Ann worked as a travel agent, specializing in international travel arrangements for musicians, including the Cincinnati Symphony Orchestra. Wanting to spend more time with her children by working from home, Nancy Ann, along with her husband Tom Wartman, joined Usborne in 1994 and has enjoyed success there, winning the President's Award and being named Supervisor of the Year. Ruth joined Usborne in 1995 and gained similar recognition. Due to their excellent sales records, both sisters have earned dozens of the company's incentive trips, sharing international travel experiences with their friends and family. Ruth has also served as a board member for the International Bluegrass Music Association Foundation, an organization dedicated to preserving the future of bluegrass music via educational and artistic activities.

Through their work in the classroom, each member of the McLain Family Band has given back to the music that brought him or her so much enjoyment. Such commitment helps to ensure the future of bluegrass music. In fact, by 2019 the number of institutions across the country that offer bluegrass music programs had grown to more than forty.[39] The careers of now-established performers like the Price Sisters and Sam Gleaves owe a great deal to the patience and attention the McLains continue to practice in the classroom and in their everyday lives. As Sharon White observes, "The most important thing we can do now is to pour into the ones that come behind us, and we need to be intentional about it. That's the beauty of what the McLain family has done. They've continued to expand individually, play with other people, and do other things with their music."[40]

Rhonda Vincent points out that the McLains' careers as instruc-
tors is "a continuation of their ambassadorship. What an incredible
thing to pass that on to others. I see how they influence their students
continuously with their music, their attitude, and really everything
that they do."[41] In this sense, the McLains have carried on a mission
that seems to be part of their DNA. As educators they have followed
in the footsteps of their parents and their grandparents, their careers
providing living proof to John Dewey's notion that education is not
just preparation for life, but life itself.[42]

Celebrating Life and Fifty Years Together

⊶◆⊷

The year 2018 was a momentous one for the McLain Family Band. To celebrate their fiftieth anniversary as a group, the McLains released their first album in thirty-two years and embarked on tours at home and abroad. Highlighting their domestic schedule was a return to Bean Blossom on June 13, where they joined old friends including Ricky Skaggs, Larry Sparks, Doyle Lawson, Bobby Osborne, Jesse McReynolds, and Little Roy Lewis. Other appearances of note included performances at the Mountaineer Opry House in Milton, West Virginia, and with the Bluegrass Pops in Lexington, Kentucky.

In August the band performed a concert in support of the Singing Bird Music School in Berea, an initiative spurred by the actions of Belle Jackson, Donna Lamb, and Sam Gleaves. Designed to ensure that the torch of Appalachian music is passed to future generations, Singing Bird features workshops on traditional instruments (guitar, fiddle, banjo, and mandolin) and also serves to introduce attendees to important aspects of the area's culture, such as storytelling and square dancing.

Also in 2018, the McLains resumed their tradition of taking bluegrass music to foreign shores. In late June and early July, the band played concerts in seven Danish cities before heading to the Emerald Isle to perform in Limerick, Westport, Bruff, Kilworth, and other Irish communities. Morehead State graduates Leanna and Lauren Price joined them there for several dates, showcasing their trademark harmonies and trading licks with performers whose musical heritage helped give birth to bluegrass.

Closer to home, the McLains collaborated with Michael Johnathon on his children's book, *Mousie HiWay: The Adventures of Banjo Mouse in the Appalachian Mountains.* The illustrated fable demonstrates a theme already familiar to McLain Family Band devotees: how music can help to bring strangers together. In Johnathon's book, these include Fiddle Fox, Doggy Dobro, Mando Moose, Kitty Guitar, and Little Bitty Beaver. In the best tradition of children's literature, Johnathon effectively supplements the engaging story with educational messages. At the bottom of each page is an interactive "Hey Kids" section that provides background information on the various instruments each character plays. Lesson plans for grades K–4 and 5–7 are included for teachers who want to employ the work as part of their curriculum. Included with the book is a CD that includes a spoken version of the story and a performance of the "Mousie Hiway Song." Noted Dobro player Rob Ickes joins Johnathon and the McLain Family Band on the rollicking track.

Celebrate Life (2018)

After an absence of more than thirty years, the McLain Family Band returned to the studio in 2017 to lay down tracks for *Celebrate Life.* Recorded at the studio of the Kentucky Center for Traditional Music at Morehead State University, the project was designed to help celebrate the band's fiftieth anniversary tour for the following year. Raymond W., Ruth, Alice, and Al are joined here by Daxson Lewis, who plays banjo and guitar. Lewis graduated from Morehead State in 2016, having taken classes with both Raymond W. and Ruth. Born in West Liberty, Kentucky, Lewis cites J. D. Crowe, Sonny Osborne, and Raymond W. as the banjo players who have most directly influenced him. When hand surgery left Raymond W. temporarily unable to play the banjo, he identified Daxson as a possible replacement.

"I count on him on the same level as I do the rest of my family,"[1] Raymond W. stated in 2018. In addition to his musical roles on banjo and guitar, Daxson looks after the group's social media presence and handles bookings and merchandise. He has also joined Raymond W. and Ruth as an instructor at the Morehead State Kentucky Center for Traditional Music.

Celebrate Life features seven original numbers, three traditional tracks, a Carter Family song, and a new rendition of Patsy Montana's "I Want to Be a Cowboy's Sweetheart." While characteristically joyful in tone, the album also reflects the fact that the performers have reached a new stage in their lives. Two tracks, Al's "You Can't Find Love If It Just Isn't There" and Raymond W.'s "Nightbird," are thought-provoking meditations on life. The cover photo by Frederick Parks is a formal portrait that shows group members holding their instruments. Raymond W. stands in the center, flanked on his right by Alice and Daxson and on his left by Ruth and Al. As a nod towards continuity, Raymond F.'s woodcut lettering is retained to spell out the name of the group.

Celebrate Life kicks off with the band revisiting Ruth's "Come On Out Tonight," first recorded for the *Family Album* forty years previously. While the original featured Raymond W. on lead vocals, here Ruth sings lead, and Daxson Lewis introduces himself with a powerful banjo break. The band learned the following track, "Kitty Alone," from the Armstrong Sisters. Often sung as a lullaby, the McLains offer a much more upbeat interpretation, with Al handling lead vocals and playing clawhammer banjo.

Following these two numbers, Raymond W.'s "Nightbird" comes as a complete surprise. Wanting to explore "the deep reach of love," Raymond W. sought help from friend and fellow songwriter, Sasha Colette. The result of a lengthy gestation period, "Nightbird" is certainly one of his best compositions. The melody and arrangement were finalized long before the lyrics. While he generally knew the story and feelings he wanted to convey through the song, he sought help from Colette to put his feelings into words. Having heard a story about the difficulties a newly widowed man felt when faced with the prospect of having to go to bed alone for the first time in seventy years,

Raymond recrafted the idea into a love song for his wife, Diane. The result of McLain's continuous rumination is a piece unlike anything else he or the band had ever recorded. Set to a sparse accompaniment, it is what Raymond W. likes to call a "crooked song"—one that is not strictly uniform musically or lyrically. This characteristic is well suited to the initially hesitant but eventually resolute conclusion the narrator reaches: the timelessness of a love that even death cannot threaten. Told from the point of view of a recently deceased man, "Nightbird" relates how love remains, both in the afterlife and in the dreams we experience while still on earth. Indeed, dreams and dreaming are central to the song, earning mention eight times. Unlike Hamlet's fear of haunted slumbers, the sleep that accompanies the narrator's death is filled with dreams of reunion with his wife. In a loving but busy life, "it's been so long since we felt we could dance," but in this new, everlasting dream, "our dance can last forever."

The song is far more artistic than McLain's previous compositions. The use of repeated words, images, and phrases (angels, sleep, dreams, dancing) lends thematic stability to the piece, and the figure of the titular Nightbird is subtle and fascinating. The appearance of the Nightbird heralds death ("the Nightbird cries, yes sleep is near"), yet the sentence he passes brings not pain but peace ("Now the Nightbird's quiet, yes sleep is here"). Like any good work of art, the song is clear but also open to various interpretations. It is a song that newly rewards the listener each time it is played.

Following such a tour de force is difficult, but the strength of Ruth's title track ensures that no momentum is lost. In the liner notes, one learns that the song was "inspired by those who celebrate life, even when times are tough." Like many gospel songs, "Celebrate Life" concerns finding your strength, having the courage to carry on, and then passing along this fortitude to others. The simple, effective chorus drives the number and is a tidy summation of how the McLains view life.

The medley "Marie's Wedding/Cooley's Reel/Carried Out of Buckley's" is comprised of two traditional Irish tunes, paired with an instrumental composed by Al that was inspired by Buckley's Pub in Ireland. Al's contribution fits seamlessly with the other tunes and betrays his deep knowledge of traditional music. His spritely fiddling is a highlight of this toe-tapping track.

The third recording of family favorite "Kentucky Wind" is also the longest at nearly four minutes. Alice, Ruth, and Raymond W. sing the song as a trio, before Ruth takes the last verse by herself. Daxson's banjo solo is appropriately thoughtful. His playing is flashier on the next track, "Bully of the Town." This traditional song was made famous by Gid Tanner and His Skillet Lickers and was later covered by many others, including Jerry Reed, the Everly Brothers, and Norman Blake. Here the McLains play the song as an instrumental, somewhat in the manner of the Stanley Brothers.

The McLains again show their affection for the Carter Family by covering "Sweet Fern," a song included on the pioneering group's first Camden recording. Like many of their covers, the McLains' interpretation is respectful of the original but still sounds fresh. Set to a slightly slower tempo than the original, this track features Ruth's vocals and solos on guitar (Al) and mandolin (Ruth). The theme is one common to all popular music: pondering the fidelity of a distant lover.

"Going Down," Raymond W.'s second original composition on the album, is a straightforward song about the worries and insecurities that plague many relationships, and thus it contrasts with "Nightbird." The track is more pop oriented than most of the McLains' compositions and has a late 1950s Everly Brothers feel to it. Al White's "You Can't Find Love If It Just Isn't There" is even more somber in tone. The liner notes describe this song as portraying the feeling you get "when what you wish with your whole heart just isn't there." Coming to terms with reality in this way is a difficult but necessary skill we must all acquire in order to keep moving forward in life. On an album of fine original and traditional songs, this track stands out and displays Al's growing stature as a songwriter. A number of effective musical rests seem to mimic the narrator's heart as it occasionally skips a beat.

The mood changes with Ruth's new recording of "I Want to Be a Cowboy's Sweetheart," first included on *Troublesome Creek*. Al's mandolin and Daxson's driving banjo provide effective backing to Ruth's vocals and add verve to a composition already brimming with life. Al's double-barreled instrumental, "Jake's Ramble/Big Wheel Reel," brings the album to its conclusion in catchy fashion. Al's fiddle carries the piece, occasionally giving way to Daxson's banjo.

THE LEGACY OF THE MCLAIN FAMILY BAND

If there is one word that describes the essence of the McLain Family Band, it is "joy." Though many of their songs celebrate secular values, their catalog can truly be described in the words of Psalm 98: "Make a joyful noise unto the Lord, all the earth: make a loud noise, and rejoice, and sing praise." In simple terms, for fifty years the group has played and sung in praise of life. Even when acknowledging the challenges we all face, they elected to put a positive spin on our existence, and it is this very encouragement that has led so many listeners to embrace their sound. As Sharon White puts it, "That was their approach to music: every song was going to make you feel good."[2]

While people turn to music for many purposes, chief among them must be to find enjoyment. From our earliest days, humans have demonstrated a need for music and dance, a rhythm to accompany us as we experience the sorrows and delights that are the components of life. In caves all over the world, archaeologists have discovered evidence of flutes made of bone and hides stretched to make drums. Music is primal and central to the human experience. In recent years, several authors have attempted to explain the neurological basis of our need for and love of music. Daniel Levitin's 2006 work, *This Is Your Brain on Music*, for example, is both thought provoking and accessible. The body of the work includes explanations of how every region of the brain is involved in processing music, but perhaps the most enjoyable parts of the book are the dozens of examples Levitin cites from the worlds of classical, jazz, pop, rock, and country music to explain why music is so attractive to humans and why it has become such a central part of our existence. In a chapter that discusses why we like certain kinds of music or specific performers and composers, Levitin states, "We surrender to music when we listen to it—we allow ourselves to trust the composers and musicians with a part of our hearts and our spirits; we let the music take us somewhere outside of ourselves."[3] When listeners hear the music of the McLain Family Band, they find this external source of comfort and joy. They temporarily leave behind the cares of the world and find something to smile about.

Besides promulgating joy, McLain Family Band songs often express universal needs and desires. The phrase "we need each other, yes we do" from "Can't We Get Together Once Again?" simply but effectively captures our core reliance on others. That music can help address this need is communicated throughout the group's oeuvre. "It takes sweet music every day / To keep those lonesome blues away" from "You Sing for Me" provides one example, while "Foolish Pleasure" presents a similar message: "I know there can't be any greater treasure / Than the melody that brings me close to you." Yet songs from the pens of Raymond K. and his sister Rosemary also acknowledge that life is mysterious and transitory. In "Our Song" and "I Got High Hopes," Rosemary hints at the fleeting nature of our time on earth and demonstrates the uniquely human knowledge of our mortality. Raymond K.'s musings in "Kentucky Wind" hint at the enigmatic nature of our time on earth: "whatever song it seems to want to sing us / It's not in our experience to know."

For all its challenges, however, the McLains firmly believe that life is to be enjoyed and embraced. Nowhere is this more evident than in the title track to their 2018 comeback album, where the narrator expresses her thanks and gratitude to both a higher power and her earthly friends who "give us strength to carry on." The simple chorus ("celebrate life, celebrate life") is repeated five times, leaving no doubt as to the song's ultimate message.

If the McLains are cognizant of the support they have received from others throughout the years, they have themselves served as friends and mentors to hundreds of students and fellow musicians. While some (most notably the Price Sisters and Sam Gleaves) have begun to enjoy very successful careers, one suspects that it is the less celebrated among their charges, like Samantha Cunningham, who bring the greatest satisfaction to Raymond W., Ruth, Michael, and Al White. Rhonda Vincent picks up on their contributions by stating, "I admire that they are influencing these kids."[4]

Through their frequent international tours, the McLain Family Band made new friends and brought their joyful brand of bluegrass to many who had never heard anything like it. They excelled in their role as bluegrass ambassadors due to their warm personalities and engaging performance style. For, as British journalist Walter Bagehot observed, "an ambassador is not simply an agent; he is also a spectacle."[5] Or, as Cheryl White puts it, "They busted down the walls, is what they did!"[6] Rhonda Vincent concurs, making special note of their distinctive innovations. "They didn't pattern themselves after anyone. They didn't set any limits for themselves. They created their own style, their own songs. When you heard them, you knew it was the McLain Family Band."[7] The wording on the Distinguished Achievement Award plaque the IBMA awarded them in 2013 further speaks to their legacy: "In recognition of pioneering accomplishments that have fostered bluegrass music's image and broadened its recognition and accessibility."

Raymond K.'s children are quick to credit him with the success they enjoyed for so many years. Yet they are not alone in this estimation. Cheryl White speculates that one of the secrets to the group's success is that Raymond K. never placed any restrictions on his children. "I wonder if they really had any rules when they started learning stuff. It seemed like they didn't. Whatever they did, it worked. They colored outside the lines. They weren't afraid of the boundaries. Bluegrass was a music that was expected to be a certain way, back in those days."[8] Michael Johnathon notes the band's compositional talents, stating that they are "musically better than most of the bluegrass bands even today. They had chord changes that were beyond bluegrass. They weren't doing the typical three chord thing."[9]

Perhaps Nathan Kiser sums up the McLain Family Band's career most succinctly. "If you look at everything that they've achieved in their lifetimes, it's almost hard to believe. They were able to take bluegrass music to all the other cultures, they were able to incorporate other cultures in their music, they played with orchestras, they really kind of extended what was bluegrass music. And then there are their educational efforts on top of that. There are people who are really good performers and people who are really good educators, but it's hard to find people who do both. They were kind of the whole package."[10]

APPENDIX A

Interpretations

———◦◆◦———

This appendix examines traditional songs the McLain Family Band recorded, as well as the numbers they covered that were written by their peers and predecessors. These selections informed the creation of their original pieces described earlier in this work and represent nearly two-thirds of their recorded repertoire.

INSTRUMENTALS

Instrumental selections are an important part of any bluegrass band's repertoire. In a genre known for its virtuosity, these numbers allow group members to show off their chops and stretch their legs. Over the years the McLain Family Band recorded twenty-four instrumentals, including an entire album of country dance tunes.

Playing for dances formed an important part of the group's early stage career, and numerous studio tracks indicate that they retained a strong interest in this music as the years passed. "Grand Square" (*Country Ham*) is typical of the band's team-based approach, as it features Raymond W.'s Dixieland-style banjo, inventive mandolin work by Alice, and solid guitar runs by Raymond K. "Fair Jenny" (*Country Dance Album*) is a lengthy (4:35) jig composed by Peter Barnes. "I actually wrote this tune on the fiddle," Barnes says, "when I was trying to teach myself that instrument in the mid-seventies. I made it easy to play on the violin, which may account for its totally unexpected popularity."[1] One of the group's favorite waltzes, "Georgiana Moon" (*Big*

Hill) was composed by Clayton McMichen and originally recorded by the Georgia Wildcats in 1937. Raymond W.'s fiddle playing dominates the dignified-sounding piece. His baroque variations the third time through the number are remarkable for their ingenuity.

Raymond W. included "Boil Them Cabbage Down" (*Country Dance Album*) in his instructional book for beginning fiddlers (*Fiddle A Little*), but none of his students would be able to play this traditional number at anywhere near the speed he does here. Michael contributes an excellent banjo break, and Al follows suit on guitar. Not to be left out, Ruth includes a bass solo. Finally, Raymond W. sings a short snatch of the famous tune near the end of this extraordinary performance. This cut shows the band at their rip-roaring best. A long medley simply named "Hoedown" closes the *Country Dance Album*. Here the band stitches together "Hell Broke Loose in Georgia," "Pigtown Fling," "Come On Out Tonight," "Sugarfoot Rag," and "Katy Hill" in a track that is nearly ten minutes long. Raymond W. plays mandolin on "Sugarfoot Rag," where he enjoys trading licks with his brother Michael on banjo. Short sung snatches of both "Sugarfoot Rag" and Ruth's composition "Come On Out Tonight" lend variety to the medley. The pace never lets up as the band veers from tune to tune, leaving its listeners (and any dancers who show the necessary stamina) short of breath but ready for more.

Though the McLains show tremendous stylistic range in their repertoire, they are first and foremost a bluegrass band. The tracks described below confirm this designation and were doubtless as much fun to record as they are to listen to. "Shuckin' the Corn" (*7th Album*) is credited to B. Graves, L. Certain, and G. Stacey. While theirs are not household names, dozens of fine bluegrass groups have covered this composition. These include Flatt and Scruggs and the fine contemporary supergroup, the Earls of Leicester, whose name puns on their bluegrass heroes. Raymond W. liked the tune so well that he would rerecord it on his *A Place of My Own* album years later. He and his brother Michael combine to good effect on "Kentucky Chimes" (*All Natural Ingredients*), a duet written by Wendy Miller that is in some ways similar to their work on "Troublesome Creek." Ruth and Michael Riopel add variety to the piece with their lovely work on mandolin and lead guitar, respectively, before the banjos return to center stage.

On "Dixie Breakdown" (*Family Album*), the band employs overdubs, one of the few times they found this practice necessary. Here it was required because Raymond W. plays both banjo parts. Interestingly, Ruth begins the piece with a lengthy bass solo before her brother launches into his attack. The guitar and the mandolin join the fun, too, on this Don Reno composition. Influenced by the playing of Snuffy Jenkins, Reno developed his own instantly recognizable three-finger style and was one of Raymond W.'s banjo heroes. In the late 1940s, Reno joined Bill Monroe's Blue Grass Boys and later formed a famous partnership with Red Smiley. In 1974, Raymond W. got a chance to work with his idol in the studio, recording "Dixie Breakdown" with Reno on his *River and Roads* album.

Otto Wood and his wife Marguerite are the source of "Blue Ridge Mountains of Virginia" (*All Natural Ingredients*). Otto was a fiddler from Grand Rapids, Michigan, who also called dances; Marguerite played piano and accordion. Here, perhaps in tribute to Marguerite, Raymond K. introduces the piece on piano. Though he played mainly rhythm guitar on the group's albums, Raymond K. was most proficient on piano, and it must have been gratifying for him to tickle the ivories on this piece. The number is primarily an instrumental, though Ruth sings a brief verse near its conclusion.

One of the best-known and most recognizable compositions in bluegrass and country music, "Orange Blossom Special" (*In Concert at Carnegie Hall*) was composed by Ervin T. Rouse (1917–1981). Sometimes referred to as the fiddle player's national anthem, the piece was inspired by the passenger train that shares its name. While many fiddlers extend the piece to show off all their licks, here Raymond W. humbly limits himself to two minutes of magic. His bowing delighted the Carnegie Hall crowd, many of whom had probably been hoping that the chestnut would be included before the curtain went down on the McLains' performance.

"Old Joe Clark" is another song nearly everyone knows, but Raymond W. imparts his own spin to the piece. Though he quickly gained a reputation as one of the best banjo players on the circuit,

"Joe Clark's Dream" (his take on the traditional piece) proves he is nearly as talented on the mandolin. Raymond W.'s performance is an exotic twist on the old classic that was inspired by hearing Bill Monroe experimenting with tuning the strings of his mandolin to eight different pitches late one night at a festival in Colorado. In this inventive arrangement, Raymond W. nicely builds and releases musical tension in a performance that is worthy of Monroe in its intensity and originality.

Raymond K.'s fondness for ragtime piano music is evident in the fact that the family band recorded no fewer than five "rags." Characterized by syncopated or "ragged" rhythm, such pieces were especially popular in the first quarter of the twentieth century but are rarely performed by bluegrass groups. Their inclusion in the McLains' oeuvre is another factor that sets them apart from most of their contemporaries. In his liner notes to *Kentucky Wind*, Raymond K. speculates that the title of "Hattie Call Rag" may refer to Hadacol, a quack medicine sold during earlier times to hopeful but naïve patients. The band learned the number from J. T. Perkins, a friend from Alabama. Raymond W.'s fiddle is in fine voice here, and Ruth provides one of her signature bass solos as well. "Bugle Call Rag" (*Big Hill*) was composed by Jack Pettis, Billy Meyers, and Elmer Schoebel. Benny Goodman, Duke Ellington, and Glenn Miller are among the many to cover the piece. The McLains' interpretation features dueling banjos, played in a number of styles. Also included on *Big Hill*, "Peacock Rag" is a Fiddlin' Arthur Smith number that Raymond W. learned when he was moonlighting with Reno, Smiley, and Harrell. The mandolin and fiddle take turns leading the piece before Ruth contributes one of her characteristic bass solos. "Levi Jackson Rag" (*Country Dance Album*) is driven by Raymond W.'s fiddling, but it also includes a nice banjo break from his brother Michael and some fine lead guitar from Al White.

If rags are unusual in bluegrass music, marches are even more so. Once again risking the wrath of genre traditionalists, the McLain Family Band recorded two numbers more typically played by trombones, tubas, and trumpets than banjos, fiddles, and mandolins. What genre a number might originate from mattered little to the McLains.

Audiences were no doubt surprised to hear a bluegrass band play jazz pieces or a march, but it's hard to imagine that any of them did not enjoy the variation and the quality of the performances. "Under the Double Eagle" (originally recorded for *Big Hill* and also performed on the group's *In Concert at Carnegie Hall* album) became a favorite of "The March King," John Philip Sousa (1854–1932), but it was composed by the Austrian military bandmaster Josef Franz Wagner (1856–1908). The percussive opening employed by the McLains is typically inventive, and when performed in concert, Nancy Ann would include a clog dance to add visual appeal to the march.

The McLains first performed Sousa's "Stars and Stripes Forever" in 1977 on Flag Day as part of the Kin and Communities symposium held in Washington, DC. Raymond K. excelled at arranging pieces, and his sure touch is shown to good effect on the recording included as part of the *Family Album*. Driven by his accordion, the rousing track is a prime example of how easily the McLains could transition from straight bluegrass to other types of music. Raymond K. may have been inspired by Wilene Forrester to include the accordion on this and other pieces. Forrester was the wife of Blue Grass Boy fiddler Howdy Forrester and played accordion on "True Life Blues" and some other sides for Bill Monroe's famous group in the early 1940s. Scholars have also noted that Forrester was the first woman to appear as a regular member of a bluegrass band, thus paving the way for Alice, Ruth, and hundreds of others. On "Stars and Stripes Forever," Ruth's bass aptly answers her brother's banjo interjections, and the group brings the piece to a suitable climax with immaculate timing.

Two other McLain Family Band tracks merit mention here as examples of the group's willingness to paint outside the lines of bluegrass music. Raymond W. won many banjo contests by playing "The Bells of St. Mary's" (*Kentucky Wind*). His highly imaginative interpretation of this famous piece no doubt impressed judges, many of whom would have been surprised both by McLain's choice of material and his execution of it. The effect he uses for the chimes ringing in the second verse is but one example of his artistry. The song was composed in 1917 by A. Emmet Adams and lyricist Douglas Furber after they visited St. Mary's Church in Southampton, England. It has been sung by many, including a famous rendition by Bing Crosby for the movie of the same name. Raymond W. worked up his arrangement of the song in conjunction with Raymond K. and has stated that he often thinks of his father when he performs it. The banjoist also acknowledges the influence of guitarist Bob Saxton's use of harmonics when he recorded the piece. Ruth's bass provides nice backing throughout this lovely track, rerecorded in 1992 for Raymond W.'s *A Place of My Own* solo album.

"Jesusita En Chihuahua" is a lively polka known by many other names in English, including "The Jesse Polka," "The J.C. Polka," and "The Cactus Polka." It was written by Quirino Mendoza y Cortés, an officer who served during the Mexican Revolution. Pancho Villa is said to have particularly favored the piece, often ordering his bands to play it before and even during battle. The polka was a tribute to the "soldaderas," women who supported the troops on campaign. Its fame has endured, appearing in movies including *Three Amigos*, *Like Water for Chocolate*, and even *Love Laughs at Andy Hardy*. That the McLains elected to record a piece most often associated with Mariachi music again shows their willingness to experiment and their disregard for bluegrass purists who might not deem it suitable. Raymond K.'s accordion appears once more, but it's the mandolin work here that stamps the piece as a McLains number.

GOSPEL SONGS

Gospel songs have formed an important element in bluegrass music from its very beginnings. As Neil Rosenberg observes, "Religious songs constituted, on the average, 30 percent of the recorded and published (in songbooks) output of the most influential early bluegrass bands—Monroe, Flatt and Scruggs, the Stanley Brothers, and Reno and Smiley."[2] Some have speculated that since the predominant faith of the Appalachian people, fundamentalist Protestantism, does not require strict church attendance in order for its practitioners to gain salvation, music has come to play a proportionately larger role as an expression of their faith than is the case for other sects. Howard Wight Marshall believes, for example, that because Protestants have no equivalent to Catholicism's confessional, gospel music allows adherents to "feel 'saved' and to express belief in salvation."[3] In an article entitled " 'Keep on the Sunny Side of Life:' Pattern and Religious Expression in Gospel Music," Marshall finds five prevalent themes in bluegrass gospel: "individual salvation, life's rocky road, the maternal hearth, grief for the deceased, and the good Christian's 'action orientation.' "[4] Robert Cantwell takes a slightly different view of the music, stressing that "The idyllic world is the basis of an entire bluegrass gospel tradition, in which fond recollection of a childhood spent in a cabin home among rolling green hills, secure in the love of parents, brothers, sisters, and friends, provides an image of the heavenly world to which death will someday restore us."[5]

The gospel songs the McLain Family Band covered touch on all of these themes. Restoration, for example, is certainly found in what is perhaps the most famous of all gospel numbers, "Amazing Grace," which the group recorded on two separate occasions. The band's interpretation on *Country Ham* is really two songs. The first half harkens back to the folk tradition, while the second, spurred on by Raymond W.'s banjo, places it firmly in the world of bluegrass. Again, the band's accompaniment and approach enhance the lyrics nicely: the wretched narrator starts out in an unsure, hesitant manner, but once he finds faith, his strength and commitment are renewed. Their performance on *Sunday Singing* is quite different. While Ruth again sings lead, this time the band includes up-tempo samples of "I've Just Begun to Live" on two occasions to supplement the original lyrics. This idea works well, lending some pep and variety to a song already so familiar to listeners.

The McLains learned "Sweet Rivers of Redeeming Love" (*Country Life*) from Minnie Bates of Hazard, Kentucky. Their performance provides a good demonstration of three-part harmony singing. The mandolin part is interesting and creatively performed, and Raymond W.'s ascending and descending banjo runs are supplemented by strikingly diverse variations. Sam Gleaves, later a student of Al White at Berea College, struggles to express his admiration for Raymond W.'s banjo work on the song. "When you listen to him play the banjo on 'Sweet Rivers of Redeeming Love,' it's like . . . I don't know what that is. I know I like it, and I know that it's amazing, but I don't know what that is."[6] In his liner notes for *Country Life*, Raymond K. describes the banjo as "well suited to describe Satan's ragings in the third verse." Both assessments of Raymond W.'s performance are sound.

An entirely different instrumental approach is used on "Angel Band" (*Family Album*), as Raymond K.'s accordion drives the number. The song was obviously important to the family patriarch since he had earlier employed the titular phrase when he set lyrics to "Back Up and Push." Written by the remarkably prolific Haldor Lillenas (1885-1959), "I Will Arise and Go to Jesus" was a favorite of Raymond K.'s grandmother, Minnie Belle Kane. The group's lovely interpretation of this melodic song features Ruth on lead vocal.

"Lonesome Valley" (*All Natural Ingredients*) is a good example of how the McLains made an often-recorded number their own. While classically trained folk singer Richard Dyer-Bennet's powerful and dramatic interpretation stressed the high stakes of potential salvation, the tempo changes and call and response vocals employed by the McLains lend the song a lighter and more optimistic feel. Raymond K.'s recorder provides "Garden Hymn" and "How Firm a Foundation" (both from *Sunday Singing*) with a peaceful texture and again demonstrates the group's innovative approach to bluegrass music. The flashy use of guitar, fiddle, and banjo on "The Old Landmark" (*Sunday Singing*) finds the band returning to a more traditional approach.

The theme of faith as a foundation for a good life is explored in three songs the McLains recorded over the years. Raymond W. handles lead vocals on "I'm Working on a Building," copyrighted by A. P. Carter and included on *Sunday Singing*. Stuart Hamblen, one of radio's first singing cowboys, wrote "This Old House," a #1 hit for Rosemary Clooney. Hamblen was apparently inspired to write the piece after happening upon the body of a man in a mountain hut during a hunting trip. In his liner notes for *All Natural Ingredients*, Raymond K. describes the song as telling a universal story, that one's earthly body ultimately gives way to the soul. As the oldest member of the group, it is appropriate that Raymond K. sings lead here, and he delivers a strong performance to a piece that also features some fine fiddling and mandolin work. Hank Williams's "House of Gold," also included on *All Natural Ingredients*, reflects the inner conflict between earthly lucre and more lasting riches that the composer and so many others have experienced. Ruth learned the song from Buck White at the McLain's Family Festival one year. The song has a challenging vocal range, which Ruth handles well.

The McLains chose to close their gospel album with another Williams composition, "I Saw the Light." Apparently inspired by a remark made by the writer's mother, the song's melody has its base in the old Scottish song "Bonnie Charlie," also known as "Will Ye No Come Back Again?" Here Raymond W. features on lead vocals, joined by his siblings during the track's unaccompanied finale. Like so many of Williams's songs, "I Saw the Light" leaves the listener satisfied but also yearning for more.

Besides Williams, the McLains looked to a number of other twentieth-century composers for their gospel material. Family friend Joe Carter (1927–2005) wrote "Little David Played His Harp," recorded by the group on *Sunday Singing*. Son of A. P. and Sara Carter, Joe was a talented guitarist who followed in his family's vast musical tradition, often performing with his sister, Janette. Nancy Ann sings lead on the song, and Michael Riopel appropriately plays his harmonica. A jazzy banjo introduction kicks off this fine retelling of the David and Goliath story.

Dot Swan wrote "Let the Light Shine Down on Me," recorded by Bill Monroe for *The Gospel Spirit* album. Unlike many of the other songs included on *Sunday Singing*, this number is straight-ahead, banjo-powered bluegrass. It sounds as if the performers can't wait to get to the next verse, not to mention the next instrumental break.

Carter Stanley's "The Darkest Hour" is a fine example of what came to be known as "mountain soul." Carter's brother Ralph described his feelings for gospel music as distinctive and different: "I can put more in a sacred song than I can in just an ordinary song."[7] Ruth's vocals on the track, recorded for the McLains' *7th Album*, perfectly capture this feeling, as well as the message of the song, while the mandolin and fiddle work together just as effectively. An enduring piece, "The Darkest Hour" has been covered by many bluegrass artists, including Ricky Skaggs, who included it on his 1999 gospel album, *Soldier of the Cross*.

Former Blue Grass Boy Peter Rowan wrote "Dancing with the Angels," the track that kicks off *Sunday Singing*. Now a practicing Buddhist, Rowan released an album titled *Dharma Blues* in 2014. "Dancing with the Angels," however, is strictly out of the Christian tradition. A peppy number with a catchy chorus, the composition starts the album in high gear and is a good showcase for the group's vocal stylings.

Jean Ritchie wrote "Let the Sun Shine Down on Me" (not to be confused with Swan's "Let the Light Shine Down on Me"), recorded as part of the McLains' 1982 Carnegie Hall concert. Like the best gospel songs, its lyrics are simple and memorable. More complex, but equally memorable, is Albert Brumley's famous tribute to the power of the wireless in spreading the word of God, "Turn Your Radio On." Brumley wrote hundreds of songs in his lifetime, including this classic and the well-known "I'll Fly Away." The band's interpretation on *Kentucky Wind* features Raymond K.'s accordion, Raymond W.'s guitar, and strong, imploring vocals by Ruth.

Related in spirit to gospel songs are those that celebrate Christmas. The stately "Babe of Bethlehem" (*Sunday Singing*) employs Raymond K.'s recorder and a guitar tone that resembles a harp, lending the piece a feel not often heard on a bluegrass album. Steve and Elizabeth Rhymer's "Light of the Stable" from *Big Hill* is a gentle piece whose "alleluias" showcase the band's vocal talents. Cheryl and Sharon White performed this song at the McLain Family Band Festival, and it quickly became a favorite of the hosts. They liked it so much, in fact, that the band performed the piece to help celebrate Raymond W.'s Christmastime wedding in 1979.

TRADITIONAL SONGS

The majority of the traditional songs that the McLains covered are well known to bluegrass fans. "Pig in the Pen" (*Big Hill*) is an energetic piece that, like so many of the group's selections, recounts the joys of country life and southern cuisine. In his liner notes to the *Family Album*, Raymond K. notes that "Rabbit in a Log" imparts a lesson that "what you want often appears just beyond reach." Never ones to give up easily, the McLains, like the inventive hunter in the song, are persistent and find ways to solve life's little problems. Bluegrass giants including the Stanley Brothers and Bill Monroe recorded the song, while mandolin wizard and *Prairie Home Companion* host Chris Thile has also introduced it to a more contemporary audience.

"Two Dollar Bill" (*7th Album*) was recorded by the Stanley Brothers, as well as J. D. Crowe and the New South. Tim Owen's banjo stylings are sassy here, and Raymond W.'s fiddle puffs emulate the engine described in the song. "New River Train" (*On the Road*) continues the railroad theme.[8] Whereas the Monroe Brothers included six verses on their interpretation of the song and Pete Seeger nine, the McLains are typically laconic, contenting themselves with four. As discussed earlier, a great many of their recorded tracks do not exceed two minutes in length. Their decision to practice such economy leaves the listener wanting more, rather than lamenting unnecessary padding. There's still plenty to like in such brief pieces, however. Here Ruth includes one of her trademark slap bass solos. In 1974 she was named Most Promising Bass Player by *Muleskinner News*, and in 2018 she was nominated by the International Bluegrass Music Association (IBMA) as Bass Player of the Year. The vital role of bass players in bluegrass music is often overlooked. While most are content to play a support role behind the scenes, the McLains often featured Ruth front and center. In fact, as Murphy Henry points out in *Pretty Good for a Girl*, her bass was in many ways an additional lead instrument for the group.

"Walkin' in My Sleep" (*7th Album*) has a complex provenance. It is credited on the album to Asa Martin and is an adaptation of the Civil War era song, "Shear 'Em." It also resembles a 1937 recording by country blues guitarist Casey Bill Weldon. Finally, Fiddlin' Arthur Smith gained a copyright on the song that same year, though his claim seems rather dubious given the fact that it had been recorded by the Dixie Reelers one year previously. No matter how the song originated, it is certainly an enjoyable number as performed by the McLains. Three short, playful verses are punctuated by some first-rate fiddling and a solid mandolin solo.

Love and courting are, of course, common themes in traditional music. The McLains chose to open their Carnegie Hall concert with the Stanley Brothers favorite, "How Mountain Girls Can Love." "Curly Headed Baby" (*Kentucky Wind*) provides a portrait of one such beauty. Popularized by North Carolina's Callahan Brothers in the 1930s, the song was written by L. Leatherman and has been covered by a diverse range of performers from Doc Watson, Roy Acuff, the Louvin Brothers, Pete Seeger, and Paul Robeson to Dinah Shore. Raymond W. drives the song nicely with fine vocal and banjo work. It is his fiddle that lends punch to the group's interpretation of "Shady Grove," recorded for the *Family Album*. Ruth and Alice provide the kind of tight-knit vocal duet that only sisters can create, and Al White contributes a rollicking guitar solo to a wonderful performance that proves the validity of Raymond K.'s liner notes statement: "You can't beat mountain tunes (with a stick, or touch them with a ten foot pole)!"

The family patriarch sings lead on "Farewell, Sweet Jane," worked out by the band in their car while on tour in Germany and learned from Isom Ritchie back home in Knott County. In some ways this song from the band's debut album is a pastiche of several traditional songs, including two motifs commonly used in folk music: "who will glove your hand, who will shoe your foot, and who will kiss your ruby red lips," and a lonesome dove flying from pine to pine. Lovely harmonies provide support for Raymond K.'s voice on the higher parts of the song, and Raymond W.'s banjo nicely speaks the part of the mournful dove. Alice's mandolin break offers a change from the expected banjo solo and lends the piece an old-time feel.

The McLains often used "The Girl I Left Behind Me" (*Country Life*) to open live sets. Another example of the group's remarkable economy, the track clocks in at only one minute and twenty-five seconds. Though dozens of verses exist, here the McLains content themselves with only three. On such a short piece, they still manage to convey the essence of the story and fit in two very good, driving solos, one on banjo, the other on mandolin. This performance shows the group at its most assured. It is a demonstration of how powerful they could be when they wanted to step on the gas, and how seamlessly they meshed with each other.

The sadder side of love is represented by "Fair and Tender Ladies" (*7th Album*) and "Lonesome Day" (*On the Road*). The former is one of the band's vocal masterpieces. According to Raymond K., the McLains worked on the piece "for years until we thought we could sing it well enough to sustain the feeling."[9] Their patience paid dividends, as the band's gentle accompaniment (featuring outstanding mandolin work by Raymond W.) allows Ruth's vocal to take center stage. Her reading of the oft-performed number is heartbreaking in its emotional power. Her tonal modulations show how far she has come as a singer and perfectly fit the tenor of the song. This is a true McLain Family Band classic.

The group displays its skill at singing harmonies on the similarly aching "Lonesome Day." As they have on several other occasions, the band here chooses to begin the song with unaccompanied singing. This artful device perfectly reflects the tone of loneliness inherent in the piece. Ruth's lead vocals are strong and appropriately plaintive. The song featured one of Raymond W.'s earliest fiddle contributions, and here he already sounds like a veteran on the instrument, using it to mimic the church bells referred to in the lyrics. Alice contributes solid mandolin work to a number that certainly falls into the high, lonesome category and serves to refute some critics' claims that the McLains could not produce the goods in this respect.

"Married Me a Wife" (*Country Life*) and "Pretty Little Reckless Boy" (*On the Road*) show an entirely different side of the band and demonstrate their keen sense of humor. The group learned "Married Me a Wife" from Frankie Duff of Decoy, Kentucky. Known in some versions as "The Wife Wrapped in the Wether's Skin," the song would not find favor today, condoning as it does spousal abuse. Still, the exact details of the song belie its playful tone, and the McLains' interpretation doesn't come off as particularly offensive. Raymond W.'s lead vocals are quite expressive. Numerous asides ("I should have left her alone, too, buddy") punctuate the verses and show solidarity with an imagined audience of male listeners. His exchanges with Alice lend humor to the piece, and she closes the song wonderfully with her own comments: "Cook? What's that? My cousin's old man got her a maid!" In sum, the number is an anachronism, but a fairly harmless one.

"Pretty Little Reckless Boy" most likely stems from the song "Nicoll a Cod" that dates from the seventeenth century and was a staple in the repertoire of New Hampshire's famed Hutchinson family. In the 1920s, Ernest Stoneman performed the song with his wife Hattie as "Mountaineer's Courtship." Peggy Seeger voices both parts in her performance of the piece. Here, Raymond W. plays the title character, Ruth his would-be bride. Her question, "When are we gonna get married?" is at first answered only by Raymond W.'s prevaricating fiddle. The fact that they are already arguing like an old married couple leads one to wonder if the reckless boy really has five children ("six if the weather's all right!"), or if his lover's nagging prompts him to invent them as a way out of the woman's clutches. The fiddle's concluding laugh echoes the reckless boy's relief at having apparently dodged a bullet. Again, the song may not suit modern sensibilities, but it needs to be understood as a period piece.

A classic that has stood the test of time, "In the Pines" (*Troublesome Creek*) has been recorded by dozens of artists but is most often associated with Huddie Ledbetter, better known as Lead Belly, who popularized the piece in the 1930s. The Price Sisters, who studied with both Raymond W. and Ruth at Morehead State, have recorded the song and it is a staple of their concert performances. Raymond W. sings lead and his fiddle nicely picks up the wind motif employed throughout the number.

"Pretty Polly" is another familiar number. First recorded on the McLains' debut album, it also was part of their set list for the Carnegie Hall concert. In his liner notes to that album, Raymond K. states that his mother Bicky petitioned the band to include their interpretation of this traditional murder ballad for the occasion. A staple of both old-time and bluegrass music, murder ballads occur with rather alarming frequency in the repertoire of most bands from the genre. While it is difficult to imagine the sweet-tempered Raymond W. delivering the song believably, he is certainly up to the task. "I dug on your grave the best part of last night" is truly one of the most chilling lines in all of music, and Raymond W.'s phrasing and tone lend the words a very convincing malevolence.

"Jump Josie" (*On the Road*) and "Goin' to Boston" (*7th Album*) again reflect the McLains' origins as a country dance band. The former is based on a game from Tennessee that helps children experience two rhythms and learn how to double numbers. Alice has lead vocal duties on this song, one well suited to her eventual profession of elementary schoolteacher. "Goin' to Boston" came from the famous Ritchie family of Kentucky. In her book, *Folk Songs of the Southern Appalachians*, Jean Ritchie notes that " 'Boston' is at the top of every play-partner's list, having one of the finest tunes combined with the best of the running-set figures."[10] The group's energetic cover of the song offers a fine banjo introduction and a pulsing mandolin solo. The real star of the show, however, is Raymond W.'s expressive fiddling. His fills are particularly delightful on this number.

"Me and My Gal Sal" from *Country Ham* stands as the sole recitation in the McLains' recorded catalog. Raymond W.'s natural charm is on full display in this rapid-fire tall tale. His breath control and vocal dexterity are worthy of an auctioneer—or a twenty-first-century rapper. The number's youthful high spirits and playfulness made it a crowd favorite in concert.

SONGS OF THE CARTER FAMILY AND OTHER TWENTIETH-CENTURY SONGWRITERS

It is difficult to adequately state the influence the Carter Family exerted on twentieth-century music. Together with Jimmie Rodgers, they established what eventually became known as country music. The dozens of songs A. P. Carter collected and recorded with his wife Sara and his sister-in-law Maybelle created a kind of great American songbook for artists, not only in country music but also in bluegrass and folk. The songs of the Carters combine simple but powerful lyrics with distinctive harmonies and a trademark guitar method that came to be known as the "Carter scratch." The McLain Family Band felt great admiration for the Carters' music and established lasting friendships with A. P. and Sara's children, Janette and Joe. After the Carter Fold was established in Hiltons, Virginia, in 1974 as a venue to honor the legacy of the Carters and host musical acts that carried on their spirit, the McLains accepted frequent invitations to play there. Raymond K. summed up the entire family's veneration for the foundational group by simply stating in his liner notes for *Troublesome Creek*, "Oh, the Carter Family, pioneer musicians!"

Besides "I'm Working on a Building" described above, the McLains covered five additional Carter Family songs. "Storms Are on the Ocean" (*Kentucky Wind*) features Raymond W. on vocals and guitar in a suitably unadorned performance. While he often gained plaudits for his prowess as an instrumentalist, Raymond W.'s singing can also be extraordinary. His tenor is light but clear, and he understands that singing is first and foremost about matching one's voice to the emotions evoked in the song. "East Virginia Blues" was chosen to kick off the band's *7th Album*. Again, the reading is respectful but fresh. Raymond W. opens the song with his fiddle and sings lead vocal. Tim Owen's banjo is also immediately apparent, with his fingers dancing up and down the neck in spritely fashion.

The McLains dedicated *Big Hill* to Janette Carter, so it is only fitting that they include two Carter Family songs on the album. Ruth's lead vocals perfectly capture the desperate nature of the narrator's plight in "I Never Will Marry," while "Worried Man Blues," sung by Raymond W., betrays similar anguish. "You Are My Flower" was included on *Will the Circle Be Unbroken*, the Nitty Gritty Dirt Band's 1972 recording that reinvigorated bluegrass music and introduced classic songs like this to a new generation of listeners. The McLains cover the song on *Troublesome Creek*, lending their sweet harmonies to the gentle piece.

Inspired by the examples of the Carters and Woody Guthrie, hundreds of other performers began to record their own compositions after World War II. The so-called Tin Pan Alley model of song creation thus slowly began to be replaced by this more grassroots model. Like all musicians, The McLains were avid listeners as well as performers. To create album tracks, they mined the rich veins of both country and bluegrass songwriters and occasionally forayed into the related genres of blues and western swing.

Though most associate "Footprints in the Snow" with Bill Monroe, he was not its original composer. The song's original author appears to be Harry Wright, who composed it around 1880 with the title "Footmarks in the Snow," and the piece was first recorded in 1931 by

Ernest Branch & the West Virginia Ramblers as "Little Footprints."[11] Whatever its origin, the song's lyrics are quite intriguing. Though the narrator's sweetheart is now deceased, he concentrates on happy memories of her, invoked every time it snows. That she is now dead is not as important as the joys she provided during her life. The memories she and the snow evoke are what remain paramount. As Robert Cantwell has pointed out, here "innocence is joined metaphorically through snow to death."[12] The McLains' fine interpretation features Nancy Ann on mandolin and a lengthy fiddle introduction by Raymond W., who also sings lead.

The group dedicated *Country Life* to Bill Monroe and included his "Rose of Old Kentucky" on the album. The song was derived from a minstrel song of the same title and has been recorded by dozens of performers, including Doc Watson, Barbara Mandrell, and Del McCoury. The McLains' interpretation is a cheerful tribute to a woman whose love has bloomed before the eyes of her admiring husband and has subsequently stood the test of time. The band omits one verse from Monroe's original and lends it a slightly peppier feel. Raymond W. demonstrates his frailing technique on banjo to provide the song its drive.

The McLains learned "Blue Railroad Train" (*All Natural Ingredients*) and "Big River Blues" (*On the Road*) from the recordings of another seminal act, the Delmore Brothers. Michael Riopel's harmonica opens the former track, and he also contributes a lengthy and inventive solo on the instrument later in the piece. Raymond W.'s guitar work nicely complements his brother-in-law's harp break, while his vocals reach the top of his range when the train's whistle blows. The group's unaccompanied vocal close to the track is smoothly executed. Typically, their version of "Big River Blues" is shorter than the original, as they omit the first verse. Ruth's bass is wonderfully prominent here, with her sister Alice noting in the diary she kept of their 1975 Alaskan tour that "Ruth's break is in the style of Jesse McReynolds' mandolin playing." During the same tour, the group spent an hour rehearsing the song one night before taking the stage to debut it.

Written by Buck Graves, Josh Graves, and LeRoy Mack of Kentucky Colonels fame, "If You're Ever Gonna Love Me" (also from

On the Road) is typically energetic and features Raymond W. on lead vocals. It is hard to imagine the object of the singer's affection being able to turn him down after such an earnest and charming approach. The interpretation by Little Roy Lewis and Lizzy Long shows many similarities to this performance.

Family friend Don Reno wrote "Emotions" (*Troublesome Creek*), an expressive song that is closer to pop than any other number in the group's repertoire. The lyrics "if you confess, I bet you have emotions, too" recall Rosemary's "I am confessing, guessing you feel the same" from "Love, Love, Love." The rather basic guitar solo mirrors the simple structure of this song that treats feelings so central to the human experience.

Three waltzes, each composed by Kentuckians, comprise *All Natural Ingredient's* "Waltz Medley." "The Tennessee Waltz" was written by Redd Stewart (lyrics) and Pee Wee King (melody) and proved a hit for Patti Page in 1950. Here, Nancy Ann sings lead vocals. The band then segues into one of Bill Monroe's first compositions and biggest hits, "The Kentucky Waltz." Finally, a faster tempo is introduced for Monroe's "Blue Moon of Kentucky," famously covered by Elvis Presley early in his career at Sun Studios. As the tune slows again, Raymond W. provides some fancy banjo licks before relinquishing center stage to Ruth's vocals. The vision for and execution of this medley demonstrate once again the McLains' artistic approach to material covered so often in the past by others.

The group portrays its appreciation for country music composers in the following nine songs. On Jimmie Rodgers's "California Blues" (*Country Ham*), the McLains pay homage to the singing brakeman. The McLains' interpretation is performed in a livelier manner than Rodgers's original (also titled "Blue Yodel #4") and features a confident lead vocal by Raymond W. His father's rhythm guitar sounds more insistent on this track than on most others recorded by the band. Ernest Tubb's "Walking the Floor Over You" from *All Natural Ingredients* features another lead vocal performance by Nancy Ann. Her inflections nicely pick up the measure of solace Tubb's lyrics provide, leaving the listener with a sense of hope that belies the tenor of the song's title. Willie Nelson recorded Scott Wiseman's "Remember

Me" for his landmark 1975 *Red Headed Stranger* album. On *Big Hill*, Ruth lends her gentle touch to Wiseman's song, a fitting finale to an album that runs a wide range of emotions.

Ruby Rose Blevins, better known as Patsy Montana, wrote "I Want to Be a Cowboy's Sweetheart" in 1935, and it became the first country song written by a female artist to sell more than a million copies. Ruth does wonderful justice to the high-spirited and romantic number, lending it one of her best vocal performances. Her yodeling is extraordinary, and she hits the final high note in the piece with real precision. Echoing his efforts on "Kentucky Wind," Raymond W.'s banjo nicely emulates the wind in the singer's face mentioned in the second verse.

In his liner notes to *Troublesome Creek*, Raymond K. speculates that composer Tom T. Hall may have written "Shoeshine Man" in 1970 as a tribute to Rufus "Tee Tot" Payne, the street musician who served as a mentor to Hank Williams. Hall, in turn, may have been influenced by Johnny Cash's 1959 hit "Get Rhythm," which also features a cheerful shoeshiner. Here, the McLains omit Hall's spoken introduction to the song. Michael Riopel's harmonica sounds as busy as the title character, and Raymond W.'s fiddle solo adds to the fun.

Former Blue Grass Boy Clyde Moody (1915–1989), known in some circles as the "Hillbilly Waltz King," offered "Pretty Flowers" to the band, and they certainly do it justice on *Country Life*. Alice's lead vocal is plaintive and heartfelt and lends just the right sense of resignation to the song, while her siblings provide wonderful harmonies and backup singing. All in all, "Pretty Flowers" is one of the group's recordings that is most high and lonesome sounding.

"Bringing in the Georgia Mail" (*All Natural Ingredients*) was written by Fred Rose (1887–1954), who formed a famous music publishing partnership with Roy Acuff. The percussive opening that the band employs emulates the gradual buildup of a steam train getting ready to leave the station. As is their standard practice, the McLains do not include all the verses others have, and the track clocks in at less than one and a half minutes. George Linus Cobb (1886–1942) and lyricist Jack Yellen (1892–1991, famous for writing the words to "Happy Days Are Here Again" and "Ain't She Sweet?") collaborated to write "Alabama Jubilee," a Tin Pan Alley piece, first published in 1915. The band is obviously enjoying themselves as they race through the performance on *Troublesome Creek*. The fiddle introduces the track, which also features some fine guitar and one of Ruth's patented bass solos. Finally, Raymond W. delivers the old woman's admonition to "watch your step, watch your step!" in a charming manner. The final flourishes on the banjo and fiddle conclude a high-spirited and memorable performance.

Recorded for the Carnegie Hall concert, "Fried Chicken and a Country Tune" once more shows off the band's humorous side. Written by C. Harwell and made popular by Billy Edd Wheeler, the composition merits mention in John T. Edge's book that celebrates this cherished American dish, *Fried Chicken: An American Story*. The crowd's reaction confirms how much fun Raymond W. is having as he sings the ditty. Much more somber in nature is John Jacob's Niles's "Go Away from My Window," also recorded for the concert. Born in Kentucky in 1892, Niles played an important role in the American folk revival in the 1950s and 1960s. This powerful song, remarkably composed when Niles was still a teenager, has been recorded by a long list of famous singers, including Joan Baez. Raymond W.'s lead vocal is not nearly as melancholy as on Baez's interpretation but still evokes the emotions its creator intended. Another native Kentuckian, Jean Ritchie, wrote "(Way Down in a) Cedar Swamp," which also features on the 1982 live recording. In her book, *Folk Songs of the Southern Appalachians*, Ritchie associates the song with her school days. Raymond K. sings lead vocals, and his daughters help on the chorus.

If many of the songs the McLains covered came from established pens, others are diamonds in the rough. The melancholy "Dark Hollow" (*Troublesome Creek*) was written by singer-songwriter Bill Browning in 1958 and gained new exposure when the Grateful Dead recorded it in 1973. Here Raymond K. again sings lead vocal, lamenting a theme common to bluegrass songs: the narrator's regret over moving from the country to the city. A rare lead vocal from Michael Riopel is featured on "That's How I Can Count on You," composed by Bob Newman and Shorty Long (born Emidio Vagnoni), a classically trained violinist who surprised his parents by becoming a country-western musician. The song's theme of reassurance ("Like a baby can count on his mother") is one quite common in the McLains' repertoire. Written by Sam King, "Banjo Pickin' Fool" from the band's debut album is upbeat and playful. Raymond W.'s ebullient personality and his lovely tenor voice are on full display here. Appropriately enough, the song features no fewer than three banjo breaks.

The spirited "Lovely Dove" (*Country Ham*) was written by family friend Sonya Yancey from Hazard, Kentucky, for her grandfather, Preacher Bates. The singing on the track is especially strong and assured, and Raymond W.'s banjo nicely matches his sisters' ascending vocals. Glenn Lawson, one of Raymond K.'s first students at Berea College, wrote the title track to the McLains' third album as a class assignment. One assumes he received an A for his efforts. Lawson went on to enjoy a successful career in music, playing with the Bluegrass Alliance, and then J. D. Crowe. His lyrics certainly fit vocalist Raymond W.'s experiences: "I've been halfway round this world, and I know what's in store / For a rambling boy like I used to be." Raymond K.'s guitar provides a solid underpinning to the piece, and the banjo and mandolin solos are equally skillful. This is a standout piece on a standout album.

SONGS FROM RELATED GENRES

The fact that the McLains enjoyed western swing is evident in their recording of "Blue Bonnet Lady" on the *7th Album*. Written by Woody Paul, the song name checks Bob Wills's "San Antonio Rose" and has been popularized in recent years by the cowboy group Riders in the Sky. Yet it was Al White's marriage into the family that is responsible for the other numbers from the genre that the family recorded. The first recording to include Al, 1978's *Family Album*, includes three songs from his native Southwest. Vernon Dalhart's "Prisoner's Song" has been recorded by the likes of Hank Snow, Bill Monroe, Del McCoury, and Mac Wiseman. The brief mandolin quotation from a naval tune is a nice feature of the performance and typical of the band's ability to add small ornaments to oft-recorded numbers. Al White takes his lead vocal bow on James Talley's "West Texas Sun." In a letter from 1977, Ruth notes that Al taught the group this song in Africa. His smooth, relaxed vocal delivery that recalls

Tony Rice fits his laid-back personality and lends even more variety to an act already gifted with great diversity. A hit for Bob Wills and the Texas Playboys in 1941, "Take Me Back to Tulsa" is a somewhat playful inclusion here, given that the line from the chorus ("I'm too young to marry") is sung by Al, a newlywed. Another song about a traveling musician, this number features a sassy fiddle introduction, two nice guitar solos by Al, and a bass solo from Ruth for good measure. It's clear to the listener just how much the band enjoys playing the piece and how seamlessly Al fit into the group's well-established sound. Finally, when Al rejoined the band for their *Country Dance* album, they recorded Bob Wills's "Beaumont Rag" for the occasion.

As Raymond K. points out in his liner notes to the *Country Life* album, bluegrass music has a lot of blues. "Milk Cow Blues," penned by Kokomo Arnold in the 1930s, is a classic from the genre. On their cover of the tune for the *Family Album*, Raymond W. sounds completely at ease, encouraging the band in two separate asides to "play it together!" and then, near the conclusion, to "take it home!" Indeed, the guitar, mandolin, and bluesy fiddle come together with good effect at numerous times throughout the recording. The rather salacious double entendres so often found in the blues seem a bit out of character for the wholesome family band, but their performance again demonstrates their range. Harmonica great Little Walter wrote "Blue and Lonesome." The McLains' interpretation on their *7th Album* is driven by mandolin and includes a fiddle part that evokes the train mentioned in the lyrics. "Columbus Stockade Blues" (*All Natural Ingredients*) includes some yodeling and a short banjo break from Michael McLain.

Finally, the McLains occasionally included children's songs on their recordings. "Mister Frog," a somewhat truncated version of "Frog Went A-Courting," was recorded for the band's debut album and features a happier ending than is typical for the tale. While the polliwog groom often ends up being eaten in other versions, here the song simply ends with the bride's uncle going to town to buy her wedding gown. Some percussive use of wooden-bodied instruments and hand clapping nicely mimics the sound of the groom riding to see his intended. The arrangement features Raymond K. on lead vocal.

In his liner notes he muses, "I used to sing this to the children as they were growing up. Now to have them sing it with me is a satisfaction I never expected from life." Clocking in at only one minute and five seconds, the band's interpretation of "Old Dan Tucker," included on *Country Ham*, is even more abbreviated than "Mister Frog." While many versions of the song run to four verses, the McLains include only two. During a concert thematically linked by songs about food, the McLains included "Momma's Little Baby Loves Short'nin' Bread" on stage at Carnegie Hall. Its simple charm recalls the joys of childhood and found favor with the audience, many of whom no doubt delighted in the chance to momentarily forget their adult cares and revel in the group's performance of the song.

The nature and scope of material any band chooses to cover says a great deal about its roots and aims. Equally significant, of course, is the musical spin artists add to pieces that did not originate with them and that listeners have often heard before. Through the recordings detailed above, the McLain Family Band showcased favorites and honored those songwriters whom they most admire. That they were able to make these recordings come alive for their audience and stand on their own, not as staid replicas but as distinct and vibrant interpretations, speaks to both their taste and their creativity. Songwriter Nick Lowe has stated that when he finds a cover song that he likes, he will work on it until he almost comes to believe that he wrote it himself.[13] The care the McLains took with other people's songs indicates that they, like Lowe, approached material from any source with respect but then strove to make it uniquely their own.

Solo Recordings

The McLain Family Band curtailed their touring schedule in 1989 in order to devote time to their families, careers in education, and new musical ventures. They would not record another album together until 2018's *Celebrate Life*, but individual members of the group remained busy with a number of other projects. Raymond W., Ruth, Alice, Al, and Michael provided musical support on a multitude of recordings by artists such as Jim and Jesse and the Virginia Boys, the Price Sisters, Michael Johnathon, Bill Clifton, Mike Stevens, Claire Lynch, the Berea Castoffs, Sarah Wood and Thomas Albert, the Woodsheep, Becky Alfrey, Michelle Canning, Samantha Jean Cunningham, Alisa Jones, Ramona Jones' Family & Friends, Southland Drive, the Berea College Bluegrass Ensemble, and the Mountain Music Ambassadors. They also found time (under a variety of band names) to record seven albums of their own between 1992 and 2016. While each has its own character, these albums share many characteristics of the family band: excellent musicianship, innovative approaches to material, interesting song selection, and an optimistic approach to life.

A Place of My Own (1992): Raymond W. McLain

Raymond W. recorded his first solo album in Nashville. At the time he was playing with Jim and Jesse McReynolds and the Virginia

Boys, and both brothers feature prominently on this project. Jesse's distinctive cross-picked mandolin is heard to good effect on most tracks, and Jim lends his smooth baritone to "Ain't Gonna Work Tomorrow." In 1988, the McReynolds heard Canadian harmonica player Mike Stevens, were immediately intrigued by his distinctive sound, and invited him to perform with them whenever his schedule permitted. Raymond W. and Stevens quickly became friends and found that Stevens' lightning fast runs on the harmonica deftly complemented Raymond's banjo and fiddle work.

While the harmonica is not an instrument often featured in bluegrass, Stevens' long career is testament to how well it can be incorporated into the genre when played in the right style. "I had no idea the harmonica wasn't supposed to be in bluegrass," Stevens says. "A band was calling for auditions, and I went in with a harmonica and saw a look of horror in their eyes when I came in, but I got the job."[1] The Canadian's energetic playing employs a difficult-to-master technique called "overblowing." In essence, overblowing creates a jump in pitch and allows skilled harmonica players to coax three and a half octaves out of a ten-hole diatonic harmonica.

Raymond W. produced *A Place of My Own* for Flying Fish Records, with help from his brother Michael, Jesse McReynolds, and legendary sound engineer Bil VornDick. The cover shows a smiling Raymond, all by himself, holding his banjo. This is, of course, appropriate, since the album represents what liner notes' author Mike Fleischer calls "a musical home that Raymond McLain can truly call his own." This home is one where instrumentals dominate, a place where the musician experiments with varying combinations of instruments and accompanists until, to borrow a line from the old Shaker hymn, he reaches "a place just right."

On his first solo album, Raymond W. revisits previously recorded McLain Family Band selections including "On the Road," "Silver Creek," "The Bells of St. Mary's," "Shuckin' the Corn," and "Raymond's Breakdown," but he also includes eight new tracks that characterize his approach to bluegrass. The gentle title track was composed with the help of his brother Michael and is reminiscent of Stephen Foster's work. Featuring fiddler Glen Duncan, "A Place of My Own" illustrates its composer's intent to draw attention to his music rather than to himself. Another original composition, "Windswept," returns to the theme of the breezes that blow through our lives. Here Jesse McReynolds' fluttering mandolin nicely emulates the zephyrs and seems to answer the questions posed by Raymond W.'s banjo. "Kitten on the Keys," composed as a ragtime piano solo by Zez Confrey (1895–1971), was, in fact, inspired by the composer hearing a feline traipsing across the ivories. Raymond K. had frequently played this piece on the piano at home. While Raymond W.'s banjo takes the lead throughout with typical flourishes and ornamentation, his work is nicely underpinned by Ruth's bass and Michael's guitar.

David Royko's glowing review stresses the freedom Raymond W. must have felt while recording the album. "Emancipated from being strictly a sideman, he now has a place of his own, and what a pad it is, each room unique, inviting, impeccably designed and decorated, and all adorned with surprising and delightful details." The reviewer lauds McLain's "soaring improvisations" on "Shuckin' the Corn," which, he writes, lead him "into realms only hinted at by Flatt, Scruggs, and Graves." Royko also has high praise for McLain's original compositions, describing "Silver Creek" as scorching and "Windswept" as a "showpiece for McLain's lyricism."[2]

Kentucky Mountain Banjo (1995): Raymond W. McLain

Subtitled "Old Time Songs and Instrumentals," Raymond W.'s second solo album found him returning to the Country Life Records label. *Kentucky Mountain Banjo* was recorded in Nashville in 1994 and features many of the same musicians who played on *A Place of My Own*. These include Jim and Jesse McReynolds, fiddler Glenn Duncan, Mike Stevens, and Raymond's siblings Michael and Ruth. The cover photograph by Larry Hill shows Raymond W. in profile, with his banjo. In the liner notes, famed old-time musician John Hartford adroitly observes that "there is some fancy playing on this recording, but not for the sake of tricks. It's music first. It's about the spirit and the feeling. This recording is Raymond McLain following his heart."

The album's title track is an up-tempo and engaging reminder that Raymond W. can still play bluegrass banjo with the best of them when he has a mind to. "Hot Stuff," composed by Raymond W. and Mike Stevens, is a brief (1:37) banjo and harmonica duet. The listener feels as if he has just happened upon the pair as they're playing for pleasure on their front porch one fine summer evening. While the medium-tempo piece sounds informal and improvised, it is obvious the pair has practiced it until they can play it perfectly. The track serves as a preview of sorts to the *Old-Time Mojo* album Raymond would record with Stevens some years later.

Besides fun tunes like "Why Don't You Haul Off and Love Me," "Cindy," and Jimmy Driftwood's "Baby O," *Kentucky Mountain Banjo* also includes a lovely medley titled "Tennessee Blues/Tennessee Lonesome Blues." Clocking in at over six minutes, the first half of this volunteer state medley was written by swamp-rock pioneer Bobby Charles (1938–2010). It is a plaintive song, far removed from Charles's more typically lighthearted pieces and describes the narrator's understandable desire to find a place he can stay that is free from all worries. Ruth supplies lovely vocal support on the chorus, while Stevens augments the song's mournful tone with his harp. The second half of the pairing is a Jesse McReynolds composition that features an excellent fiddle break by Glenn Duncan and first-rate harmonica work from the Canadian master.

"The Dance in Old Kentucky" is the album's standout track. Michael McLain and John Hartford helped Raymond W. write this wonderfully spirited song that pays homage to the days when Raymond K. would take him to dances in his home state. "I really like this one because it's kind of personal to me," Raymond recalls. "It's about musical experiences I had playing for country dancing when I was young. Things I did with Daddy. Going to play music with him was just bigger than life. Doing things with your father—those can be the best times you ever had."[3] The number threatens to boil over with excitement at some stages, especially when Raymond declares that "some rowdy boys are coming in, it's Jim and Jesse and all of them." Duncan's energetic fiddling drives the number, which also includes exciting mandolin and guitar solos. Both nostalgic and contemporary, "The Dance in Old Kentucky" quickly became a staple at McLain Family Band reunion concerts.

More Fun Than We Ought to Have (1998): The McLains

This album was released by a group known as the McLains, consisting of Raymond W., Michael, and his wife Jennifer Banks McLain. Recorded in Nashville for Pinecastle Records, it was coproduced by all three group members. The cover shot by Hank Widick shows Jennifer framed by her husband and Raymond W. The album's title was inspired by Widick's chance remark during the shoot that "This is a fun group. They seem to have more fun than they ought to have." Music journalist Stephanie Ledgin wrote the liner notes. Ledgin had known the McLain Family Band for years, having interviewed them for *Pickin'* in July 1977. Here she introduces this most recent iteration of the band by stating, "If the name McLain is in the band, you can be sure you've got the instruments and voices of time-honored experience, top-notch talent, and seasoned showmanship."

The lineup for the album's opening song, "It'll Come to Me," forms a model for many of the tracks. Raymond W. contributes vocals, banjo, and fiddle; Michael plays guitar and adds harmony vocals; and Jennifer picks her mandolin and provides harmony vocals. While the song's composer, Beth Nielsen Chapman, is perhaps best known for the haunting "Sand and Water" composed after her husband's death, here she has written a song from the opposite end of the emotional spectrum. This is a lighthearted, joyful piece about patience and kicks off the album in fine fashion.

Two train-oriented songs provide an interesting contrast. Fred Eaglesmith's "(I Wish I Was a) Freight Train" uses the locomotive metaphor to illustrate a troubled relationship. Mike Stevens guests on the track, and his use of a handheld microphone of his own design lends an appropriately haunting feel to the cut. "My Baby Thinks He's a Train," on the other hand, is much breezier. Even though Leroy Preston's song describes an unfaithful lover, Jennifer's reading sounds more resigned than brokenhearted. The narrator seems to retain a soft spot for the man even though, like a train, he's "always giving some old tramp a ride."

Jennifer's vocals on "Lips That Lie" are much more plaintive. The Stanley Brothers also covered this Fred Stryker and Don Byrd song that describes a sweet-talker whose actions don't live up to his words.

Jennifer combines with her husband to sing "Through the Garden," a pretty song about a childhood sweetheart who's gone away. Michael sings the first two verses from the male point of view before Jennifer concludes the piece by stating her hopes for a reunion. The group shows off its harmonies on the chorus, while Michael (guitar) and Raymond (fiddle) add lovely solos. Michael offers a rare solo vocal turn on the catchy "Take Me in Your Lifeboat," and his rich baritone is heard to good effect throughout.

The younger McLain brother's "Gracie" is the only original McLain composition on the album and features him on banjo. A driving instrumental, the tune also features guests Al White on mandolin and Mike Stevens on harmonica. On "Dizzy Fingers," Raymond W. and Michael reprise their double-barreled banjo attack, first heard on "Troublesome Creek." A relaxed instrumental written by jazz and ragtime composer Edward Confrey (1895–1971), the piece features guest Jim Hurst on guitar and sounds as if it could have come from *A Place of My Own*. It's a crooked, unpredictable number and sounds great in this unusual arrangement. The album concludes with the A. P. Carter classic, "Foggy Mountain Top." After largely featuring the works of contemporary songwriters, the McLains show their roots by closing with a traditional rendition of the chestnut. The group's unaccompanied vocal harmonies during the chorus help make the piece their own.

Old-Time Mojo (2004): Raymond W. McLain and Mike Stevens

After working together on the road and in the studio for years, Raymond W. and Mike Stevens decided in 2004 that it was time for them to record an entire album together. The project's title reflects a unique take on old-time material and shows their desire to create a sound that infuses some contemporary swagger into the music they grew up with. Speaking in 2001, Raymond W. accurately describes the sound he and Stevens create together as something new: "I don't think anyone has ever done this before."[4] Stevens' high-powered harmonica style certainly partners well with Raymond's fiddle, banjo, and guitar. "What Mike does," Raymond W. explains, "is incorporate the harmonica in the fundamental sound of the band in terms of backup, rhythm, and lead, playing melody, harmony, and improvisation."[5] Stevens returns the compliment by stating, "Raymond's musicianship is totally honest and real. He's lived with and learned from a lot of the real creators and pioneers of this music."[6]

"Old-time" is a term not usually paired with the contemporary slang term "mojo," which is usually defined as designating a magic charm, spell, talisman, or, more recently, sex appeal. The music on the album, coproduced by McLain and Stevens, is often sparse but always innovative. Every track reflects an enjoyable, newfound freedom in each musician's playing. Larry Towell's black and white cover photograph of Stevens "planking"[7] sets the tone before a single track has been played.

The album includes three new versions of songs first recorded on McLain Family Band albums. Raymond W. veers into western swing with Bob Wills's "Take Me Back to Tulsa" and adds some interesting fiddle work to both "In the Pines" and "Footprints in the Snow." "I'm Always in Love with You" is Raymond W.'s sole original composition on the album and is a lovely and gentle tribute to the woman who patiently awaits the return of an itinerant musician. It is the reassurance of her love that helps maintain the narrator's peace of mind as he travels his lonely path. A song that all road-weary performers can relate to, "I'm Always in Love with You" is one of Raymond W.'s best lyrical compositions. Stevens adds a mournful harmonica introduction and lengthy solo to supplement McLain's heartfelt vocals.

The Canadian's mouth harp nicely emulates the train celebrated in "The Wabash Cannonball," the A. P. Carter classic made famous by Roy Acuff. Acuff, in fact, first heard Stevens play on stage at the Grand Ole Opry. "Roy was on stage when I started to play," Stevens remembers. "All of a sudden he comes over and just sort of stares at me."[8] Over the years, many fans and musicians besides the King of Country Music have been similarly impacted by Stevens' unique sound. Here Raymond W. plays banjo and sings while Stevens takes listeners on a musical ride they're not likely to soon forget.

It is no wonder that the duo chose to include Jesse McReynolds' "Blowing Up a Storm" on their album. Both McLain and Stevens played extensively with Jim and Jesse and the Virginia Boys and are quick to sing their praises. "They have such incredibly high standards as far as how they treat their fans and friends," says Stevens. "And their music is as real as their commitment to their fans. No one can ever copy what they've done." Raymond W. is similarly effusive in his regard for the brothers. "They've always been on the edge, haven't they? They are not playing the way anyone else did before them or since."[9] Here McLain and Stevens do justice to the original recording of the up-tempo piece. Raymond W.'s banjo work is fiery, and Stevens demonstrates his ability to play sixty-fourth notes on the harp. The result on both this track and their cover of "Dueling Banjos" is akin to two maestros duking it out. As the often-heard piece heats up and gains momentum, one is astonished that the harmonica can keep pace with McLain's five-string attack. This astonishing performance shows the duo at the height of their abilities.

In 1965, Jim and Jesse recorded *Berry Pickin' in the Country*, their salute to the music of Chuck Berry. No doubt inspired by their friends' effort, McLain and Stevens here dust off their rock-and-roll chops on a cover of Berry's most famous song, "Johnny B. Goode." Raymond W. drums on the head of his banjo and provides Sonny Terry-like vocal whoops to lend the piece further distinction.

The introduction to the album's final track, "Blues Stay Away from Me," features a sample of an actual locomotive before Stevens provides his own take on the diesel engine's whine. "Blues Stay Away from Me" is a traditional song most often associated with the Delmore Brothers, who recorded it in 1949. Again, McLain and Stevens' interpretation is quite unusual and wholly different from anything heard before. Stevens speaks the lyrics in a soulful bass and is accompanied throughout by Raymond's pizzicato fiddle. Stevens makes one final run on his harp to conclude this innovative and enjoyable album.

Let the Mountains Roll (2013): Al, Alice, and Ruth

Recorded at Michael McLain's studio, *Let the Mountains Roll* features Al White on guitar, banjo, and fiddle, his wife Alice on bass and mandolin, and his sister-in-law Ruth on mandolin. All three take turns singing lead and join their voices in bluegrass harmonies throughout. Like many projects family members recorded, the CD has a distinctly rural feel, highlighting the countryside they grew up in and stressing the joys of country life. The album cover shows an inset photo of the trio taken on the steps of Uncle Sol's cabin at the Hindman Settlement School, superimposed onto a shot of green, rolling mountains.

The strong presence of Jean Ritchie can be felt throughout the album. A passage from Genesis 3:8 ("Then the man and his wife heard the sound of the Lord God as he was walking in the garden in the cool of the day, and they hid from the Lord God among the trees of the Garden") inspired her to write "Cool of the Day." In three short verses, Ritchie manages to convey a number of varied messages: the importance of freedom, a reverence for God, and how vital it is to protect the environment.

The McLains became familiar with the playful dance song "Killy Kranky"[10] during their childhood through the recordings of Jean Ritchie, and Alice sounds delighted to be singing it once again. Ruth and Michael add solos on mandolin and guitar, while Al plays his banjo clawhammer style. According to the album's liner notes, Ritchie's father, Balis, sang the beautiful Scots-English ballad "Foreign Lander" to his future bride, Abigail, as a proposal of marriage. The song's narrator has conquered all his enemies on the battlefield but has, in turn, been conquered by the beauty of his dearest. Virtually a solo performance, Al's moving and soulful vocals lend just the right tone to the touching song.

Quite different in mood are "My Lazy Day" and "When the Storm Is Over." The former was written by Smiley Burnette (1911–1967). Best known as Gene Autry's sidekick in numerous movies, Burnette was also a talented musician and prolific songwriter. Ruth sings lead here and adds a mandolin solo. "My Lazy Day" is a fun track that illustrates the notion that on some days even a pastime as relaxing as fishing simply requires too much effort. In the liner notes, the group notes that Bob Lucas's "When the Storm Is Over" reminds them of spring days on horse farms in Kentucky. Another happy number that celebrates rural pleasures, it features Michael McLain on guitar, Al on clawhammer banjo, Ruth on mandolin, and Alice on bass.

Besides "Cool of the Day," three other gospel pieces appear on *Let the Mountains Roll*. Sadie Faircloth, a friend of the family, found "Angel Gabriel" (dated 1875) in the Berea College archives. It has a catchy melody, sung here by Ruth and supplemented by guitar work from Al White and Michael McLain. Peter Rowan's "Dancing with the Angels" was recorded by the McLain Family Band on their *Sunday Singing* album. This interpretation is slightly longer, a bit less rambunctious, and features Michael on three-finger banjo and Al on guitar. Ruth sings lead on "Wondrous Love," sometimes known as "What Wondrous Love Is This," a melody American composer Samuel Barber liked so well that in 1958 he penned a piece that utilizes variations on the tune.

While the band covers traditional tracks like "Shady Grove" and "Polly Put the Kettle On," they also tackle more contemporary numbers like "Pans of Biscuits." Based on "Palms of Victory," a religious song from the 1920s recorded by Uncle Dave Macon, the tune was further employed by Bob Dylan as "Paths of Victory" in the 1960s. A song of sympathy for the plight of hardworking farmers, "Pans of Biscuits" is a protest song of sorts, and Al's world-weary vocals are well suited to its theme.

The album's title track concludes the recording and also contains elements of protest. "Let the Mountains Roll" was composed by Berea College graduate Billy Edd Wheeler, known for writing the Johnny Cash hit, "Jackson," and "Coward of the County," the basis for a 1981 film. Here Wheeler's narrator expresses an understanding of the economic need for coal mining but simultaneously pleads for us to spare the mountains. Alice's lead vocal is straight from the heart and perfectly captures the song's plea. The unaccompanied vocal conclusion lends power to this moving performance.

'Tis a Gift (2014): Al, Alice, and Ruth

The trio had long wanted to record a Christmas album, and in 2014 they finally found time to realize their dream. Michael McLain engineered and mastered the CD, whose cover (created by Neil Di Teresa) depicts an angel holding a holiday wreath. Only eight tracks long, *'Tis a Gift* features five original songs by McLain family members, two from twentieth-century songwriters, and the Shaker hymn "Simple Gifts," which is performed in suitably unadorned fashion. Al sings lead on "Bells are Ringing," a joint composition by Mary Carpenter and John Jennings that movingly details how faith can restore peace in the heart, no matter one's material situation. The guitar and mandolin effectively emulate the bells of the song's title. "Light of the Stable" was written by Steven and Elizabeth Rhymer in 1975 and has been covered by Emmylou Harris and Ricky Skaggs. Here Ruth has lead vocal duties on the song, whose theme recalls "We Three Kings of Orient Are."

Rosemary McLain's "Follow the Light" was first recorded on *Sunday Singing*. On this performance, the trio remains faithful to the original, the major difference being Al's clawhammer banjo accompaniment. Alice wrote "Caroling in the Snow," a gentle song that recalls the joys of singing the songs of the season: happy hearts, good friends, and a cup of hot chocolate afterwards. "The First Christmas Day" is also her composition and describes the Nativity. Spoken passages introduce each verse of this brief but eloquent piece.

Ruth's original compositions for the album are similarly strong. "Starlit Lullaby" once again picks up the theme of reassurance, evident in McLain Family Band songs like "Kentucky Wind" and "Blow the Candle Out." Though Ruth wrote "I Wonder What It's Like (in Heaven Today)" as a tribute to her mother, its sentiments are, of course, universal. The narrator misses a loved one who has passed and thinks of that person most at this time of year, the holiday season, recalling a favorite sweater worn by the deceased and finding comfort in the thought that he or she is among friends in heaven. Lasting art features personal stories that most everyone can relate to, and here Ruth employs this formula quite movingly.

Hit the Road and Go (2016): Michael and Jennifer McLain

Michael and Jennifer assembled a very talented band to record their first joint album, which they also coproduced. The couple had been performing live shows for years, but here their sound is more expansive. The cover shot shows Michael and Jennifer flanked by young bass player Kori Caswell and veteran fiddler Dan Kelly. Other musicians who contributed to the project include five-time IBMA bass-player-of-the-year Mike Bub, his former bandmate from another famed bluegrass family, Ronnie McCoury, on mandolin, and Nashville session player Wanda Vick Burchfield on Dobro.

Jennifer is in fine voice throughout the recording. She is equally at home on lively songs like Ray Charles's "This Old Heart (Is Gonna Rise Again)," more intimate numbers like "Do I Ever Cross Your Mind?" and the jazzy "Up This Hill and Down." On the title track, she effectively captures the determined spirit of the narrator. The zest has gone out of her relationship, but instead of passively moping she's moving on to something better. Jennifer also captures the good-time vibe of Marty Stuart's "Busy Bee Café," where people hang out more for the music than the diner's consumables.

Jennifer collaborated with her mother, Reva Banks, to write the touching "Boom Town." Like Bruce Springsteen's "My Hometown" and "Our Town" by Iris Dement, this composition describes a small community that once had a future but has now largely been deserted by folks who have "moved to the city to break new ground." On an album that features the work of so many fine songwriters, this original piece more than holds its own.

Michael's instrumental, "McIntosh," is similarly accomplished in composition and has a Celtic feel to it. Inspired by the neighborhood he lived in (Apple Valley) at the time of the piece's composition, it features some fine picking by its composer, as well as guest performances by Ronnie McCoury on mandolin and Corrina Logston on fiddle. And, in the best McLain tradition, Michael and Jennifer transform "Lady of Spain" into a banjo duet. During the penultimate stanza, Michael shows off some fancy licks, using a distinctive roll pattern that mimics the sound of an accordion to give the interpretation a personal touch.

"Southbound," written by Doc and Merle Watson, features a rare performance by Michael on lead vocals. His understated delivery is well suited to a song that celebrates a number of classic southern themes—trains, hoboing, and picking the blues. Supplementing Michael's vocals is his extended guitar solo and Burchfield's Dobro stylings. Finally, Jennifer's vocals mimic the whistle of the train that is taking the native son home again.

In the album's liner notes, Michael recalls that he was present at the 1991 Nashville session that produced the hit cover of Carl Perkins' "Restless" for Mark O'Connor's New Nashville Cats, a studio super-group that included Steve Wariner, Vince Gill, and Ricky Skaggs. Michael was working as a guitar tech for Skaggs at the time and was asked to come to the studio to help with Ricky's equipment. Michael remembers sitting with Wariner as he worked out the twin part for the guitar shoot-out featured at the end of the classic recording. Dan Kelly also has a unique connection to the song. As part of Wariner's band, Dan played fiddle on this piece dozens of times on the road. Here Jennifer sings lead, Michael provides banjo support, while Kelly reprises his fiddle part. The song's theme is a common one: the narrator has itchy feet and wants to move on to where the living's easy and he can make a fresh start.

If most of the album's selections describe the rollercoaster nature of secular life, *Hit the Road and Go* also includes two gospel songs—Albert Brumley's touching "Jesus, Hold My Hand" and Hazel Houser's "I'm Ready to Go Home"—included on the Louvin Brothers album, *Satan Is Real*. An appropriate final track, this song details how the narrator's faith in Jesus has helped him bear all life's burdens with grace. Jennifer's vocals reveal both how arduous life's journey has been and how sweet her newfound home will be.

Reviews for the album were positive. Writing for *Bluegrass Unlimited*, Bill Wagner notes that the "fun and highly listenable" recording hearkens back to the "soft, gentle and direct approach of the late 1960s and early 1970s."[11] In his review of the album for Roughstock.com, Matt Bjorke notes that *Hit the Road and Go* "blends everything a listener loves about the genre. It's both expanding on the roots defined by Bill Monroe and his Blue Grass Boys decades ago and also showcases where Bluegrass can go in the 21st century."[12] Writing for Gashouseradio.com, Michael Saulman praises Jennifer's vocals, noting that "her voice does a fantastic and deeply felt job of exploring a variety of emotions and stances throughout this release."[13]

Ventsmagazine.com reviewer Lydia Hillenburg describes the album's production as "warm and intimate" and characterizes the duo's approach to their material as "relaxed, yet studied." She has special praise for the album's final track, noting that "it's difficult with such emotionally fraught material to embody feelings like welcoming death without casting a downbeat note, but the McLains do an exceptional job."[14] Hillenburg's apt observation of the McLain's ability to inject joy into their music once again underscores the family's attitude towards life. It is precisely this approach that has endeared them to audiences for more than fifty years.

CHRONOLOGY

1905	Raymond Francis McLain born.
1906	Beatrice Kane born.
1928	Raymond Kane McLain born (April 18, 1928).
1928	Elizabeth Winslow born (November 8, 1928).
1934	Rosemary McLain born (July 12, 1934).
1950	Raymond K. graduates from Denison University.
1952	Raymond K. marries Elizabeth Winslow.
1952	Al White born (May 25, 1952).
1953	Raymond Winslow McLain born (December 18, 1953).
1954	Raymond K. becomes recreation director at the Hindman Settlement School.
1955	Raymond F. becomes president of American University in Cairo, Egypt.
1956	Raymond K. becomes executive director of the Hindman Settlement School.
1956	Rose Alice McLain born (August 14, 1956).
1958	Ruth Helen McLain born (May 18, 1958).
1965	Nancy Ann McLain born (January 8, 1965).
1967	Michael Kane McLain born (March 20, 1967).
1968	McLain Family Band formed.
1968	McLain Family Band begins weekly TV show on WKYH in Hazard, Kentucky.
1968	McLain house fire on December 31, 1968.
1969	Single of "Cimarron" and "Charlie Brown" released under band name of the Bluegrass State.

1970   The McLain family moves to Berea. Raymond K. begins
        teaching at Berea College.

1971   Gian Carlo Menotti sees the McLain Family Band perform
        in Berea.

1972   McLain Family Band appears at Festival of Two Worlds in
        Spoleto, Italy.

1972   McLain Family Band tours Germany, Italy, and Belgium.

1973   *The McLain Family Band* LP released.

1974   McLain Family Band premiers Rhodes' *Bluegrass Concerto*.

1974   McLain Family Band tours England, Romania, Hungary,
        Spain, Sweden, Norway, Finland, and Iceland.

1974   McLain Family Band debuts on the Grand Ole Opry.

1974   *Country Ham* released.

1975   *Country Life* released.

1975   McLain Family Band tours Alaska, Japan, Taiwan, the
        Philippines, Indonesia, Burma, Laos, India, Nepal, Iran,
        Afghanistan, Egypt, Tunisia, Lebanon, Hungary, Romania,
        Austria, Poland, and Czechoslovakia.

1976   McLain Family Band tours Haiti, Guatemala, Costa Rica,
        Curaçao, Surinam, Venezuela, Brazil, Uruguay, Chile, Peru,
        Ecuador, Bolivia, and Columbia.

1976   *On the Road* released.

1977   Alice marries Al White.

1977   McLain Family Band tours Tanzania, Zambia, Mauritius,
        Cameroon, Chad, Kenya, and Spain.

1977   *Kentucky Wind* released.

1977   The McLain Family Band Festival held for the first time.

1978   McLain Family Band tours France, Algeria, Egypt, North
        Yemen, Oman, UAE, Qatar, and Bahrain.

1978   *Family Album* released.

1979   *7th Album* released.

1979   McLain Family Band tours Mexico.

1980   McLain Family Band tours Rwanda, Burundi, Congo, Zaire,
        Central African Republic, Benin, Liberia, and Morocco.

1980   *Big Hill* released.

1981   *Concerto for Bluegrass Band and Orchestra* released.
1981   Raymond F. McLain dies.
1982   McLain Family Band performs at Carnegie Hall. *In Concert at Carnegie Hall* released.
1983   *All Natural Ingredients* released.
1984   *Sunday Singing* released.
1984   McLain Family Band premiers "Far Away from Here," written for them by Peter Schickele.
1985   McLain Family Band performs at Carnegie Hall as part of "A Folk Celebration."
1985   *Troublesome Creek* released.
1986   *McLain Family Band Country Dance Album* released.
1989   McLain Family Band ceases active touring.
1992   Raymond W. releases *A Place of My Own.*
1995   Raymond W. releases *Kentucky Mountain Banjo.*
1998   Raymond W., Michael, and Jennifer Banks McLain release *More Fun Than We Ought to Have* as the McLains.
2003   Raymond K. McLain dies.
2004   Beatrice Kane McLain dies.
2011   Betty McLain dies.
2013   Al, Alice, and Ruth release *Let the Mountains Roll.*
2013   McLain Family Band honored by the International Bluegrass Music Association (IBMA) with "Distinguished Achievement Award."
2014   Al, Alice, and Ruth release *'Tis a Gift.*
2016   Michael and Jennifer McLain release *Hit the Road and Go.*
2016   McLain Family Band honored by the LEXI Awards with "Lifetime Achievement Award."
2017   McLain Family Band resumes active touring schedule.
2018   McLain Family Band celebrates fiftieth anniversary.
2018   *Celebrate Life* released.

DISCOGRAPHY

1969 The Bluegrass State (Troublesome Records)

- "Cimarron"
- "Charlie Brown"
  45 (Single)

Raymond W. McLain: banjo, vocals
Raymond K. McLain: guitar, vocals
Alice McLain: vocals
Ruth McLain: bass, vocals

 MCLAIN FAMILY BAND RECORDINGS

1973 *The McLain Family Band* (Country Life Records CLR 2)

- "My Very Sunshine"
- "Banjo Pickin' Fool"
- "Please, Mr. Sunshine"
- "Raymond's Breakdown"
- "Farewell, Sweet Jane"
- "Gather Together"
- "Take One Step at a Time"
- "Mister Frog"
- "Bubble Gum Baby"
- "Christmas on the Farm"
- "Silver Creek"
- "Sweet Tomorrow"
- "Pretty Polly"

Raymond W. McLain: banjo, vocals
Raymond K. McLain: guitar, vocals
Alice McLain: mandolin, vocals
Ruth McLain: bass, vocals

Recorded at Malaco Studios, Jackson, Mississippi. Engineer: Jerry Puckett.

1974 *Country Ham* (Country Life Records CLR 3)

- "I Got High Hopes"
- "Grand Square"
- "Old Dan Tucker"
- "Live It Up, Honey"
- "Bad News Blue"
- "Country Ham"
- "Lovely Dove"
- "Hiking Down the Interstate"
- "California Blues"
- "Me and My Gal Sal"
- "Moving On to Higher Ground"
- "Amazing Grace"

Raymond W. McLain: banjo, vocals
Raymond K. McLain: guitar, vocals
Alice McLain: mandolin, vocals
Ruth McLain: bass, vocals

Recorded at Rite Records Productions, Cincinnati, Ohio. Engineers: Lan Ackley and Carl Burckhardt Jr.

1975 *Country Life* (Country Life Records CLR 4)

- "Wild Honey"
- "Married Me a Wife"
- "Sweet Rivers of Redeeming Love"
- "Blue Licks Breakdown"
- "Pretty Flowers"
- "Rose of Old Kentucky"
- "Country Life"
- "Straightaway to Jesus"
- "Joe Clark's Dream"
- "The Girl I Left Behind Me"
- "Let Time Walk By and Lose Me"
- "Love, Love, Love, Love"

Raymond W. McLain: banjo, vocals
Raymond K. McLain: guitar
Alice McLain: mandolin, vocals
Ruth McLain: bass, vocals

Recorded at Malaco Studios, Jackson, Mississippi. Engineers: Jerry Puckett and Ed Butler.

1976 *On the Road* (Country Life Records CLR 6)

- "New River Train"
- "Old Maid Song"
- "Lonesome Day"
- "Pretty Little Reckless Boy"
- "If You're Ever Gonna Love Me"
- "A Heavenly Song"
- "On the Road"
- "Jump Josie"
- "Believe Me"
- "Brown Eyed Baby"
- "Big River Blues"
- "Can't We Get Together Once Again?"

Raymond W. McLain: banjo, vocals
Raymond K. McLain: guitar
Alice McLain: mandolin, vocals
Ruth McLain: bass, vocals

Recorded at Malaco Studios, Jackson, Mississippi. Engineer: Jerry Puckett.

1977 *Kentucky Wind* (Country Life Records CLR 7)

- "You Sing for Me"
- "Kentucky Wind"
- "Hattie Call Rag"
- "Storms Are on the Ocean"
- "Sail Away"
- "Curly Headed Baby"
- "Back Up and Push"
- "My Name's Music"
- "Turn Your Radio On"
- "Follow the Light"
- "Bells of St. Mary's"
- "Always"

Raymond W. McLain: banjo, vocals
Raymond K. McLain: guitar
Alice McLain: mandolin, vocals
Ruth McLain: bass, vocals

Recorded at Malaco Studios, Jackson, Mississippi. Engineer: Jerry Puckett.

1978 *Family Album* (Country Life Records CLR 8)

- "Rabbit in a Log"
- "Down Home Waltz"
- "Milk Cow Blues"
- "Prisoner's Song"
- "West Texas Sun"
- "Come On Out Tonight"
- "Dixie Breakdown"
- "Shady Grove"
- "Foolish Pleasure"
- "Take Me Back to Tulsa"
- "Angel Band"
- "Bound for Gloryland"
- "Stars and Stripes Forever"
- "Today is Gone"

Raymond W. McLain: fiddle, banjo, mandolin, guitar, vocals
Al White: lead guitar, vocals
Alice McLain White: mandolin, vocals
Raymond K. McLain: guitar, accordion
Ruth McLain: bass, vocals

Recorded at the Mississippi Recording Co., Jackson, Mississippi.

1979 *7th Album* (Country Life Records CLR 9)

- "East Virginia Blues"
- "Walkin' in My Sleep"
- "Goin' to Boston"
- "Shuckin' the Corn"
- "The Darkest Hour"
- "Jesusita En Chihuahua"
- "Fair and Tender Ladies"
- "Blue and Lonesome"
- "Two Dollar Bill"
- "Blue, Blue Bonnet Lady"
- "I'm Bound for Gloryland"

Raymond W. McLain: fiddle, banjo, mandolin, vocals
Raymond K. McLain: guitar, accordion
Ruth McLain: mandolin, bass, vocals
Nancy Ann McLain: bass
Tim Owen: banjo

Recorded at the Mississippi Recording Company of Jackson, Mississippi.

1980 *Big Hill* (Country Life Records CLR 10)

- "Big Hill"
- "I Never Will Marry"
- "Pig in the Pen"
- "I Will Arise and Go to Jesus"
- "Georgiana Moon"
- "Alaska Airlines"
- "Light of the Stable"
- "Bugle Call Rag"
- "Under the Double Eagle"
- "Casey at the Bat"
- "Peacock Rag"
- "Our Song"
- "Dickenson County"
- "Worried Man Blues"
- "Remember Me"

Raymond W. McLain: fiddle, banjo, lead guitar, vocals
Raymond K. McLain: guitar, piano
Beverly Buchanan McLain: banjo, guitar
Ruth McLain: mandolin, bass, vocals
Nancy Ann McLain: bass
Michael McLain: mandolin, tambourine

Recorded at the Mississippi Recording Company of Jackson, Mississippi.

1981 *Concerto for Bluegrass Band and Orchestra* (Country Life Records CLR 11)

- *Concerto for Bluegrass Band and Orchestra*
    - I. "Breakdown"
    - II. "Ballad"
    - III. "Variations"
- "You Sing for Me"
- "Silver Creek"
- "Back Up and Push"
- "On the Road"
- "I'm Bound for Gloryland"
- "Movin' on to Higher Ground"

Performed by the McLain Family Band and the Carleton Orchestra; Jeremy Balmuth, conductor
Raymond W. McLain: banjo, fiddle, vocals
Raymond K. McLain: guitar, accordion
Ruth McLain Riopel: mandolin, bass, vocals
Michael Riopel: guitar
Nancy Ann McLain: bass, mandolin
Michael McLain: mandolin, tambourine

Recorded and mastered at Sound 80 Recording Studio, Minneapolis, MN.

1982 *The McLain Family Band in Concert at Carnegie Hall* (Country Life Records CLR 12)

- "How Mountain Girls Can Love"
- "Pretty Polly"
- "Let the Sun Shine Down on Me"
- "Troublesome Creek"
- "Quicksand"
- "Beaver Creek"
- "Back Up and Push"
- "Under the Double Eagle"
- "Chicken Medley"
- "Fried Chicken and a Country Tune"
- "Momma's Little Baby Loves Short'nin' Bread"
- "Country Ham"
- "Way Down in a Cedar Swamp"
- "Go Away from My Window"
- "Orange Blossom Special"
- "Sweet Tomorrow"
- "I Don't Want to Go"

Raymond W. McLain: banjo, guitar, fiddle, vocals
Raymond K. McLain: guitar, accordion, bass, vocals
Ruth McLain Riopel: mandolin, bass, vocals
Nancy Ann McLain: bass, mandolin, vocals
Michael K. McLain: mandolin, banjo, guitar
Michael J. Riopel: lead guitar, harmonica

Recorded live at Carnegie Hall, New York, April 26, 1982. Onsite recording engineer: Dale Ashby. Mixed and edited by Jerry Puckett, Mississippi Recording Company, Jackson, Mississippi. Mastered by Lan Ackley, Rite Record Productions, Cincinnati, Ohio.

1983 *All Natural Ingredients* (Country Life Records CLR 13)

- "Bringing in the Georgia Mail"
- "Blue Railroad Train"
- "Footprints in the Snow"
- "Waltz Medley"
- "This Old House"
- "Lonesome Valley"
- "Kentucky Chimes"
- "Walking the Floor Over You"
- "Skaggs' Rag"
- "House of Gold"
- "Blue Ridge Mountains of Virginia"
- "Columbus Stockade Blues"
- "Blow the Candle Out"

Raymond W. McLain: fiddle, banjo, mandolin, guitar, whistle, vocals
Raymond K. McLain: guitar, piano, sand blocks, vocals
Ruth McLain Riopel: mandolin, bass, wood block, vocals
Michael McLain: banjo, mandolin, guitar
Nancy Ann McLain: mandolin, bass
Michael Riopel: guitar, harmonica

Recorded at Malaco Studios, Jackson, Mississippi. Engineer: Jerry Puckett.

1983   *The Charlotte Bluegrass Festival* (Old Homestead OHS 90160)

Various performers. The McLain Family Band performs the following tracks:
- "Jesse Polka"
- "This Lonesome Valley"
- "Troublesome Creek"
- "Baptism in Beaver Creek"
- "Medley of Chicken Songs"

Recorded live at the Charlotte Bluegrass Festival, June 1982. Sound Recording: Dave McPherson. Remixed by John Morris.

1984   *Sunday Singing* (Country Life Records CLR 14)

- "Dancing with the Angels"
- "Garden Hymn"
- "Little David Played His Harp"
- "Amazing Grace"
- "Take One Step at a Time"
- "Green Pastures"
- "Straightaway to Jesus"
- "I'm Working on a Building"
- "How Firm a Foundation"
- "The Old Landmark"
- "Follow the Light"
- "Babe of Bethlehem"
- "Let the Light Shine Down on Me"
- "I Saw the Light"

Raymond W. McLain: banjo, fiddle, vocals
Raymond K. McLain: guitar, recorder, vocals
Ruth McLain Riopel: mandolin, bass, vocals
Michael McLain: guitar
Nancy Ann McLain: bass, vocals
Michael Riopel: guitar, harmonica

Recorded at the Mississippi Recording Company. Engineer: Jerry Puckett.

1985 *Troublesome Creek* (Country Life Records CLR 15)

- "Troublesome Creek"
- "Kentucky Wind"
- "You're Why I Try"
- "I Want to Be a Cowboy's Sweetheart"
- "In the Pines"
- "Fine Times at our House/Guilderoy"
- "Alabama Jubilee"
- "Show Me That You Know Me"
- "Emotions"
- "That's How I Can Count on You"
- "Dark Hollow"
- "Shoeshine Man"
- "You Are My Flower"
- "Cherry Road"

Raymond W. McLain: banjo, fiddle, guitar, mandolin, vocals
Raymond K. McLain: piano, guitar
Ruth McLain Riopel: bass, mandolin, vocals
Nancy Ann McLain: bass, mandolin, vocals
Michael McLain: banjo, mandolin, tambourine
Michael Riopel: harmonica, guitar

Recorded at the Mississippi Recording Company. Engineer: Jerry Puckett.

1986 *The Country Dance Album* (Country Life Records CLR 16)

- "Levi Jackson Rag"
- "Yesterday's Waltz"
- "Fair Jenny"
- "Big Hill/Fiddle-a-Little"
- "Boil Them Cabbage Down"
- "Beaumont Rag"
- "October Rose"
- "Goin' to Boston"
- "Hoedown: Hell Broke Loose in Georgia/Pigtown Fling/Come On Out Tonight/Sugarfoot Rag/ Katy Hill"

Raymond W. McLain: fiddle, guitar, banjo, mandolin
Michael McLain: banjo
Raymond K. McLain: piano
Ruth McLain: bass
Al White: guitar, mandolin, banjo
Alice McLain White: mandolin

Recorded at Track 16, Lexington, Kentucky. Engineers: Michael McLain and Tom Tandy.

2004 *In Performance at Carleton* (1975–2003): Music of Phillip Rhodes, Composer in Residence, Carleton College (No Label)

- *Concerto for Bluegrass Band and Orchestra*

Performed by the McLain Family Band and the Carleton Orchestra; Jeremy Balmuth, conductor
Raymond W. McLain: banjo, fiddle, vocals
Raymond K. McLain: guitar, accordion
Ruth McLain Riopel: mandolin, bass, vocals
Michael Riopel: guitar
Nancy Ann McLain: bass, mandolin
Michael McLain: mandolin, tambourine

Recorded and mastered at Sound 80 Recording Studio, Minneapolis, MN.

2018 *Celebrate Life* (Country Life Records CLR 22)

- "Come On Out Tonight"
- "Kitty Alone"
- "Nightbird"
- "Celebrate Life"
- "Marie's Wedding/Cooley's Reel/Carried Out of Buckley's"
- "Kentucky Wind"
- "Bully of the Town"
- "Sweet Fern"
- "Going Down"
- "You Can't Find Love If It Just Isn't There"
- "I Want to Be a Cowboy's Sweetheart"
- "Jake's Ramble/Big Wheel Reel"

Raymond W. McLain: fiddle, guitar, mandolin, vocals
Ruth McLain: mandolin, bass, vocals
Alice McLain White: bass, mandolin, vocals
Al White: guitar, mandolin, banjo, fiddle, vocals
Daxson Lewis: banjo, guitar

Recorded at the Kentucky Center for Traditional Music, Morehead State University, Morehead, Kentucky. Engineer: Jesse Wells.

⦿ OTHER RECORDINGS BY MCLAIN FAMILY BAND MEMBERS

Raymond W. McLain

1992   *A Place of My Own* (Flying Fish FF-70597)

- "On the Road"
- "A Place of My Own"
- "Cotton Eyed Joe"
- "Silver Creek"
- "Windswept"
- "Wild Fiddler's Rag"
- "Bells of St. Mary's"
- "Raymond's Breakdown"
- "Cannonball Blues"
- "Kitten on the Keys"
- "Ain't Gonna Work Tomorrow"
- "Shuckin' the Corn"
- "Maiden's Prayer"

Raymond W. McLain: banjo, guitar, vocals
Ruth McLain: bass, harmony vocals
Michael McLain: guitar
Glen Duncan: fiddle
Jesse McReynolds: mandolin
Jim McReynolds: guitar
Blaine Sprouse: fiddle
Mike Stevens: harmonica

Recorded at Music Row Audio and Video, Nashville, TN. Engineer: Bil VornDick. Produced by Raymond W. McLain, with Michael McLain, Jesse McReynolds, and Bil VornDick.

Raymond W. McLain

1995   *Kentucky Mountain Banjo* (Country Life Records CLR-18-CD)

- "Shady Grove"
- "Why Don't You Haul Off and Love Me"
- "Hot Stuff"
- "Kentucky Mountain Banjo"
- "Tennessee Blues/Tennessee Lonesome Blues"
- "Cindy"
- "Playing Possum"
- "The Dance in Old Kentucky"
- "Boil Them Cabbage Down"
- "Baby-O"
- "Dixie Hoedown"
- "My Old Kentucky Home"
- "Night Runner"
- "Brown's Ferry Blues"

Raymond W. McLain: banjo, vocals
Michael McLain: guitar
Ruth McLain: bass
Mike Stevens: harmonica
Jesse McReynolds: mandolin
Glen Duncan: fiddle

Produced by Raymond W. McLain. Recorded at Music Row Audio, Nashville, Tennessee. Engineer: Hank Tilbury.

The McLains

1998   *More Fun Than We Ought to Have* (Pinecastle Records PRC-CD-1086)

- "It'll Come to Me"
- "Lips That Lie"
- "Star of Munster"
- "Take Me in the Lifeboat"
- "(I Wish I Was a) Freight Train"
- "My Baby Thinks He's a Train"
- "Dizzy Fingers"
- "Through the Garden"
- "The Winner's Circle"
- "Little Darlin' "
- "Gracie"
- "Foggy Mountain Top"

Raymond W. McLain: banjo, fiddle, guitar, vocals
Michael McLain: guitar, banjo, vocals
Jennifer Banks McLain: mandolin, vocals
Todd Phillips: bass
Dennis Crouch: bass
Al White: mandolin
Mike Stevens: harmonica
Jim Hurst: guitar

Produced by the McLains. Recorded at Eleven O Three Studio, Nashville Tennessee. Engineer: Hank Tilbury.

Mike Stevens and Raymond McLain

2004   *Old Time Mojo* (BCD162)

- "I Am a Pilgrim"
- "Cash on the Barrelhead"
- "Blowin' Up a Storm"
- "Wabash Cannonball"
- "Don't Let Your Deal Go Down"
- "Boil Them Cabbage Down"
- "I'm Always in Love with You"
- "Dueling Banjos"
- "Take Me Back to Tulsa"
- "In the Pines"
- "Footprints in the Snow"
- "Johnny B. Goode"
- "Blues Intro"
- "Blues Stay Away from Me"

Raymond W. McLain: banjo, fiddle, guitar, vocals
Mike Stevens: harmonica, vocals

Recorded at "The Cottage." Engineer: Scott Merritt. Produced by Mike Stevens and Raymond McLain.

Al, Alice, and Ruth

2013   *Let the Mountains Roll* (Country Life Records)

- "When the Storm Is Over"
- "Cool of the Day"
- "Dancing with the Angels"
- "Foreign Lander"
- "My Lazy Day"
- "Killy Kranky"
- "Wondrous Love"
- "Green, Green Rocky Road"
- "Polly Put the Kettle On"
- "Pans of Biscuits"
- "Angel Gabriel"
- "Let the Mountains Roll"
- "Shady Grove"

Al White: guitar, mandolin, banjo, fiddle, vocals
Alice McLain White: bass, mandolin, vocals
Ruth McLain Smith: bass, mandolin, vocals
Michael McLain: banjo, guitar

Produced by Al, Alice, and Ruth. Engineer: Michael McLain.

Al, Alice, and Ruth

2014   *'Tis a Gift* (Country Life Records CLR-20)

- "Follow the Light"
- "I Wonder What It's Like (in Heaven Today)"
- "Bells are Ringing"
- "Caroling in the Snow"
- "Starlit Lullaby"
- "The First Christmas Day"
- "Simple Gifts"
- "Light of the Stable"

Al White: guitar, mandolin, banjo, fiddle, vocals
Alice McLain White: bass, mandolin, vocals
Ruth McLain Smith: bass, mandolin, vocals
Jennifer Banks McLain: harmony vocals

Engineer: Michael McLain.

Michael and Jennifer McLain

2016   *Hit the Road and Go* (Big Pick Productions)

- "This Old Heart (Is Gonna Rise Again)"
- "Do I Ever Cross Your Mind?"
- "Restless"
- "Jesus, Hold My Hand"
- "Southbound"
- "Up This Hill and Down"
- "McIntosh"
- "Hit the Road and Go"
- "Busy Bee Café"
- "Boom Town"
- "Lady of Spain"
- "I'm Ready to Go Home"

Jennifer McLain: banjo, mandolin, vocals
Michael McLain: banjo, guitar, vocals
Dan Kelly: fiddle
Mike Bub: bass
Ronnie McCoury: mandolin
Wanda Vick Burchfield: Dobro
Corrina Rose Logston: fiddle
Joel Whittinghill: fiddle
Todd Cook: bass
Christy Sutherland: harmony vocals
Dale Ann Bradley: harmony vocals

Produced by Michael and Jennifer McLain. Recorded at Big Pick Productions, Nashville, Tennessee. Engineer: Alex McCollough.

NOTES

INTRODUCTION

1. Fickling, "Bluegrass Bands Enjoy."
2. Saunders, review of *Country Life*.
3. Vincent, interview by Hoffman.
4. Stafford, interview by Hoffman.
5. Rockwell, "What Is Bluegrass Anyway?"
6. Goldsmith, *The Bluegrass Reader*, 1.
7. Rosenberg, *Bluegrass: A History*, 3.
8. Sharon and Cheryl White, interview by Hoffman.
9. Osborne, interview by Hoffman.
10. Kochman, *Big Book of Bluegrass*.
11. Kochman, *Big Book of Bluegrass*, 113–114.
12. Fickling, "Bluegrass Bands Enjoy."
13. McLain Family Band, interview by MacDonald.
14. McLain Family Band, interview by MacDonald.
15. Ritchie and Orr, *Wayfaring Strangers*, 268.
16. Al White, interview by Gleaves.
17. Godbey, "McLain Family Band," 16.
18. Raymond W. McLain, interview by Jenkins.
19. Sharon and Cheryl White, interview by Hoffman.
20. Vecsey, "Country Family Plays the City."
21. Sharon and Cheryl White, interview by Hoffman.
22. Vincent, interview by Hoffman.
23. Henry, *Pretty Good for a Girl*, 177.
24. Henry, *Pretty Good for a Girl*, 177.
25. Vincent, interview by Hoffman.

CHAPTER 1

1. Raymond W. McLain, interview by Jenkins.
2. King, "Making Its Mark."
3. Murphy, *American University in Cairo*, 133.
4. Murphy, *American University in Cairo*, 133.
5. Murphy, *American University in Cairo*, 134.
6. Murphy, *American University in Cairo*, 125.

7. Murphy, *American University in Cairo*, 125.
8. Murphy, *American University in Cairo*, 126.
9. Murphy, *American University in Cairo*, 125.
10. Murphy, *American University in Cairo*, 126.
11. Murphy, *American University in Cairo*, 140.
12. Murphy, *American University in Cairo*, 137.
13. McLain Smith, "McLain Family Band."
14. McLain Smith, "McLain Family Band."
15. McLain Smith, "McLain Family Band."
16. Stoddart, *Challenge and Change in Appalachia*, 1.
17. "Hindman Settlement School."
18. The McLain children were named after family and friends. Raymond Winslow McLain's middle name was in honor of his mother's maiden name; Rose Alice was named after Raymond K.'s sister Rosemary and a Hindman Settlement School nurse, Alice Beaman; Ruth Helen was named after Bicky's sister Ruth and her grandfather Charles Wallace Winslow's sister Helen and also Hindman's music teacher, Ruthie White; Nancy Ann was named after Nancy Ann Ritchie from Knott County, Kentucky; Michael Kane was named after Bicky's father, Michael Kane.
19. Cline, "The McLain Family."
20. Cline, "The McLain Family."
21. Alice McLain, interview by Hoffman.
22. Alice McLain, interview by Hoffman.
23. Alice McLain, interview by Hoffman.
24. Alice McLain, interview by Hoffman.
25. Alice McLain, interview by Hoffman.
26. Alice McLain, interview by Hoffman.
27. Raymond W. McLain, email message to author, January 24, 2019.
28. Alice McLain, interview by Hoffman.
29. Alice McLain, interview by Hoffman.
30. Cline, "The McLain Family."
31. Cline, "The McLain Family."
32. Cline, "The McLain Family."
33. Stoddart, *The Quare Women's Journals*, 88.
34. Raymond K. McLain, "Folk Music at Hindman," 14.
35. Raymond K. McLain, "Folk Music at Hindman," 14.
36. Raymond K. McLain, "Folk Music at Hindman," 15.
37. Raymond K. McLain, "Folk Music at Hindman," 16–17.
38. Gohl, "The Appalachian Region."
39. Stoddart, *Challenge and Change in Appalachia*, 158.
40. Stoddart, *Challenge and Change in Appalachia*, 158.
41. McLain Family Band, interview by MacDonald.
42. Alice McLain, interview by Gleaves.
43. Alice McLain, interview by Gleaves.
44. Shrubsall, "Raymond McLain," 5.
45. Shrubsall, "Raymond McLain," 6.
46. Shrubsall, "Raymond McLain," 7.
47. Shrubsall, "Raymond McLain," 8.

48. Shrubsall, "Raymond McLain," 8.
49. McLain Family Band, interview by MacDonald.
50. Alice McLain, interview by Gleaves.
51. Alice McLain, interview by Hoffman.
52. Alice McLain, interview by Hoffman.
53. Alice McLain, interview by Hoffman.
54. Shrubsall, "Raymond McLain," 7.
55. Alice McLain, interview by Gleaves.
56. Alice McLain, interview by Gleaves.
57. Ruth McLain, interview by Gleaves.
58. Alice McLain, interview by Gleaves.

CHAPTER 2

1. Alice McLain and Ruth McLain, interview by Gleaves.
2. Wilson, *Berea College*, 1.
3. Wilson, *Berea College*, 1.
4. Wilson, *Berea College*, 2.
5. Wilson, *Berea College*, 92.
6. Wilson, *Berea College*, 103.
7. Wilson, *Berea College*, 153.
8. Wilson, *Berea College*, 164.
9. Dinwiddie, "Where Have All the Fiddles Gone?," 10.
10. Mielke, *Teaching Mountain Children*, xiii.
11. Dinwiddie, "Where Have All the Fiddles Gone?," 12.
12. Dinwiddie, "Where Have All the Fiddles Gone?," 12–13.
13. Davis, "Bluegrass Family," 6.
14. Davis, "Bluegrass Family," 6.
15. Davis, "Bluegrass Family," 5.
16. Davis, "Bluegrass Family," 5.
17. Alice White, Ruth McLain Smith, Raymond W. McLain, and Al White, interview by Hoffman and Jenkins.
18. Raymond W. McLain, interview by Jenkins.
19. Alice White, Ruth McLain Smith, Raymond W. McLain, and Al White, interview by Hoffman and Jenkins.
20. Alice White, Ruth McLain Smith, Raymond W. McLain, and Al White, interview by Hoffman and Jenkins.
21. Alice White, Ruth McLain Smith, Raymond W. McLain, and Al White, interview by Hoffman and Jenkins.
22. Alice McLain, interview by Hoffman.
23. Alice McLain, interview by Hoffman.
24. Alice McLain, interview by Hoffman.

CHAPTER 3

1. Sharon and Cheryl White, interview by Hoffman.
2. Price, *Old as the Hills*, 60.
3. Alison Krauss is a huge fan of the group and helped arrange for the album to be finished.

4. Family bluegrass bands continue to flourish in the twenty-first century. I cannot, of course, list all of them here.
5. The band was headed by mother Debi, who played guitar, sang, and wrote songs for the group. Daughters Sara (bass, Dobro, banjo, vocals), Jade (mandolin, vocals), and Eden (fiddle) rounded out the lineup.
6. Jenkins, "The Wells Family."
7. Vincent, interview by Hoffman.
8. Vincent, interview by Hoffman.
9. Osborne, interview by Hoffman.
10. McLain Family Band, interview by MacDonald.
11. Fleischhauer and Rosenberg, *Bluegrass Odyssey*, 130.
12. Dillon, "Kin and Communities," 3.
13. Dillon, "Kin and Communities," 3.
14. Novak, "Family Out of Favor," 37.
15. Rosenberg, *Bluegrass: A History*, 205.
16. Hillinger, "Bighill, Ky., Plays Host."
17. Hillinger, "Bighill, Ky., Plays Host."
18. Sharon and Cheryl White, interview by Hoffman.
19. Sharon and Cheryl White, interview by Hoffman.
20. Sharon and Cheryl White, interview by Hoffman.
21. Vincent, interview by Hoffman.
22. Hillinger, "Bighill, Ky., Plays Host."
23. Using the pseudonym of Christopher North, John Wilson wrote in his 1829 work *Noctes Ambrosianae* about "His Majesty's dominions, on which the sun never sets."
24. Lane, "An Economic Impact Analysis."
25. Crompton and McKay, "Motives of Visitors."
26. Johnathon, interview by Jenkins.
27. All statistics included here were found in original documents housed in the McLain Family Archives at Berea College.
28. Rosenberg, *Bluegrass: A History*, 277.

CHAPTER 4

1. Rhodes, "Bluegrass Concerto."
2. Rhodes, "Bluegrass Concerto."
3. Mootz, "Review of 'Bluegrass Concerto.' "
4. Mootz, "Review of 'Bluegrass Concerto.' "
5. Mootz, "Review of 'Bluegrass Concerto.' "
6. Gidwitz, letter to McLain Family Band, October 1973.
7. McLain Family Band, interview by MacDonald.
8. Veinus, *The Concerto*, 1.
9. Roeder, *History of the Concerto*, 13.
10. Godbey, "McLain Family Band," 16.
11. Rhodes, "Bluegrass Concerto."
12. Rhodes, "Bluegrass Concerto."
13. Keyes, "Orchestra's Super Pops."
14. Keyes, "Orchestra's Super Pops."

15. Shrubsall, "Raymond McLain," 8.
16. Rhodes, "Bluegrass Concerto."
17. Ball, "Review of Bluegrass Concerto."
18. Wigler, "Review of Bluegrass Concerto."
19. Monson, "Review of 'Far Away from Here.'"
20. McLellan, untitled review.
21. Cooklis, "Talent Was There."
22. Sharon and Cheryl White, interviewed by Hoffman.
23. While most readers are familiar with the work of McEuen and O'Connor, some may not be familiar with Crary, an excellent guitarist who cofounded the Bluegrass Alliance and Spontaneous Combustion, a bluegrass/rock fusion group founded in 1986.
24. Osborne, interviewed by Hoffman.
25. Osborne, interviewed by Hoffman.
26. Osborne, interviewed by Hoffman.
27. Osborne, interviewed by Hoffman.
28. Godbey, "McLain Family Band," 16.

CHAPTER 5

1. Raymond W. McLain, interviewed by Jenkins.
2. Sharon and Cheryl White, interviewed by Hoffman.
3. Acme (Cincinnati), Arrow (Columbia, Kentucky), as well as London, Laurel, Lemco, King Bluegrass, and Pine Mountain (all run by A. L. Phipps of Barbourville, Kentucky) were in business at the time.
4. Alice McLain, interviewed by Hoffman.
5. Raymond W. McLain, interviewed by Jenkins.
6. Raymond W. McLain, interviewed by Jenkins.
7. The McLain Family Band also performed at Carnegie Hall in 1985 as part of an event billed as "A Folk Celebration."
8. Raymond W. McLain, interviewed by Jenkins.
9. Raymond W. McLain, interviewed by Jenkins.
10. Saunders, "Review of *Country Ham*," 18.
11. Saunders, "Review of *Country Life*," 23.
12. Saunders, "Review of *Kentucky Wind*," 23.
13. Griffith, "Review of *On the Road*," 38.
14. Hatlo, "On Record," 46.
15. Palmer, "Bluegrass."
16. Roemer, "Review of The McLain Family Band in Concert at Carnegie Hall."
17. Tallmadge, "All Natural Ingredients."
18. Fox, "Review of *Sunday Singing*," 38.
19. Spottswood, "Review of *Troublesome Creek*," 34.

CHAPTER 6

1. Raymond W. McLain, interviewed by Jenkins.
2. See Heintz, *Pinkhoneysuckle*, 250.
3. Raymond W. McLain, interviewed by Jenkins.

CHAPTER 7

1. Raymond W. graduated from Berea College with a degree in communications.
    Alice supplemented her Berea degree in home economics with a master's
    degree in elementary education from Eastern Kentucky University. Ruth's BA
    from Berea was in art design. Michael received a bachelor of music degree
    from Belmont University.
2. McLain Family Band, *The McLain Family Band*, 41.
3. The band's most active international touring years were 1972–1980. In 1988
    they toured Brazil, and in 2018 as part of their fiftieth anniversary the group
    traveled to Denmark and Ireland. In the years in between, the McLains
    performed in China, Wales, Scotland, Switzerland, Australia, and the
    Netherlands.
4. See Malone, *Bill Clifton*.
5. Ewing, *Bill Monroe Reader*, 111.
6. Raymond W. McLain, Alice McLain, Ruth McLain Smith, and Al White,
    interviewed by Hoffman and Jenkins.
7. Alice McLain, letter to C. Robert Dickerman, December 26, 1973.
8. Betty McLain, letter to Alice McLain, February 17, 1974.
9. Ruth McLain, letter to Betty McLain, April 12, 1976.
10. Ruth McLain, letter to Betty McLain, March 4, 1974.
11. *Independent Helsinki Daily*, April 16, 1974.
12. *Independent Helsinki Daily*.
13. Alice McLain, letter to Betty McLain, February 12, 1974.
14. Pete Sayers, letter to McLain Family Band, August 1, 1977.
15. Raymond W. McLain, Alice McLain, Ruth McLain Smith, and Al White,
    interviewed by Hoffman and Jenkins.
16. Raymond W. McLain, Alice McLain, Ruth McLain Smith, and Al White,
    interviewed by Hoffman and Jenkins.
17. Alice McLain, Diary of 1975 tour.
18. Alice McLain, Diary of 1975 tour.
19. Alice McLain, Diary of 1975 tour.
20. Alice McLain, Diary of 1975 tour.
21. Raymond W. McLain, Alice McLain, Ruth McLain Smith, and Al White,
    interviewed by Hoffman and Jenkins.
22. Alice McLain, Diary of 1975 tour.
23. Alice McLain, Diary of 1975 tour.
24. Alice McLain, Diary of 1975 tour.
25. Alice McLain, Diary of 1975 tour.
26. Alice McLain, Diary of 1975 tour.
27. Alice McLain, Diary of 1975 tour.
28. Alice McLain, Diary of 1975 tour.
29. Raymond W. McLain, Alice McLain, Ruth McLain Smith, and Al White,
    interviewed by Hoffman and Jenkins.
30. Raymond W. McLain, Alice McLain, Ruth McLain Smith, and Al White,
    interviewed by Hoffman and Jenkins.
31. Alice McLain, Diary of 1975 tour.

32. Alice McLain, Diary of 1975 tour.
33. Berea Police Department, letter to unknown Brazilian officials, March 12, 1976.
34. Alice McLain, letter to Betty McLain, November 30, 1978.
35. Ruth McLain, letter to Betty McLain, March 4, 1974.
36. Ruth McLain, letter to Betty McLain, November 25, 1975.
37. Ruth McLain, letter to Betty McLain, May 13, 1975.
38. Raymond W. McLain, Alice McLain, Ruth McLain Smith, and Al White, interviewed by Hoffman and Jenkins.
39. Cline, "The McLain Family."
40. James Burns, letter to McLain Family Band, June 17, 1976.
41. Ross, American Embassy Report.
42. Jack Perry, letter to McLain Family Band, June 6, 1975.
43. Ruth McLain, letter to Betty McLain, April 21, 1976.
44. Ruth McLain, letter to Betty McLain, May 16, 1976.
45. McLain Family Band, interviewed by MacDonald.
46. Raymond W. McLain, Alice McLain, Ruth McLain Smith, and Al White, interviewed by Hoffman and Jenkins.
47. McLain Family Band, interviewed by MacDonald.
48. McLain Family Band, interviewed by MacDonald.
49. McLain Family Band, interviewed by MacDonald.
50. Ruth McLain, letter to Betty McLain, March 4, 1974.
51. Akila Bellahouel, letter to McLain Family Band, November 26, 1978.
52. Martha Cristian, letter to McLain Family Band, September 6, 1976.
53. Peter Kandler, letter to McLain Family Band, September 16, 1972.
54. Carlen Kreutzer, letter to McLain Family Band, December 7, 1978.
55. Leland Cross, letter to McLain Family Band, March 11, 1982.
56. Raymond W. McLain, Alice McLain, Ruth McLain Smith, and Al White, interviewed by Hoffman and Jenkins.
57. McLain Family Band, interviewed by MacDonald.
58. Raymond W. McLain, Alice McLain, Ruth McLain Smith, and Al White, interviewed by Hoffman and Jenkins.

CHAPTER 8

1. Shrubsall, "Raymond McLain," 9.
2. Shrubsall, "Raymond McLain," 9.
3. Shrubsall, "Raymond McLain," 9.
4. Shrubsall, "Raymond McLain," 10.
5. Raymond W. McLain and Forbes, *Fiddle a Little*, 5.
6. Shrubsall, "Raymond McLain," 6.
7. Raymond W. McLain, interviewed by Jenkins.
8. Vincent, interviewed by Hoffman.
9. Raymond W. McLain, interviewed by Jenkins.
10. Accessed March 21, 2019, https://www.mheducation.com/prek-12/explore/music-studio/spotlight-on-music.html.
11. Raymond W. McLain, interviewed by Jenkins.

CHAPTER 9

1. Tottle, "Reflections on Bluegrass."
2. Tottle, "Reflections on Bluegrass."
3. Buller, "Raymond McLain," 38.
4. Buller, "Raymond McLain," 38.
5. Tottle, "Raymond McLain: An Appreciation," 46.
6. Buller, "Raymond McLain," 38.
7. Buller, "Raymond McLain," 41.
8. Buller, "Raymond McLain," 41.
9. Buller, "Raymond McLain," 41.
10. Buller, "Raymond McLain," 41.
11. Buller, "Raymond McLain," 41.
12. KTCM Mission Statement.
13. Cardwell, "Don Rigsby," 41.
14. Cardwell, "Don Rigsby," 42.
15. Kiser, interviewed by Hoffman.
16. Kiser, interviewed by Hoffman.
17. Hobert and Nichols, "I Have to Finish This Song."
18. Kiser, interviewed by Hoffman.
19. Ruth McLain, email message to Paul Jenkins, January 15, 2019.
20. Jenkins, "The Price Sisters."
21. Jenkins, "The Price Sisters."
22. Jenkins, "The Price Sisters."
23. Belmont School of Music Mission Statement.
24. Michael McLain, course syllabus, 2012.
25. Michael McLain, course syllabus, 2012.
26. Amanda Combs, email message to author, December 14, 2016.
27. Maggie White, email to author, January 4, 2017.
28. Dinwiddie, "Where Have All the Fiddles Gone?," 11.
29. Dinwiddie, "Where Have All the Fiddles Gone?," 13.
30. Dinwiddie, "Where Have All the Fiddles Gone?," 13.
31. Al White, interviewed by Gleaves.
32. Al White, interviewed by Gleaves.
33. Al White, interviewed by Gleaves.
34. Gleaves, interviewed by Hoffman.
35. Gleaves, interviewed by Hoffman.
36. Gleaves, interviewed by Hoffman.
37. Al White, interviewed by Gleaves.
38. Mission Statement.
39. In July 2019, Nancy Cardwell, IBMA Foundation administrator, provided a list from the following link that names these institutions: http://bluegrassfoundation.org/programs/.
40. Sharon and Cheryl White, interviewed by Hoffman.
41. Vincent, interviewed by Hoffman.
42. The actual phrasing of this often-used quotation is "Cease conceiving of education as mere preparation for later life, and make it the full meaning of the present life," from Dewey's 1893 work, *Self-Realization as the Moral Ideal.*

CHAPTER 10

1. Leach, "Plucked from West Liberty."
2. Sharon and Cheryl White, interviewed by Hoffman.
3. Levitin, *This Is Your Brain on Music*, 242.
4. Vincent, interviewed by Hoffman.
5. Bagehot, "Works and Life of Walter Bagehot."
6. Sharon and Cheryl White, interviewed by Hoffman.
7. Vincent, interviewed by Hoffman.
8. Sharon and Cheryl White, interviewed by Hoffman.
9. Johnathon, interviewed by Jenkins.
10. Kiser, interviewed by Hoffman.

APPENDIX A

1. Peter Barnes, accessed November 28, 2016, https://thesession.org.
2. Rosenberg, *Bluegrass: A History*, 231.
3. Marshall, " 'Keep on the Sunny Side of Life,' " 28.
4. Marshall, " 'Keep on the Sunny Side of Life,' " 24–26.
5. Cantwell, *Bluegrass Breakdown*, 226.
6. Gleaves, interviewed by Hoffman.
7. Marshall, " 'Keep on the Sunny Side of Life,' " 21.
8. For more on "New River Train," see Noah Adams, *Far Appalachia* (New York: Delacorte Press, 2001), 51–52.
9. Kochman, *Big Book of Bluegrass*, 112.
10. Ritchie, *Folk Songs of the Southern Appalachians*, 19.
11. If you want to track down the original recording, see N 17795-A, "Little Foot Prints," Superior 2688 (released July 1931), County CD-3519. For more information, see Supplement to "Footprints in the Snow: The Intercontinental Journey of a Song," by Julay Brooks, *Old-Time Herald* 13, no. 4 (December 2012).
12. Cantwell, *Bluegrass Breakdown*, 236.
13. Nick Lowe, accessed February 19, 2019, https://quotefancy.com/quote /1625936/Nick-Lowe-When-I-find-a-cover-song-that-I-like-I-ll-work-away -at-it-until-I-kind-of.

APPENDIX B

1. Jenkins, "Sharing a Gift," 12.
2. Royko, "Review of *A Place of My Own*."
3. Jenkins, "Sharing a Gift," 6.
4. Jenkins, "Sharing a Gift," 6.
5. Jenkins, "Sharing a Gift," 6.
6. Jenkins, "Sharing a Gift," 6.
7. For those unfamiliar with the term, "planking" is an isometric core strength exercise.
8. Jenkins, "Sharing a Gift," 12.
9. Jenkins, "Sharing a Gift," 12.
10. Killiecrankie is a village in Perth, Scotland.

11.   Wagner, Review of *Hit the Road and Go*, 53.
12.   Bjorke, "Album Review."
13.   Saulman, "Review of *Hit the Road and Go*."
14.   Hillenburg, "CD Review."

BIBLIOGRAPHY

Bagehot, Walter. "The Works and Life of Walter Bagehot." Vol. 5. Accessed October 11, 2019. https://oll.libertyfund.org/titles/bagehot-the-works-and-life-of -walter-bagehot-vol-5.

Ball, Becky. "Review of Bluegrass Concerto." *Oak Ridger*, May 25, 1982.

Belmont School of Music Mission Statement. Accessed November 12, 2016. www .belmont.edu.

Bjorke, Matt. "Album Review: Michael & Jennifer McLain—Hit the Road and Go." Accessed February 10, 2017. www.roughstock.com.

Buller, Becky. "Raymond McLain: Sharing the Pleasures of Music." *Bluegrass Unlimited*, July 2001, 38–41.

Cantwell, Robert. *Bluegrass Breakdown: The Making of the Old Southern Sound.* Urbana: University of Illinois Press, 1984.

Cardwell, Nancy. "Don Rigsby: Midnight Caller." *Bluegrass Unlimited*, October 2007, 40–44.

Cline, Erin. "The McLain Family." Accessed April 12, 2004. http://www.mclains .com.

Cooklis, Ray. "Talent Was There, but Mix Was Not." *Cincinnati Enquirer*, December 5, 1983.

Crompton, John L., and Stacey L. McKay. "Motives of Visitors Attending Festival Events." *Annals of Tourism Research* 24, no. 2, 1997.

Davis, Chandler. "Bluegrass Family—Family Bluegrass." *Bluegrass Unlimited*, October 1972, 5–8.

Dinwiddie, Joseph. "Where Have All the Fiddles Gone?" *Appalachian Heritage*, Fall 1998, 6–14.

Fickling, Amy. "Bluegrass Bands Enjoy Making Music and Friends." *Dispatch*, March 28, 1980.

Fleischhauer, Carl, and Neil V. Rosenberg. *Bluegrass Odyssey: A Documentary in Pictures and Words, 1966–86.* Urbana: University of Illinois Press, 2001.

Fox, John Hartley. Review of *Sunday Singing*. *Bluegrass Unlimited*, February 1985, 38.

Godbey, Marty. "The McLain Family Band." *Bluegrass Unlimited*, February 1981, 12–16.

Gohl, Earl F. "The Appalachian Region and Its Challenges." Accessed January 25, 2019. http://www.arc.gov/noindex/newsroom/GohlSGPBCommentary 40thAnniv5-2012.pdf.

Goldsmith, Thomas, ed. *The Bluegrass Reader*. Urbana: University of Illinois Press, 2004.

Griffith, James. Review of *On the Road. Bluegrass Unlimited*, May 1977, 38.

Hatlo, Jim. "On Record." *Frets Magazine*, February 1981.

Heintz, Barbara Everett. *Pinkhoneysuckle*. North Charleston, SC: Create Space, 2011.

Henry, Murphy Hicks. *Pretty Good for a Girl: Women in Bluegrass*. Urbana: University of Illinois Press, 2013.

Hillenburg, Lydia. "CD Review: *Hit the Road and Go* by Michael and Jennifer McLain." Accessed February 10, 2017. www.ventsmagazine.com.

Hillinger, Charles. "Bighill, Ky., Plays Host to 6,000 Music Lovers." *Los Angeles Times*, August 23, 1987.

"Hindman Settlement School, 2016–2020 Strategic Plan." Accessed January 22, 2019. https://www.hindmansettlement.org/app/uploads/2016/08/HSS -Strategic-Plan.pdf.

Hobert, Christina, and Anna Nichols. "I Have to Finish This Song. The Story of a Daughter's Love." *Trailblazer*, March 17, 2016.

Independent Helsinki Daily, April 16, 1974.

Jenkins, Paul O. "Sharing a Gift: The Music of Raymond McLain and Mike Stevens." *Pow'r Pickin'*, July/August 2001.

———. "The Wells Family." *Pow'r Pickin'*, May 2003.

Keyes, Nelson. "Orchestra's Super Pops Scores Holiday Success." *Courier-Journal & Times*, December 22, 1974.

King, Mike. "Making Its Mark." *Courier-Journal*, April 27, 1982.

Kochman, Marilyn, ed. *The Big Book of Bluegrass*. New York: William Morrow, 1984.

KTCM Mission Statement. Accessed November 15, 2016. http://www2 .moreheadstate.edu/content_template.aspx?id=9467.

Lane, Kevin A. "An Economic Impact Analysis for the 2nd Annual Bluegrass, Old-Time Music and Dance Festival in the Village of Stone Mountain, Georgia." BA thesis, Eastern Tennessee State University, 2011.

Leach, Julianna. "Plucked from West Liberty to the World." Accessed November 5, 2018. http://www.thetrailblazeronline.net/life_and_arts/article_77c968ac -de31–11e8-b56a-e3692246b637.html.

Ledgin, Stephanie P. *From Every Stage: Images of America's Roots Music*. Jackson: University Press of Mississippi, 2005.

———. *Homegrown Music: Discovering Bluegrass*. Westport, CT: Praeger, 2004.

Levitin, Daniel J. *This Is Your Brain on Music: The Science of a Human Obsession*. New York: Plume, 2007.

MacDonald, John. Manuscript of interview with McLain Family Band for IBM project, conducted January 2–3, 1976. Housed in Berea College McLain Family Band archives.

Malone, Bill C. *Bill Clifton: America's Bluegrass Ambassador to the World*. Urbana: University of Illinois Press, 2016.

Marshall, Howard Wight. " 'Keep on the Sunny Side of Life': Pattern and Expression in Bluegrass Gospel Music." *New York Folklore Quarterly* 30, March 1974, 3–43.

McLain, Raymond K. "Folk Music at Hindman." *Mountain Life and Work*, 1958, 13–17.

McLain, Raymond W., and Dr. John Forbes. *Fiddle a Little: A Start from Scratch Guide to Fiddling*. Lexington, KY: KET, 1983.

McLain Family Band. *The McLain Family Band—50 Years of Music: A Pictorial History*. Berea, KY: McLain Family Band LLC, 2017.

McLain Smith, Ruth. "The McLain Family Band." Accessed April 12, 2004. http://www.mclains.com/bicky.htm.

McLellan, Joseph. Untitled review. *Washington Post*, December 17, 1984.

Mielke, David. *Teaching Mountain Children: Towards a Foundation of Understanding*. Boone, NC: Appalachian Consortium Press, 1978.

Mission Statement. Accessed May 9, 2018. http://www.usbornebooksandmore .com/home/NewConsultant.aspx.

Monson, Karen. Review of "Far Away from Home." *Baltimore Sun*, December 17, 1984.

Mootz, William. Review of "Bluegrass Concerto." *Louisville Courier Journal*, September 22, 1973.

Murphy, Lawrence R. *The American University in Cairo: 1919–1987*. Cairo, Egypt: American University in Cairo Press, 1987.

Novak, Michael. "The Family Out of Favor." *Harper's*, April 1, 1976.

Palmer, Robert. "Bluegrass: McLain Family Gives Carnegie Hall Concert." *New York Times*, April 29, 1982.

Price, Steven D. *Old as the Hills*. New York: Viking Press, 1975.

Rhodes, Phillip. Lecture on "Bluegrass Concerto." Unpublished manuscript.

Ritchie, Fiona, and Douglas Orr. *Wayfaring Strangers: The Musical Voyage from Scotland and Ulster to Appalachia*. Chapel Hill: University of North Carolina Press, 2014.

Ritchie, Jean. *Folk Songs of the Southern Appalachians*. Lexington: University Press of Kentucky, 1997.

Rockwell, Joti. "What Is Bluegrass Anyway? Category Formation, Debate and the Framing of Musical Genre." *Popular Music*, October 2012, 363–381.

Roeder, Michael Thomas. *A History of the Concerto*. Portland, OR: Amadeus Press, 1994.

Roemer, John. Review of *The McLain Family Band in Concert at Carnegie Hall*. *Bluegrass Unlimited*, May 1983.

Rosenberg, Neil V. *Bluegrass: A History*. Urbana: University of Illinois Press, 2005.

Ross, B. T. American Embassy Report. December, 1978.

Royko, David. "Review of *A Place of My Own*." Accessed July 16, 2014. http://www .davidroyko.com/mclaincd.htm.

Saulman, Michael. "Review of *Hit the Road and Go*." Accessed December 19, 2016. http://gashouseradio.com/2016/12/michael-jennifer-mclain-hit-road-go/.

Saunders, Walter. Review of the McLain Family Band: *Country Ham*. *Bluegrass Unlimited* 9, no.7, 1974, 18.

Saunders, Walter. Review of *Country Life*. *Bluegrass Unlimited* 10, no. 4, 1975, 23.

———. Review of *Kentucky Wind*. *Bluegrass Unlimited* 12, no.7, 1978, 23.

Shrubsall, Wayne. "Raymond W. McLain." *Banjo Newsletter*, October 3, 1983, 5–9.

Spottswood, Richard. Review of *Troublesome Creek*. *Bluegrass Unlimited*, February 1986, 34.

Stoddart, Jess. *Challenge and Change in Appalachia: The Story of the Hindman Settlement School*. Lexington: University Press of Kentucky, 2002.

———, ed. *The Quare Women's Journals: May Stone & Katherine Pettit's Summers in the Kentucky Mountains and the Founding of the Hindman Settlement School*. Ashland, KY: Jesse Stuart Foundation, 1997.

Tallmadge, William H. "All Natural Ingredients." *Berea Citizen*. September 1, 1983.

Tottle, Jack. "Raymond W. McLain: An Appreciation." *Bluegrass Unlimited*, August 2014, 46.

———. "Reflections on Bluegrass, Old Time and Country Music at ETSU." *A! Magazine for the Arts*, October 2016.

Vecsey, George. "A Country Family Plays the City." *New York Times*, January 7, 1977.

Veinus, Abraham. *The Concerto*. New York: Dover, 1964.

Wagner, Bill. Review of *Hit the Road and Go. Bluegrass Unlimited*, April, 2017, 53.

Wigler, Stephen. Review of "Bluegrass Concerto." *Democrat and Chronicle*, Rochester, NY, n.d.

Wilson, Shannon H. *Berea College: An Illustrated History*. Lexington: University Press of Kentucky, 2006.

INTERVIEWS

Gleaves, Sam, interview by Katie Hoffman, December 21, 2015.

Johnathon, Michael, interview by Paul O. Jenkins, August 12, 2013.

Kiser, Nathan, interview by Katie Hoffman, October 8, 2013.

McLain, Alice and Ruth, interview by Sam Gleaves, March 16, 2014.

McLain, Alice, interview by Katie Hoffman, March 13, 2013.

McLain, Raymond W., interview by Paul O. Jenkins, May 26, 2016.

Osborne, Sonny, interview by Katie Hoffman, September 11, 2014.

Stafford, Tim, interview by Katie Hoffman, June 11, 2014.

Vincent, Rhonda, interview by Katie Hoffman, September 12, 2014.

White, Al, interview by Sam Gleaves, February 11, 2014.

White, Alice, Ruth Smith McLain, Raymond W. McLain, and Al White, interview by Katie Hoffman and Paul O. Jenkins, January 10, 2016.

White, Sharon and Cheryl, interview by Katie Hoffman, September 12, 2014.

INDEX

Note: Abbreviations for three of the McLains are used in subentries: RKM for Raymond K., RWM for Raymond W., and MKM, for Michael. Photographs are indicated by italicized page numbers followed by f. Readers should also consult the Discography of the book.

Royko, David, 186
Rucker, Chuck, 34

"Sad and Lonesome Day," 80
"Sail Away" (Rosemary McLain), 8,
   12, 72, 101
Saint of Bleeker Street, The (Menotti),
   44
"Sally Goodin," 64
Sally Mountain Show, 50
"San Antonio Rose" (Wills), 131
"Sand and Water" (Chapman), 188
Saulman, Michael, 195
Saunders, Walter, 5, 79–80
Saxton, Bob, 166
Sayers, Pete, 107
Schaaf, Peter, 77
Schickele, Peter (aka P.D.Q. Bach),
   "Far Away from Here," 65
Schoebel, Elmer, 164
Seeger, Pete, 136, 171, 172
7th Album, 74, 102
"Shady Grove" (trad.), 10, 22, 172, 193
Sharp, Cecil, 27, 39, 40
"Shear 'Em" (trad.), 171
"Shoeshine Man" (Hall), 78, 179
"Show Me That You Know Me"
   (RKM), 78, 134
Shrubsall, Wayne, 127–28
"Shuckin' the Corn" (Graves, Certain,
   and Stacey), 11, 162, 185, 186
"Silver Creek" (RWM), 11, 60, 127–28,
   130, 185, 186
Silver Creek Elementary School in
   Berea, 138
Siminoff, Roger, 145–46
"Simple Gifts," 194
Singing Bird Music School, 153
Skaggs, Ricky, 14, 33, 55, 129, 146, 153,
   170, 195
"Skaggs' Rag" (RW), 129
"Slow Piece" (RKM), 22
Smiley, Red, 33, 34, 163, 164
Smith, Fiddlin' Arthur, 164, 171
Smithsonian Institution, Kin &
   Communities symposium, 52,
   165

Soldier of the Cross (Skaggs album), 170
solo recording projects, 6
   Hit the Road and Go, 194–97
   Let the Mountains Roll, 191–93
   *More Fun Than We Ought to
      Have*, 188–89
   Old-Time Mojo, 189–91
   RWJ's *A Place of My Own*,
      184–86
   RWJ's *Kentucky Mountain
      Banjo*, 186–87
   'Tis a Gift, 193–94
Songs of All Time (RKM), 22
Sousa, John Philip, 70, 165
"Southbound" (Watson), 195
Southern Appalachian Studies
   Project, 39
Spear, Abe, 140
Spottswood, Richard, 81
Stafford, Tim, 6–7, 11, 139
Stanley Brothers (Ralph and Carter),
   2, 48, 166, 171, 172, 188
   Carter, 169
   Ralph, 7, 25, 32, 33, 34, 49,
      77, 130
"Starlit Lullaby" (Ruth McLain), 194
"Stars and Stripes Forever" (Sousa),
   10, 11, 52, 165
Steffey, Adam, 139
Stevens, Mike, 184, 185, 186, 188, 189,
   190, 191
Stewart, Redd, 178
Stoddart, Jess, 28, 29
Stone, May, 23, 26
Stoneman Family, 4, 48
   Donna, 50
   Ernest V. "Pop," 50, 174
   Veronica (Roni), x, 50
Stone Mountain festival, 56–57
store opening performances, 76
"Storms Are on the Ocean, The"
   (Carter Family), 10, 176
"Straightaway to Jesus" (Rosemary
   McLain), 8, 97, 102–3, 131
Strayer, Emily, 55
Stryker, Fred, 188
Stuart, Marty, 33, 195